Contents

Introduction
page 4-5

Route Summaries:
Amsterdam routes - overview map	page 6
Randstad Circle route - overview map	pages 6-8
Northern route - overview map	page 9
Eastern route - overview map	page 10
Southern route - overview map	page 11

Dutch Cycling Culture:
1890s - 1940s: Adopting the two-wheeled life-style	page 12
1950s - 1960s: Cycling pushed to the margins	page 13
1970s: The great Dutch Cycling Revolution	page 14
1980s - present: Cycling into the 21st Century	page 15

The Dutch Cycling Network:
Traffic rules	pages 16-19
Cycle route signage and cycling below sea level	pages 20-21

Travel information:
Flying to Schiphol Airport and using Amsterdam as a base	page 22
Travelling by ferry and touring by bike & train	page 23
Preparing for your trip: weather and equipment	page 24
Dutch delights and Dutch difficulties	page 25
How to use this book: key to used symbols & abbreviations	page 26-28
Dutch language: key to common words and phrases	page 29

Amsterdam routes:
Route A: City Centre, River Amstel, greenbelts (Amsterdam Forest & Vondelpark) and Schiphol Airport	pages 30-39
Route B: River Amstel, Amstelland and East Corridor	pages 40-47
Route C: Rhine Canal, Weesp & Muiden, New Islands and Old Villages	pages 48-55
Route D: North Amsterdam, old seawall and Waterland	pages 56-61
Route E: Zaandam, Zaanse Schans windmills, Twiske	pages 62-69
Route F: Westerpark, "Garden Cities" and Vondelpark	pages 70-71

Randstad Circle route:
Route 1: River Vecht
Route 2: City of Utrecht
Route 3: The Green Heart
Route 4: Gouda & Kinderdijk windmills
Route 5: Low lands, Delft & City of Glass
Route 6: Hook of Holland & The Hague
Route 7: Holland Coast & Haarlem
Route 8: Tulip fields & Keukenhof
Route 9: Spaarndam & IJmuiden

Northern route (routes 10-12)
Eastern route (routes 13-15)
Southern route (routes 16-19)

Facility Listings

Introduction

Cycling in The Netherlands is a revelation. Not only do you have the run of **35,000 kilometers** of traffic-free **cycle path** (that is well over 20,000 miles!), you'll also be amazed that cycle paths can actually be so **smooth and comfortable** to ride! You'll be treated like a king of the road and can enjoy all those special **cycling-minded traffic rules** the locals take for granted.

Cycling in The Netherlands is for **everyone**, whether you are a **novice cyclist** taking it easy or want to do some **serious mileage**. It is especially great for families with children, as distances between places are small and there is always something to see and do. **Children** particularly love the cycle path infrastructure with its own signage, introducing them to traffic participation in a perfectly safe environment.

Thanks to a **special liability law** (making drivers automatically liable in accidents involving cyclists and pedestrians) and given the fact that most **drivers are cyclists too**, you'll also find Dutch drivers being extremely generous to cyclists.

The most liberating feeling about cycling in The Netherlands might be that **you won't be regarded as a different species** when out on the bike. The difference between "cyclists" or "drivers" just doesn't exist. We are all **people**, regardless of the means of transport we use!

In The Netherlands, **everyone** cycles. Every year, the Dutch people pedal about **15 billion kilometers** and about **14 million journeys** are made by bike **every day**. Nearly **one** out of every **three** journeys is made by bike. That is all done on around **18 million bikes**, which is about a million more than the entire population!

You'll also find that Dutch cyclists **dress for their destination** and **not for the journey.** You won't be pushed to wear yellow vests and helmets, simply because you don't need it. The **only way** to make **cycling really safe** is to **protect** it from the behaviours of **drivers**. The Netherlands has done that. With the **highest level of cycle use** in the western world and with the **lowest risks** per kilometer cycled, it is the safest place to cycle!

All routes in this guidebook can be easily cycled on a **shopper**, but you can also easily bring your **racing bike** with all the gears. Dutch cycle paths are designed for **cycling speed**, rather than walking speed. Pedestrians often have their own pavements. Even if you are a road racer and weary about cycle paths in your own country, you'll find Dutch cycle paths very comfortable.

This book is designed to be a **bridge between cultures**, taking international visitors to the heart of the Dutch cycling culture. The routes in this book allow you to **experience** what the Dutch cycling network really is about. Our routes take you through, but also away from Amsterdam's touristy historic canal belt, to places the locals treasure themselves. We guide you via all those special **landmarks** The Netherlands has on offer, we show you the **best countryside** and take you on the **finest rides** of the country.

At this point, a word of apology has to be made to those **locals** who might be disappointed that this book doesn't cover the whole country of The Netherlands. The provinces of Friesland, Groningen, Drente, Overijssel, Noord-Brabant and Limburg are not covered in this book and in Holland, the cities of Leiden and Rotterdam miss out; **their day is still to come**. Nevertheless, this book with **1,064 kms** (656 miles) of routes covers **six** of the **twelve** Dutch provinces and **three** of the **four** main Dutch cities. Also, this second and fully revised edition honours **Amsterdam** and all its cycling fame with the space it deserves.

The funny thing is that Dutch people just don't understand the excitement of international visitors about the Dutch cycling way of life. Dutch people grow up and live in a society ruled by bikes. They find it hard to imagine living with a road network ruled by cars and don't realise how special the situation in their country is. For them, scenes as pictured above are perfectly normal!

Besides scenery, landmarks and cycling infrastructure aspects, our routes are also chosen for their **connectivity**. All routes in this book link up together, always allowing you to cycle **all the way**, whether you arrive on a ferry from England, by plane at Amsterdam Airport or by train from Germany or France. Last but not least, this book tells you everything about cycling in The Netherlands you ever wanted to know. Personally, I hope this book will bring you just as much **cycling joy** as I have experienced since my childhood. Just go and be inspired!

Eric van der Horst

AMSTERDAM ROUTES

Labels on map: Koog-Zaandijk Station, E-routes, Central Station, D-routes, Lake Markermeer, Pampus (via ferry), C-routes, Weesp Station, Amstel Station, B-routes, Abcoude Station, A-routes, F-routes, Sloterdijk Station, Schiphol Airport (and Railway Station)

Route summaries

With the routes in this guidebook, you could have up to three weeks of relaxed cycling fun. Our main six routes in and around **Amsterdam** are a great first introduction to cycling in The Netherlands and allow you to make various day trips from **one base**. All Amsterdam routes start and end at Amsterdam Central station, with various lengths to please everyone.

The **Amsterdam routes** are marked A,B,C, D, E and F and their individual sections can be combined as you please. Routes A, C and F are mostly urban. Routes B, D and E take you well out of the city boundaries, with rides locals like to make on sunny days themselves. The six routes together provide 232 kms (143 miles) of cycling fun, see pages 30-71 for full info.

Once you are ready for some cycle touring (cycling from one accommodation to another), you can spend your second week in The Netherlands on our **Randstad Circle route**, which starts and ends in Amsterdam and also links with all ferry ports to/from the United Kingdom. Note this 337 kms (208 miles) circular includes various **day-trip itineraries** with easy access by train from Amsterdam, such as a **tulip fields route**, the **Holland Coast** route and the **Kinderdijk windmills** near **Gouda**, see pages 72-117.

Our **Northern**, **Eastern** and **Southern routes**, all linking with the Randstad Circle route (and thus with Amsterdam), provide another 428 kms (264 miles) of routes; good for another week of great cycling! When completing the Northern route, you could easily move onto the Eastern route, followed by one transfer by train to start the Southern route, see pages 118-155.

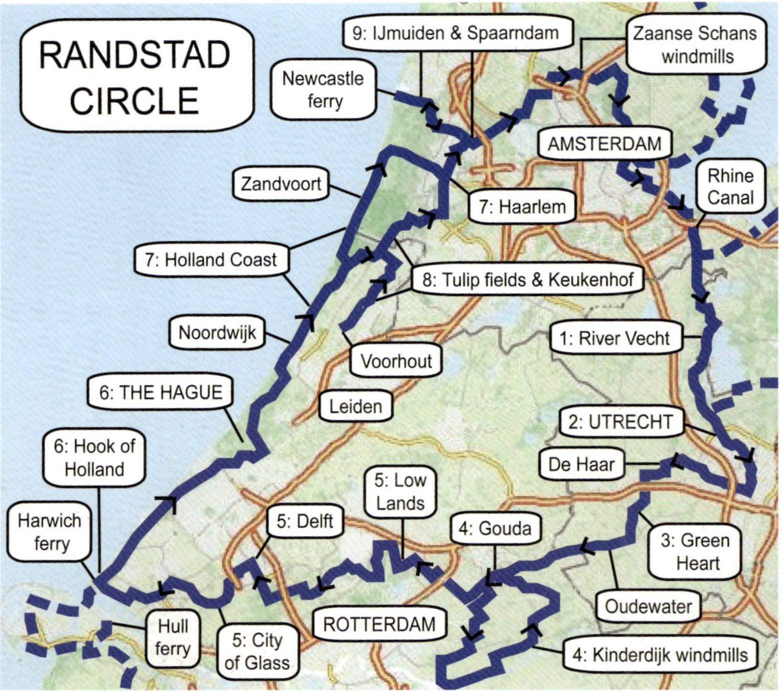

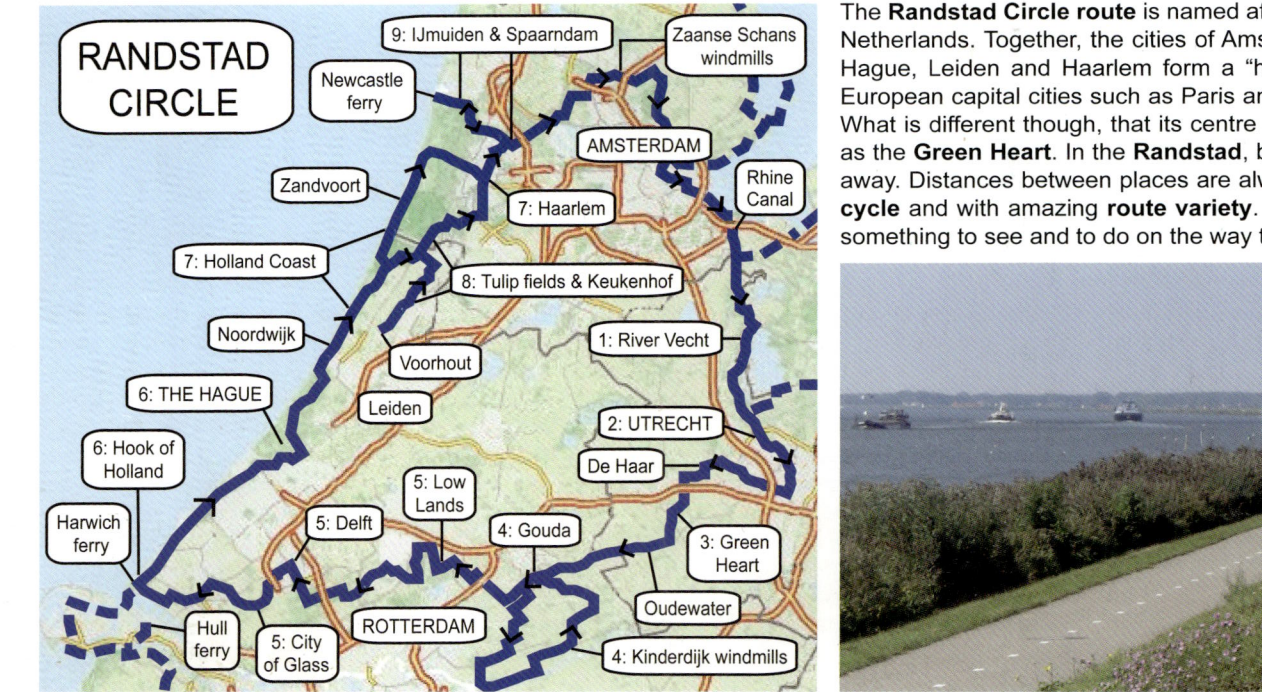

The **Randstad Circle route** is named after the central urban zone of The Netherlands. Together, the cities of Amsterdam, Utrecht, Rotterdam, The Hague, Leiden and Haarlem form a "horseshoe"-shaped city, equalling European capital cities such as Paris and London in size and population. What is different though, that its centre is **rural**. This area is aptly known as the **Green Heart**. In the **Randstad**, both urban and rural are never far away. Distances between places are always on a **human scale, easy to cycle** and with amazing **route variety**. Also for children, there is always something to see and to do on the way to break up the cycling.

RANDSTAD CIRCLE

- Zaanse Schans windmills
- Rhine Canal
- IJmuiden & Spaarndam
- AMSTERDAM
- 1: River Vecht
- 2: UTRECHT
- De Haar
- 3: Green Heart
- Oudewater
- 4: Kinderdijk windmills
- Newcastle ferry
- 7: Haarlem
- 8: Tulip fields & Keukenhof
- Voorhout
- 4: Gouda
- Zandvoort
- Leiden
- 5: Low Lands
- 7: Holland Coast
- Noordwijk
- 5: Delft
- ROTTERDAM
- 6: THE HAGUE
- 5: City of Glass
- 6: Hook of Holland
- Hull ferry
- Harwich ferry

On our **Randstad Circle route**, you'll leave Amsterdam southbound via the towpath of the **Amsterdam-Rhine Canal**, where many barges set off on their long journeys to the River Rhine and Germany. Soon, you'll swap waterways and cycle via the **River Vecht**, an idyllic stream where merchants of the Dutch Golden Age built their countryside retreats. The River Vecht route takes you to the city of **Utrecht**, where its scenic Old Canal and one of Europe's tallest medieval church towers mix with countless shopping opportunities. Then, you'll cycle into the **Green Heart**, with its majestic **De Haar Castle** and the original **Witch Weighing scales** of Oudewater.

On farms nearby the pretty city of **Gouda**, you have the opportunity to stock up on authentic Gouda **cheese**. You can also opt for the extra circular ride to the **World Heritage windmills** of **Kinderdijk**. Now heading west, you'll cycle across Holland's lowest lands (6.7 meters below sea level!) and visit another famous Dutch city, **Delft**. Pottery, royal treachery and great scenery are in the mix here, before making your way into the **City of Glass**, an area of greenhouses where the Dutch produce their famous flowers for worldwide export 365 days a year. At **Hook of Holland**, you finally hit the **Dutch coast** and can you look out over the vast **Rotterdam** docklands.

From Hook, you hit the fantastic **Dutch coastal cycling highway**, which allows you to cycle across extensive sand dune systems and with nearly continuous beach access. The city of **The Hague** provides plenty of entertainment on the way, as do seaside resorts as **Katwijk, Noordwijk** and **Zandvoort**. Choose our optional route via the **tulip fields** in April/May, when all is in full bloom, including a visit to the famous **Keukenhof Gardens**. **Haarlem** is the last great Dutch city on the itinerary, providing another great mix of medieval town squares, canals, museums and shops. Via the **Zaanse Schans windmills** the route heads back for Amsterdam.

The **Northern route** takes you from Amsterdam on the eastern shores of the North-Holland peninsula. A dam at the northern tip of the peninsula has closed off the "South Sea" **Zuiderzee bay** from the North Sea since 1932. About half of this vast water basin has been drained to become **Flevoland**. Heading north, the ride of 104 kms (64 miles) via the historic fishing harbours of **Marken** and **Volendam** and scenic towns such as **Edam** (yes, another "cheese town"!), **Hoorn** and **Enkhuizen** should entertain everyone, but the **lake crossing** to **Lelystad** and the continued ride south on the **former seabed** in Flevoland is only for those keen on serious mileage. This extra ride of 68 kms (42 miles) has long, empty and exposed stretches, truly special given its unique nature. From **Enkhuizen** and **Lelystad stations** you can take bikes back on the train to Amsterdam.

EASTERN ROUTE

Labels on map: AMSTERDAM; Breukelen; UTRECHT; 13: Utrecht Ridge National Park; 14: Grebbeberg; 14: River Nederrijn; 14: River Waal; 15: Nijmegen & Hills

The **Eastern route** takes you into the forests and moorlands of **Utrecht Ridge National Park** ("Utrechtse Heuvelrug"). A patchwork of cyclepaths will take you truly above sea level towards **Grebbeberg** and **Arnhem**. This region was involved in a lot of military action during WWII, as the rivers **Nederrijn** and **Waal** proved to be serious barriers for the Allied Forces. Today, the dykes next to these busy waters provide great vistas for cyclists, especially at the bridges into The Netherland's oldest city, **Nijmegen**. This one way ride of 123 kms (76 miles) includes a circular ride from Nijmegen into some **real Dutch hills**!

This circular of 25 kms (15 miles) takes you via the **National Liberation Museum** and is a great day ride in itself. Nijmegen is 1.5 hours by train from Amsterdam; bike rental available from Nijmegen station. Join the full Eastern route from the **Randstad Circle route** near **Breukelen station**.

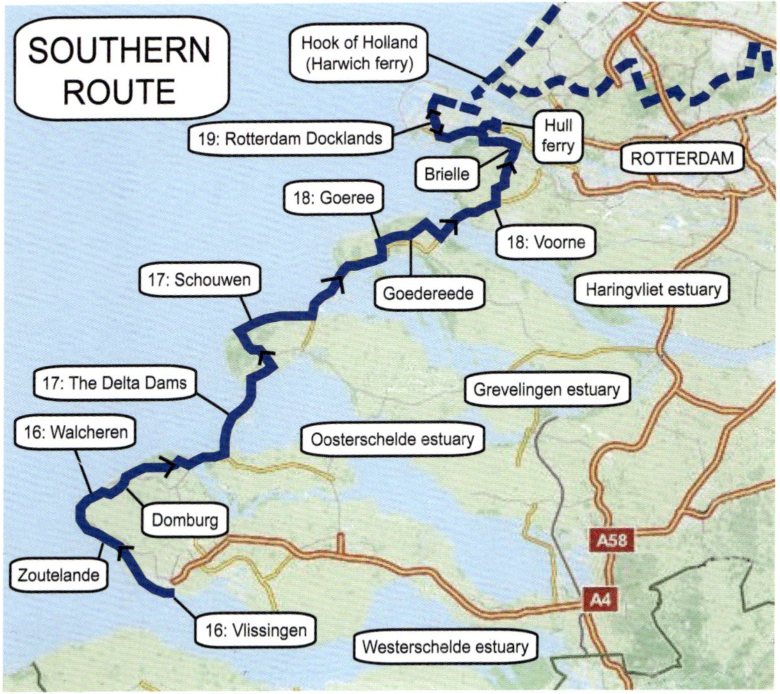

SOUTHERN ROUTE

The **Southern route** offers great coastal cycling, crossing wide estuaries via the most impressive flood barriers of the world. All barriers, built to prevent a repeat of the devestating 1953 floods, carry excellent cycle paths. This spectacular route also contains significant fine riding in sand dune reserves and forests, with plenty of beach access. Small, charming seaside resorts such as **Zoutelande** and **Domburg** can provide pleasant stays. Old towns such as **Goedereede** and **Brielle** are very scenic.

Take bikes on the train to nautic **Vlissingen** ("Flushing" in English) to be able to cycle this one way route of 133 kms (82 miles). This port is about three hours by train from both Amsterdam and Nijmegen. The route connects back onto the **Randstad Circle route** via the vast **Rotterdam Docklands** at Hook of Holland.

Dutch Cycling culture

1890s - 1940s: Adopting the two-wheeled lifestyle

Sometimes you need a stranger to look at something with fresh eyes. Such a person is American writer **Pete Jordan**. Amazed as he was about the Amsterdam cycling culture, he wanted to find out how it all came to be. Searching archives, Jordan found that there was **never** any serious research done into the history of cycling in The Netherlands, so he set off and did it himself. This resulted in the book **In the City of Bikes**, known in Dutch as **De Fietsrepubliek**. If you are interested in the Dutch cycling culture, this book is a must, as are the **"Bicycle Dutch" YouTube and Wordpress Blogs** posted by **Mark Wagenbuur**. Both authors have delivered ground-breaking research on this topic and this chapter couldn't have been written without it. Even the author of **this book** believed, as do most Dutch people, that the Dutch cycling infrastructure had "always been there". Growing up in the 1980s, he was simply not aware that he was part of a unique **cycling revolution** himself!

Logo of the "Bicycle Dutch" videos/blogs and Jordan's book

The history of cycling in The Netherlands starts in the **1890s**, when bicycles were a novelty, only affordable for the **wealthy**. The bike initially attracted the same upper class that was attracted to horse riding and the first riding schools were initiated by the same concept. Trainees practised for months in large indoor arenas before embarking out in the real world. There was a general feel of **uneasiness** with cycling, which was also experienced by the Dutch heir to the throne. Princess Wilhelmina was forbidden to learn how to ride by the government, as cycling was perceived to be dangerous (putting the continuity of the Dutch Royal family at stake!).

It was actually WWI which brought cycling to the masses. From **1918**, the Dutch could cheaply import bikes from broke neighbour **Germany**, suddenly making the bike affordable for all. In the compact Dutch cities, the bike proved to be very **practical**. Daily commutes were easy by bike, with travel times matching public transport. In a small country like The Netherlands, the bike was even suitable for intercity-travel. The flat nature of the land and the dense canal infrastructure with its many tow paths provided an incredible route choice. By the **1920s** cycling had become part of daily life. The author's grandparents are enjoying cycling in the pictures above (1930s/1940s).

1950s - 1960s: Cycling pushed to the margins

Well into the 1950s, the bicycle remained the best way to get around. A **growing economy** and **increasing wealth** also meant though that **cars** became affordable for more and more people. Just as anywhere else, the Dutch authorities saw the car as the future means of transport. Roads were built and improved. Where built **new**, roadside **cycle paths** were **incorporated** in the road design, not so much for the comfort of cycling, but to make for **comfortable driving**.

On existing roads however, there was **no space** allocated for cycling and conditions worsened quickly. By the **1960s**, most through roads in Dutch towns and cities were completely dominated by motorised traffic. Highway departments were transforming old town squares into car parks and buildings were demolished to create inner-city dual carriageways. Those who kept cycling were pushed to the margins, especially on old routes without cycle provision.

It may have been the combination of cycle paths alongside new main roads, the natural dense network of canal-side routes and the flat nature of the country that made cycling conditions still acceptable for a core group of people. Although figures of cycling participation dropped by 6% annually by the end of the 1960s, there was still a large number out on bikes. Sadly, in **1971**, **3,300 people** died in accidents on Dutch roads, of which **400** were **children** under the age of 14.

Schellingwouderbrug in Amsterdam (1957), designed with off-road cycle paths. You can cycle this bridge on Amsterdam route C6, see page 54.

Typical main road in Amsterdam in the 1960s and in the 2000s. Dual carriageways, where cyclists were forced to mix with high volume traffic, have been returned into single carriageways, with limited car parking options. By reclaiming road space, there is space for a safe cycle path and plenty of bike parking on both road sides!

1970s: The great Dutch Cycling Revolution

Stop the Child Murder became the name of a nationwide campaign calling for safer streets for children, with better conditions for walking and cycling. Petitions were signed and handed over to the authorities. Helped by the **Flower Power** and **Hippie** movements of the late 1960s, the campaign became really big. Just a handful of passionate campaigners managed to mobilise large crowds of people. Especially the **Provo political party** became instrumental with their provoking way of finding attention for the cause. In 1965, they made a first public announcement.

"Amsterdammers! The **asphalt terror** of the motorised bourgeoisie has lasted long enough. Every day, **human sacrifice** is made to the Auto-Authority. The smothering carbon monoxide is their incense; their likeness poisons the streets." The party wanted "liberation from the car monster" and stated that the bicycle "symbolises simplicity and cleanliness in contrast to the gaudiness and filthiness of the authoritarian automobile". It led to seven large-scale **cycling demonstrations** in Amsterdam from 1974. The last demonstration in 1978 was attended by 15,000 people on bikes!

Another spark to take cycling seriously was the **1973 oil crisis**. The Netherlands was denied fuel by the Middle East for political reasons. **Petrol** was **rationed** and **car free Sundays** were introduced in an attempt to make further savings. Suddenly, people were reminded how pleasant their streets used to be without cars. When announcing the fuel rationing in an **historic TV-speech**, Prime Minister Den Uyl announced that "the Dutch nation had to change its ways, had to be less dependent on energy and that this was possible without loss of quality of life".

1980s - present: Cycling into the 21st Century

The then Dutch-government deserves credit for not just talking, but also **taking action**. Both **decision makers** and **highway officials**, on **nationwide** and **local level**, showed a **true will to change**. Streets in town centres were **pedestrianised**. In 1975, **pilot projects** were set in the cities of The Hague and Tilburg, where street space was re-allocated for traffic-free cycle paths. Cycling participation on these routes shot up by 30-75%; **build it and they will come!**

Gradually, the **full Dutch road infrastructure** was reviewed. Rather than just resurfacing a road, the **function of the road** in the wider network would be assessed. On **main routes**, **cycle paths** were built to secure safety. On **minor routes**, cycling got priority, by introducing **traffic-calming**, **lower speed limits** and the **removal** of the **centre road line**. Where needed, new **by-pass roads** were built for **cars**, so the **old road** could be dedicated to **cycling**. This system now covers the whole country, ensuring you'll be looked after wherever you travel!

Dutch infrastructure in a nutshell: a road has either priority for cycling or priority for driving. If the priority is for cycling, the road is redesigned to ensure drivers behave as they should (taking drivers out of their comfort zone). If the priority is for driving, cycling is separated from the driving, still allowing comfortable cycling too!

Key to understanding Dutch infrastructure is that it is constantly under review. Also in The Netherlands, the call for more tarmac for cars has never gone away. Besides cycle paths, there are also a great many road building schemes. Within this, **cycling always has its place** though. New concepts such as **cycle streets** and **sing-a-song paths** (see pictures), are trialled all the time. To keep people cycling in today's world, it has to be extremely convenient!

The Dutch Cycling Network

Traffic rules

The Dutch cycling network is very conspicuous in the general infrastructure of The Netherlands. Therefore, its traffic rules can be considerably different in comparison to where you are from. Don't behave as a **tourist** who doesn't have a clue and **earn the respect of locals** by knowing what is what. If you want to ride a bike in The Netherlands, reading this chapter is essential!

Cycling on the right-hand side

In continental Europe you keep right on the roads, so you cycle on the right-hand side, whether you are on a road or on a cycle path. If you find cycle paths on both sides of a road, you should be on the path on the right-hand side of the road, unless the paths are designed for two-way travel (often with painted lines in the middle of the path). If you are used to riding on the left, keeping right is a serious blow to your natural reflexes. Be cautious when approaching junctions and work out for yourself where you are supposed to be cycling before making a move!

Use of cycle paths

If there is a cycle path adjacent to a main road marked with the blue round cycle path sign (see top picture left) you **must** use the path. You will not only be honked at by drivers if you don't, but can also be fined for cycling on a main carriageway. Some people may regard this is as non cycle-friendly, but you have to remember that Dutch cycle paths are designed to give you the same speed as if you were cycling on the road. You'll rarely find blind corners, sharp curves or sudden endings on Dutch cycle paths. Only when a path is marked with a sign with the text "fietspad" (see top middle picture), you can choose between the path and riding on the road.

No cycling

Obviously you are not allowed to cycle on motorways or interstates (in The Netherlands these roads have A-numbers). There are also other main roads where cycling is not allowed. In these situations you'll find the "no cycling sign" clearly displayed (see top picture right). Also watch out for **footpaths** where cycling is not allowed. These are marked with blue signs as above, either with a symbol (man walking with child) or with text ("voetpad", footpath in Dutch). Also watch out for signs with texts like "fietsen niet toegestaan", "verboden te fietsen" or "fietsers afstappen". These remarks all mean **no cycling**! Also, never cycle on road-side pavements!

Shared space paths

On cycle paths and roads it is completely acceptable to **ring your bell** to indicate to pedestrians that they should get out of your way. They will normally do this immediately, without the need for you to slow down. Occasionally though, you might find yourself cycling on a **shared space path**. These paths, where walking has priority, will be marked with signs as below, indicating that cycling is permitted ("toegestaan") or that you are a guest ("te gast") on your bike. On these paths you need to give way to walkers!

Use of on-road cycle lanes

Many Dutch roads without cycle paths will have a layout with only one lane for motorised traffic, with wide on-road cycle lanes on both sides of the road. You'll see motorised traffic straddling the cycle lanes to be able to pass each other, but drivers are NOT allowed to enter the cycle lanes if there is a cyclist there. This eliminates the risks of close overtaking from behind by drivers. On these roads you'll also find further traffic-calming in place. When cycling, you keep in the cycle lanes. If wide enough, you can cycle two abreast.

Priority issues - clearly marked junctions

If a cycle path crosses a road, it varies whether the cyclist on the crossing has priority or the traffic on the road. You'll need to get used to reading the **triangle "give way" markings**, also known as **shark teeth**. These are marked on the road surface or with "give way" signs. You'll also see these markings on junctions of cycle paths.

One of the key conveniences of Dutch cycle paths is that you often have **priority over turning traffic in and out of side roads**. This means you do not need to worry about turning traffic when on a cycle path; the drivers are trained to look for you! Be aware though that there are some busier side roads where cyclists have to give way. Once again, you'll find clear markings showing what the situation is. At **roundabouts**, you either have priority or have to give way as a cyclist. Once again, refer to the road markings!

At junctions with **traffic lights** you normally have to press a button to get a green light. If all the lights are flashing amber, it means that the lights are not in use. In that case, the on-road give way markings take over to show who has priority!

In all the examples above, the give way triangles (shark teeth) are pointing towards you. This means that you have to give way, whether it is traffic on another cycle path or the road. In the right picture, you have to press the button to flash amber. If the lights happen to flash amber, you'll need to give way; see the triangles!

This series of pictures shows how you can have priority when cycling on a cycle path, whether the path is next to a roundabout or crosses a road. In the right picture, the triangle signs in front of the car make the car wait!

Priority issues - junctions without markings

On junctions without any markings, the old "continental" rule still applies that **traffic from the right goes first**. So, even if your road or path keeps going straight on and the road or path from the right ends, traffic from the right goes first. It is very likely you'll be caught out by this, so we have included some **reminders** in our route directions, where space allows this.

In this picture, there are multiple roads from the right ending on the road straight on, but, as there are no road markings, all traffic from the right has priority!

One-way streets

On most one-way streets, you are allowed to cycle in both directions. If you see a "no entry" sign with below the text "uitgezonderd" (meaning "except") you can cycle both ways (see picture).

Tram tracks and railway crossings

Be careful crossing tram and train tracks. Steer your wheel reasonably straight across and never sharp diagonally to prevent your wheels getting stuck in the tracks. In cities, turning trams have always priority. At railway crossings, you must wait when any lights flash red. If there is a white light flashing (or none), you can cross safely.

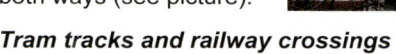

Mopeds, scooters and electric bikes

No country is perfect and the Dutch cycle network has one particular hazard; the legal use of mopeds, scooters and small cars (for use by the disabled) on most cycle paths. Also, electric bikes are becoming increasingly popular. On Dutch cycle paths, a speed limit of 45 km/h (30 mph) applies, but mopeds, scooters and electric bikes can go faster. This causes nuisance and hazardous situations, especially in urban areas.

On some paths you'll find speed bumps, also to slow racing cyclists down. There is a public campaign going to reduce the speed limit on cycle paths to 25 km/h, but it will take time until this will come into force. If you hear or see a fast scooter, moped, electric bike or racing cyclist approaching, keep cycling in a straight line and do not suddenly change direction. If turning at a junction, give a bold, clear hand signal.

Bollards

Be on your guard for permanent bollards on cycle paths. There are also bollards that sink and rise from below the road surface. You'll find these on bus routes and in shopping streets; be wary!

Cycle Route signage

Dutch signs with cycle route information form a world of their own, leaving international visitors confused and impressed at the same time. Cycling is more fun if you understand the various signage systems, so here we go!

To start, the general road signs with white lettering on a **blue** background mostly apply to motorised traffic only (see picture top left).

At nearly every junction, you'll find additional cycle route signs with **red lettering** on a **white background** (see picture bottom left). These signs often show the distance to a destination in kilometers and always show the most direct route. These routes are often not the most scenic routes. If there is a more pleasant (but longer) route to the same destination, the sign will show this in a **green italic font**. Once the name of a destination appears on a sign, you can be sure you'll be guided all the way to that destination.

In some areas, especially in the coastal sand dune reserves and moors and forests towards the east of the country, you'll find many so-called **mushroom signs**. These are signs near ground level and in the shape of a mushroom. Lettering is in a small font, so you have to slow down to be able to read them. They have the same function as the regular signs at eye height. All mushroom signs have a unique number on their base and detailed maps show these numbers.

Another system is the **LF-network**, designed for long-distance, scenic touring. All numbered LF-routes are signposted in both directions of travel, either with adjective "a" or "b". The oldest LF-route is North Sea Route LF1, originally running between Bologne Sur Mer in France and Den Helder in The Netherlands.

Another signage system that covers the whole country is the **junction-network**. In this network, junctions where multiple routes come together are numbered, rather than the routes themselves. In between the numbered junctions, you'll only find signs pointing you towards the next numbered junction. Once you've made your way to the next numbered junction, an overview map will show you various other numbered junctions nearby.

This system allows incredible route and distance flexibility in comparison to numbered routes. The numbered junctions are called **knooppunten** in Dutch. Signs with the text "u nadert knooppunt" mean "you are approaching junction". This book refers in its route directions to a knooppunt (junction) as "KP". On our maps, they are shown in the same style as on the road signs.

Sign of junction "knooppunt (KP)" 65. To get to junction 64, you go straight on, for junction 58, turn right. Below an example of an overview map at KP 47.

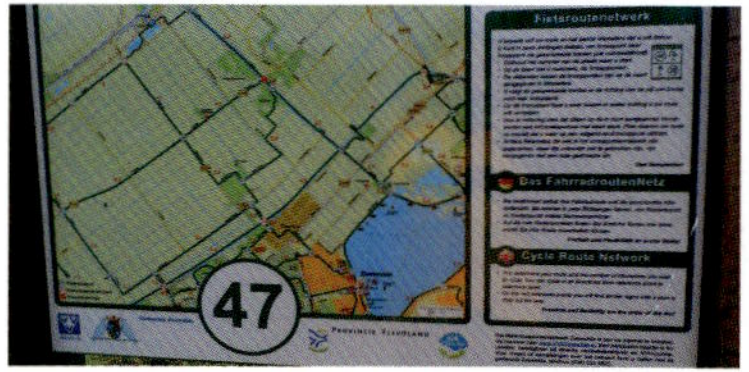

Cycling below sea level

*I was born in a valley of clay, grew up next to the cows and the hay
Where the wind blew the rye, where you looked up at the sky
Where we travelled on bikes, thanks to the dykes, dykes, dykes*
("Dankzij de dijken" by Freek de Jonge, translated from Dutch)

More than a third of the land area of The Netherlands lies well below sea level. Much of the country naturally consisted of reed swamps, protected from the North Sea by a ridge of sand dunes. These sheltered areas were gradually made suitable for agriculture, but rising sea levels and decaying peat and clay resulted in subsidence of the land. To protect the land from flooding, the first dykes were built about a thousand years ago. The creation of a unique patchwork of dams, dykes and artificially drained land had begun. The invention of the windmill in the 17th century made it possible to reclaim inland lakes into "polders". This practice continued (with modern technology) until 1968. Flevoland, "the biggest land grab of all" (see pages 9 and 126-129) became the last polder to be created.

21

Travel information

Flying to Schiphol Airport and using Amsterdam as a base

Amsterdam Schiphol Airport is one of Europe's major airports. If you wish to **bring your own bike on a plane**, your airline will require you to pack your bike in a cardboard box. You'll need to turn the handlebars and to take off the pedals and the wheels. With our **Amsterdam Route A** you can cycle between the airport and the city centre (travel time one hour, see pages 30-39). You can also take your bike on the train to/from Central Station (travel time 20 minutes). If you are looking for **bike boxes** for your flight home; these are for sale at the airport in the basement under Departure Halls 1 and 2 (€23 pp).

Of course you can also **rent a bike** in Amsterdam. Listings of bike rentals on our Amsterdam routes can be found on page 156. All have easy access by tram from Central Station. Avoid renting bikes with coaster brakes (braking by pedalling backwards). If you only intend to make short journeys over a couple of days, a 3-speed bike will do the job. If you intend to leave the city, going on longer rides, do **not** go for the cheapest. Rent a 6 or 7-speed aluminium hybrid to ensure comfortable journeys. Expect to pay up to €15 pp per day for such bikes. Be ready to leave your passport or credit card at the rental as a deposit. Also purchase the extra **theft cover**, because the risk of **bike theft** in The Netherlands is high, wherever you are. Whether you rent or ride your own, have a **good lock** on your bike. Always lock up to a secure object and obey "no bike parking" signs (see picture top right). **Guarded bike parks** (see picture left) are marked on our maps with **P**-symbols (about €1 pp or free!).

At guarded bike parks you can also **store bikes safely overnight**. You might need this service, as urban accommodations may **not** be able to store your bike overnight. Please check when making your booking. The choice of accommodation in Amsterdam is overwhelming, with all types (hotel, B&B, backpacker, camp site, home swap) available. In the context of this book, we have only listed YHA hostels and campsites near the city centre. All others can easily be searched on the internet. Try to book a place near Central Station, as all our Amsterdam routes start/finish there. Consider a stay in nearby peaceful North Amsterdam ("Noord"), with easy access via free ferries from Central Station. The **Amstel Botel** (see map page 69 and listings) is such a place, but bikes will need to be stored at Central Station.

Travelling by ferry and touring by bike & train

North Sea **ferry crossings** between The Netherlands and The United Kingdom have long sailing times (the quickest being six hours). Night crossings are most convenient, as you travel while you sleep. If you bring your own bikes from the United Kingdom, seriously consider leaving your car near your UK ferry terminal (or travel by train or cycle to the ferry). Travelling with bicycles only is easy and much cheaper than bringing a car. Wherever you sail from, all Dutch ferry ports are directly linked to our Randstad Circle Route, so you can immediately start cycling and make your way to Amsterdam by bike as you wish:

Ferry Harwich - Hook of Holland:
Southern England, South Wales & Midlands: www.stenaline.com, see page 96. *Only Hook has a station and bike rental next to the terminal!*
Ferry Hull - Rotterdam Europoort:
North Wales, Midlands, Lancashire & Yorkshire: www.poferries.com, see pages 96, 154, 155.
Ferry Newcastle - Amsterdam IJmuiden:
Northern England and Scotland: www.dfdsseaways.co.uk, see pages 114, 116.

Once you head beyond our Amsterdam routes, you are likely to be cycling from one accommodation to another. Our **services listings** from page 157 onwards provide an overview of many hotels, B&Bs, hostels, camp sites, bike repair shops and bike rentals en-route, see for further guidance pages 26-28. An alternative way of providing for your accommodations is a membership with the **Friends on the Bike** ("Vrienden op de fiets") charity. This charity's address book allows you to contact 5000 Dutch cycling enthusiasts directly and to stay overnight in their homes at a cost of max €20 pp per night. Sign up well in advance prior to your trip via www.vriendenopdefiets.nl. A membership costs just €10 pp per year.

You can easily skip route sectors by taking **bikes on trains**. Relevant railway stations are listed at the start of every route section and are shown on our maps. Dutch railways (www.ns.nl) only carry folded bikes for free. A **bicycle day ticket** ("dagkaart fiets") costs €6 pp, providing unlimited mileage on the day of purchase. No bikes on trains Monday-Friday from 6.30 - 9 am and 4.30 and 6 pm. At weekends and during July and August, you can take bikes on the train at anytime. Do **not** purchase the widely promoted "ov-chipkaart", as its system is designed for regular commuting. Just buy tickets for the day (with built-in chip) from a ticket boot or machine and validate it by "checking in" at platform gates.

Preparing for your trip: weather and equipment

If you plan to visit The Netherlands for a sufficient amount of bike riding, it is best to visit from **May to September**. The country has a moderate maritime climate with cool summers and mild winters. Hot days with high humidity, with lightning storms towards the end of the day, are increasingly common in July/August. Otherwise, rainfall is spread equally over the year, with October until February being the wettest months; always have a rain coat at hand!

If you intend to do some **urban day rides** only, you can visit anytime, but be prepared for light frost between November and March. Gloves, scarf and hat are essential during these months. Between November and February, **daylight** is limited between 8 am and 5 pm, whereas in summer, daylight lasts between 5 am and 10 pm. If you intend to visit the **blooming tulip fields** and plan your trip further in advance, you are up for a bit of a gamble. The tulips only bloom over a period of four weeks every year. This occurs anytime between March and May, depending on the "arrival of spring", see also pages 110-113.

The country may be flat, but **wind** is a serious factor that will affect your cycling. Southwesterlies are the predominant wind direction and the routes in this book have been designed to have tailwinds in exposed areas and potential headwinds in more sheltered areas where possible. Dutch cycling commuters like to make laughs about the wind, as it always seems to turn against them, making them to have to pedal against head winds during both their morning and evening journeys. Dutch weather forecasts always include wind forecasts, stating its general direction and force on the **Beaufort scale**. Any wind of scale 4 or up can make hard pedalling in exposed areas. Tail winds can be very enjoyable!

Dutch bikes always come with **mud guards, pannier rack** and **lights**. This type of bike was common everywhere until well into the 1950s, but disappeared when people stopped cycling. In many countries, the **mountain bike** became standard from the 1980s, but the reality is that the mountain bike, with its low handlebars and fat tyres, is not practical for daily or longer journeys. Think again and don't be disrespectful about the appearance of a **Dutch Granny Bike** ("omafiets"). The teenager in the picture rides an aluminium frame of this classic model, including six gears; very comfortable on the flat!

For convenient cycling, look into what is commonly referred to as a **hybrid city bike**, with light weight frame, **at least six gears** and a rack to put **pannier bags** on the rear. If you want to do camping, you might need a rack on your front wheel too, to provide for a second set of pannier bags. If you bring your own bike, a good service at your local bike shop beforehand makes for happy cycling. A puncture kit, with pump, tyre levers and patches will get you a long way.

Dutch delights and Dutch difficulties

This book is entirely focused on cycling and sight-seeing by bike. This means we couldn't include chapters on fine dining, night life and so on. Although we have included as many interesting landmarks on our routes as possible, the information about venues on the way can be very brief. For example, if you want to know more about Amsterdam's Museumplein and the famous **Van Gogh**, **Stedelijk** and **Rijksmuseum** (see page 32), we recommend you also purchase a "Lonely Planet"-style guide. What we do have on this page though is some information about **Dutch customs** of which you must be aware.

In the first place, **credit cards** are not widely accepted. The situation is gradually improving in recent years, but most shops and accommodations still only accept payments by Dutch bank card ("pinnen") or cash ("contant"). You'll end up paying cash most of the time. ATMs or cash machines ("geldautomaat"), accept Cirrus, Maestro, Visa or Mastercard and are widely available. The Dutch are in the **Euro**. You can exchange currencies at "GWK Travelex".

Secondly, **opening times** of Dutch shops are limited from 9 am until 5 pm or 6 pm on weekdays and Saturdays. Monday mornings are notorious for shops not being open until midday. "Shopping nights" are on Thursdays or Fridays (shops open until 9 pm). Trading laws are slowly relaxing, so you'll now find supermarkets open until 8 pm and also on Sundays (until 4 pm). Any other Sunday shopping is also limited to once or twice per month, except in tourist areas like in Amsterdam. 24-hour "super stores" and/or corner shops are truly unknown; shop on time!

Also, be ready for some **poor customer service** at some stage of your holiday. Shop keepers can show little interest in their customers. Change gets rounded up or down the next 5 Euro Cent and some shops even refuse to take 1 and 2 Euro Cent coins, despite it being legal tender.

Public toilets hardly exist and if these exist, you'll have to pay. Bars and restaurants will often require you to place an order, for you to be able to use their toilets. Otherwise, they'll expect you to pay by putting coins on a saucer at the toilets.

So what about the good stuff then? Well, most Dutch people speak **English** and you shouldn't have trouble finding yourself understood. You'll also enjoy the **liberal** approach to life, which reflects in various government policies. You may be pulled out by "Dutch directness" and the fact that the Dutch don't do queuing. More typical Dutch habits on www.stuffdutchpeoplelike.com.

If you want to go Dutch with **food**, you could start with chocolate sprinkles on your bread for breakfast. Dutch bakeries are a delight, with plenty of fresh choice. Have a slice of apple pie ("appeltaart") or cherry pie ("kersenvlaai") mid-morning, followed by a pizza-size pancake for lunch in a pancake restaurant. For dinner, go to a "snackbar" for chips ("patat") with mayonaise and a deep-fried meat snack from a self-service coin-operated box. The colonial era has left the Dutch with a distinct taste for Indonesian food, so you could also try a "rijst tafel" (various rice dishes combined) in a restaurant. Get some custard ("vla") from the shop as desert. On this diet, keep cycling all day to burn those calories!

How to use this book

This guidebook contains 1064 kms (656 miles) of routes. All route directions are written in such a way that you do not need a bike computer or navigation device. Just clip this book in a standard handlebars map holder and off you go!

The maps on a page always match the route directions on the same page, with visitor information scattered around it. Simply browse through the visitor information beforehand and pick the route(s) of your choice; for a summary of all routes, see pages 3 and 6-11. Once you are on your way and a route section ends, you'll always find the next connecting route mentioned (sometimes there are multiple), referring to the page(s) where you should continue reading.

Note most routes have only **one-way directions**, with the prevailing wind directions and overall connectivity in mind. Of course you can also cycle the routes in the opposite direction by using the book's maps and/or our **GPS-tracks**. GPS-tracks can be ordered from our website and can easily be downloaded via a computer, laptop or tablet onto your outdoor navigation device.

Our routes consist of two types. The six **Amsterdam main routes** are numbered A, B, C, D, E and F; all with individually numbered sub-sections, such as A1, A2, A3, etc. These individual sub-sections can be combined as you please. On the first page of every individual Amsterdam main route, you'll find suggested itineraries. For example; to cycle route F, you could do a circular route from Central Station when using sub sections E1 + F1 + A9 + A3, totalling to 15 kms (9 miles), see page 70.

The routes **away from Amsterdam** are numbered 1-19 and are either part of our **Randstad Circular, Northern, Eastern** or **Southern** routes. Of course, this network is far less dense then our Amsterdam routes, but there are still occasions on which you can choose different route options. On the Amsterdam routes, you can make up your mind on the go, but on all other routes, you'll need to **plan ahead**. Outside of Amsterdam, you'll be on your way for quite a while after making a route choice.

30 km/h (20 mph): "Safely home to your door mat"

To help you with your choice of routes, on the first page of every main route section, you'll always find **all railway stations on the way** listed. This allows you to hop on and off trains with bikes more easily, see also page 23. We also provide you with an **estimated cycle time** when cycling the **longest route option**. The **shortest time** listed is for those able to cycle 20 km/h (12 mph) or faster, allowing some time for brief stops for sightseeing. The **longest time** listed is for those cycling with younger children at a pace of 13 km/h (8 mph), with lots of stops on the way for sightseeing, picnics, etc. These timings should be used as a general indication only. Wind and weather conditions can affect your progress!

Also featuring on the first page of every main route section are some pictorials, showing the percentages of different types of cycling conditions: ⬥ (cycle path), ⬥ (quiet road), ⬥ (road with possibly fast moving traffic or regular traffic flow) and ⬥⬥ (busy main road without cycling facilities). You'll see that the first two categories have high percentages all the way, the latter only appearing very occasionally.

Note that we haven't included any **car park information** in the guidebook. We strongly discourage you to **drive** to The Netherlands, as congestion on main roads is very common and the charges of paid parking are hefty. Free on-road parking is generally only available on the outskirts of cities and towns, in residential areas.

Back to the layout of the book, you'll find that all **route directions** are in **telegram style**, using lots of symbols and abbreviations, see the next page for a full glossary. Also note how we only use **kilometers** in the directions, divide by 1.62 to get distances in miles. A cheap **bike computer** on the handlebars, set on kilometers, makes great navigating comfort. If you use a bike computer, keep resetting to zero at the start of every route section as indicated in the directions.

The scale of the **maps** vary per page and every map has the essential clarity to find your way around. The route you are on is always shown as a **continuous line**, with a **black arrow** showing the direction of travel. Connecting routes nearby and suggested routes to nearby facilities are shown as a **dotted line**.

Further, the maps always show everything that is mentioned in the text. Other information is omitted, to keep the maps easy to read. **Waypoints** of the directions are generally pinpointed on the maps, unless we felt that the maps were getting too busy. Also on the maps, you'll find circles with **alphabetical letters**, refering to the location of accommodations and bike shops, which are listed from page 156.

Please note that these **listings** don't intend to provide you with a full overview what is available. Also, the listing of a venue doesn't give any indication of the quality of the service it provides. Venues were selected on their relevancy to the cycle routes. If you find other suitable venues you can recommend or if you find venues shut down, renamed or unsuitable, please let us know (see page 2). We publish all changes (also regarding the cycle routes) on www.cyclinginholland.com. Note that places get booked up, especially in the cities and at tourist places. Book well in advance if possible or call at least ahead on the day of arrival. Travelling "on the go" without reservations is only really possible when camping.

27

Key to used symbols and abbreviations

↑	turn right
↓	turn left
←	straight on
↗	smooth turn right
↖	smooth turn left
↘	sharp turn right
↙	sharp turn left
⇉	first turn right, then immediately left
⇇	first turn left, then immediately right
🚴	cycle path or cycle lane
	quiet road
	road with possibly fast moving traffic or regular traffic flow
	busy main road; an adjacent footpath is always available!
	tourist attraction, view point or location of special interest
	beach or seafront promenade
	shop(s)
	cafe/pub with light refreshments
	pub/restaurant serving meals
	picnic area or bench(es) at prominent location
	hotel or bed & breakfast
	hostel or bunkhouse (YHA = "Stay Okay" or independent)
	campsite
	bike repair shop
P	guarded bike park (only shown on our maps in circles)

(LF 1a)	Long-distance cycle route 1 (numbered and signposted)
(KP 46)	"Knooppunt" = junction 46 (numbered and signposted)
Amsterdam	city, town, village, attraction or rural cafe/shop location
T-jct	T-junction
jct	junction
rndabt	roundabout
ep	at end of path
1st rd	first road
2nd p	second path
lhts	traffic lights
car pk	car park
imm	immediately

Key to used symbols and abbreviations in facility listings:

	quiet location with a minimum of surrounding noise
	noisy location or venue which is potentially noisy itself
	bike repair shop
hire	bike rental
gear	shop specialising in cycling touring gear

Dutch language: key to common words and phrases

To be able to understand a bit of written Dutch, you have to know that a lot of long words are made up by a string of short words. This is especially the case with street names. We have also highlighted some key phrases for conversation, ideal if you want to exchange a word or two with the locals. Your efforts will be greatly appreciated, but don't be offended if they switch to English straight away once they notice that you struggle!

Dutch words and phrases for conversation:

English	Dutch
ATM / cash machine	geldautomaat
bicycle	fiets
bicycles	fietsen
bike repair shop	fietsenmaker
breakfast	ontbijt
bye	tot ziens, dag, doei
can I	kan ik ....
- check in?	inchecken?
- pay?	betalen?
- pay in cash?	contant betalen?
- pay by card?	pinnen?
- make a reservation?	reserveren?
coffee (a coffee)	koffie (kopje koffie)
council	gemeente
cycle path	fietspad
cycling	fietsen
cyclist(s)	fietser(s)
dinner	avondeten, diner
excuse me	sorry
five people	vijf personen
four people	vier personen
good morning	goedemorgen
good afternoon	goedemiddag
good evening	goedenavond
good night	goedenacht
hello	hoi, hallo
lunch	lunch
map(s)	kaart(en)
milk	melk
money	geld
my bike is broken	mijn fiets is stuk
my bike is stolen	mijn fiets is gestolen
night/nights	nacht/nachten
no	nee
one person	één persoon
pay (I'd like to pay)	betalen (Ik wil betalen)
please	alstublieft, alsjeblieft
sugar	suiker
tea	thee (kopje thee)
ticket	kaartje
thank you	dank u, dank je
three people	drie personen
two people	twee personen
yes	ja
where is ....?	waar is ....?
wifi	say "wiffy"

Written Dutch on street signs, etc:

afgesloten	closed
andere richtingen	other directions
auto	car
baan	path, way
binnen	inside, inner
boot	ship
brug	bridge
buiten	outside, outer
burg	fort
centrum	town/city centre
dicht	closed
dijk	dyke
doorgaand verkeer	through traffic
drempels	speed bumps
eiland	island
fietsen niet toegestaan	no cycling
fietsers afstappen	cyclists dismount
gesloten	closed
gracht	canal
groot	great, large
haven	harbour
huis	house, home
kade	quay
kerk	church
klein	small
laan	avenue
langzaam	slow
markt	market
molen	windmill
nieuw	new
noord/noorden	north
omleiding	diversion
oost/oosten	east
oud	old
pad	path
perron	platform
plein	square
pont	ferry
poort	gate
schip	ship
sloot	ditch
slot	castle
slot	lock (on bike)
sluis/sluizen	lock(s) (in canal)
snelweg	motorway, interstate
spoor	tracks, railway
station	station
steeg	alley
straat	street
trein	train
veld	field
veer	ferry
verboden te fietsen	no cycling
verboden toegang	no entry
verkeer	traffic
vliegveld	airport
voetgangers	pedestrians
vracht	freight
wal	embankment
weg	road
welkom	welcome
west/westen	west
werk in uitvoering	road works
wijk	district, estate
winkel	shop
zuid/zuiden	south

29

Amsterdam Route A: City Centre, River Amstel, greenbelts and Schiphol Airport

Stations: *Amsterdam Centraal, Amsterdam Amstel, Schiphol Airport*
Route options:
- Short City Centre circular route: **9 km** (use A1 + A2 + A3)
- City Centre, River Amstel and Vondelpark: **21 km**
  (use A1 + A4 + A5 + A8 + A9 + A3)
- City Centre, River Amstel, Amsterdam Forest and Vondelpark: **28 km**
  (use A1 + A4 + A5 + A6 + A8 + A9 + A3)
- City Centre, River Amstel, both parks and Schiphol Airport: **44 km**
  (use A1 + A4 + A5 + A6 + A7 + A8 + A9 + A3)
Cycling time: 3 - 5 hours (🚴 64%, 🥾 33%, 🚆 3%)

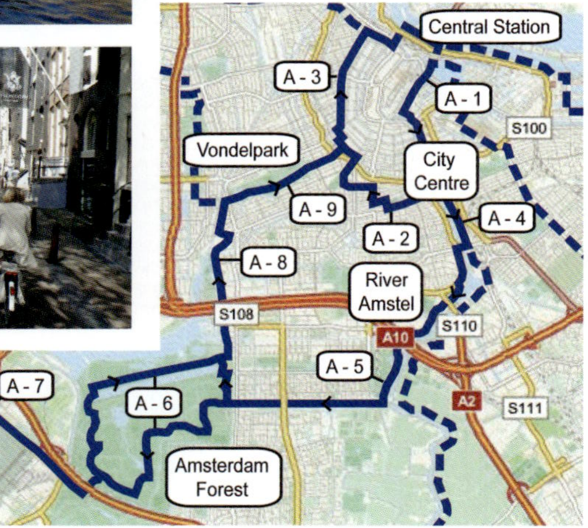

If you have only **one day** for a bike ride in Amsterdam, go for this one. It is our **very best**, taking you via the **River Amstel** into the **greenbelts** of the city and with lots of Amsterdam landmarks to take in along the way. It also provides the finest riding you can find in Amsterdam's **world heritage canal belt.** On our traffic-calmed routes, you'll hardly feel the rush of the local cyclists. The longest route option also calls at **Schiphol Airport.**

The ride starts with a journey via **Nieuwmarkt** ("New Market Square"). In medieval days, this used to be the city's boundary. An impressive city gate still stands today and now houses a stylish cafe. If you start the ride late morning, Nieuwmarkt provides plenty of lunch options. Via Amsterdam's town hall and opera building, the **Stopera**, you'll arrive at the River Amstel.

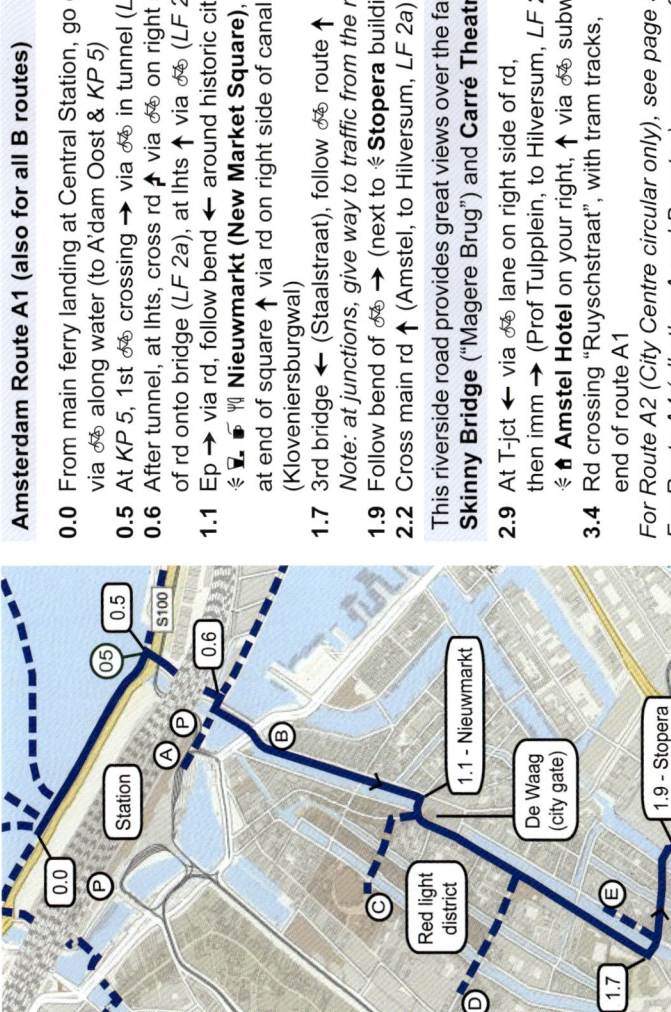

Amsterdam Route A1 (also for all B routes)

- **0.0** From main ferry landing at Central Station, go east via 🚲 along water (to A'dam Oost & KP 5)
- **0.5** At KP 5, 1st 🚲 crossing → via 🚲 in tunnel (LF 2a)
- **0.6** After tunnel, at lhts, cross rd ↱ via 🚲 on right side of rd onto bridge (LF 2a), at lhts ↑ via 🚲 (LF 2a)
- **1.1** Ep → via rd, follow bend ← around historic city gate ⛴🚻🍴🍽 **Nieuwmarkt (New Market Square)**, at end of square ↑ via rd on right side of canal (Kloveniersburgwal)
- **1.7** 3rd bridge ← (Staalstraat), follow 🚲 route ↑
  Note: at junctions, give way to traffic from the right!
- **1.9** Follow bend of 🚲 → (next to ⛴ **Stopera** building)
- **2.2** Cross main rd ↑ (Amstel, to Hilversum, LF 2a)

This riverside road provides great views over the famous **Skinny Bridge** *("Magere Brug") and* **Carré Theatre.**

- **2.9** At T-jct ← via 🚲 lane on right side of rd, then imm → (Prof Tulpplein, to Hilversum, LF 2a), ⛴🏨 **Amstel Hotel** on your right, ↑ via 🚲 subway, ←
- **3.4** Rd crossing "Ruyschstraat", with tram tracks, end of route A1

For Route A2 (City Centre circular only), see page 32.
For Route A4 (all other A and B routes), see page 34.

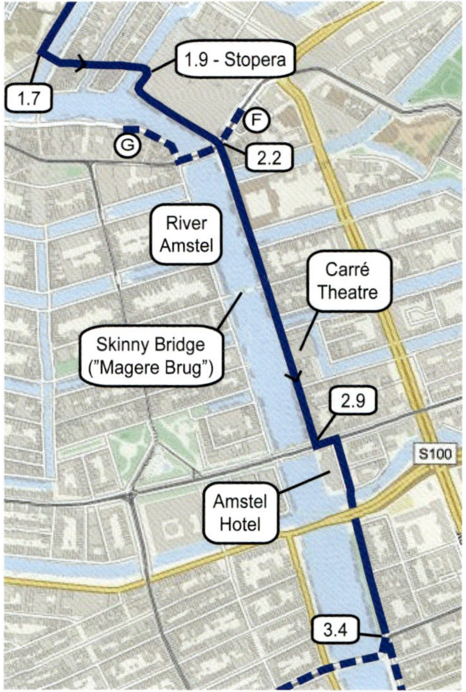

Amsterdam Route A: City Centre, River Amstel, greenbelts and Schiphol Airport

Route A2 takes you into district **De Pijp** with Amsterdam's largest street market, the **Albert Cuyp**. The original **Heineken Brewery** is also nearby. **Van Gogh**, **Stedelijk** and **Rijksmuseum** can all be visited on **Museumplein**. Of course you'll also cycle the famous historic **Rijksmuseum cycle tunnel** (see picture).

Amsterdam Route A2

- **0.0** (3.4) At rd crossing "Ruyschstraat", with tram tracks, ↗ go west via river bridge
- **0.1** After bridge, at jct with lhts, ↑ via 🚲 on right side of rd (Ceintuurbaan), keep ↑ via 🚲
- **0.9** At 2nd jct with lhts (after park on right side) → via 🚲 on right side of rd (Sarphatipark)
- **1.1** Ep (opposite pedestrian street) ← via 🚲 on right side of rd (Eerste Jan Steenstraat)
- **1.3** 1st rd → via 🚲 on right side of rd (Bolstraat)
- **1.4** At slight bend in rd ↑ via 🚲 on right side of rd *(Note:* ✦ **Albert Cuyp Street Market** *on right!)*
- **1.6** At far end of modern round square, cross rd ↓ into quiet rd "Eerste Jacob van Campenstraat" *(For* ✦ **Heineken Experience** ↑*, at lhts* →*)*
- **1.9** After canal bridge, at lhts ↑ via 🚲 onto rd ↑
- **2.1** At next jct → via 🚲 on left side of rd (wide open space ✦ **Museumplein** on your left)
- **2.2** Follow sharp bend ←, then imm → via 🚲
- **2.4** After ✦ **Rijksmuseum** 🚲 **Tunnel** ↑ at lhts
- **2.5** At next jct ← via 🚲 on right side of rd *(LF 20b)*
- **2.8** 1st rd → (Kleine Gartmanplantsoen), end of route A2

Continue with Route A3, see page 33.

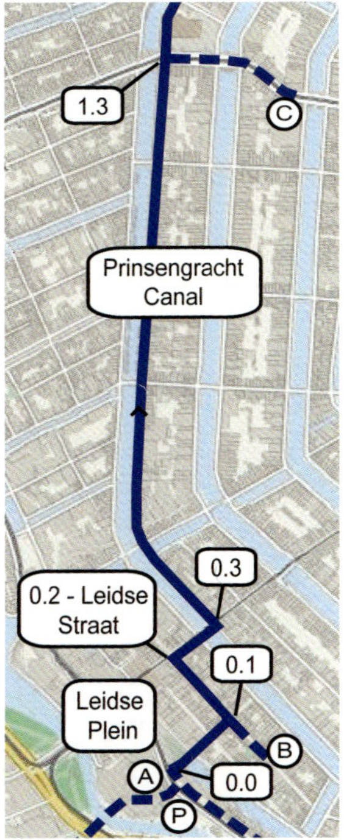

Amsterdam Route A3

The **Prinsengracht Canal** is one of three concentric half-circled canals around Amsterdam's medieval city centre, dug in the 17th century as part of a city expansion scheme. Together with the canals of the scenic **Jordaan District**, these canals are listed as **World Heritage**.

0.0 (2.2 or 2.8) 1st rd → (Kleine Gartmanplantsoen), (Note: ⚑ 🅿 ¶ **Leidse Plein square** on left!), keep ↑
0.1 2nd rd ← (Lange Leidsedwarsstraat)
0.2 *Dismount* at next jct and walk →
into shopping street ⚑ 🅿 ¶ **Leidse Straat**
0.3 After bridge imm ← (⚑ **Prinsengracht**), *start cycling*
Note: at junctions, give way to traffic from the right!
1.3 At jct with lhts, cross main rd ↑ (⚑ **Prinsengracht**)
1.4 ⚑ **Anne Frank Huis Museum** on right side of rd, ↑
2.2 At jct with busier rd → into shopping street
⚑ 🅿 ¶ **Haarlemmerstraat**
2.7 After canal bridge, imm ← via 🚲 into subway
(to Centraal Station)
2.8 Imm subway, 1st 🚲 bridge ← (to Fietsflat),
after bridge ← via 🚲 on left side of rd, into tunnel
3.0 At lhts, cross main rd, then → via 🚲 along water
3.2 Main ferry landing at Central Station, end of route A3

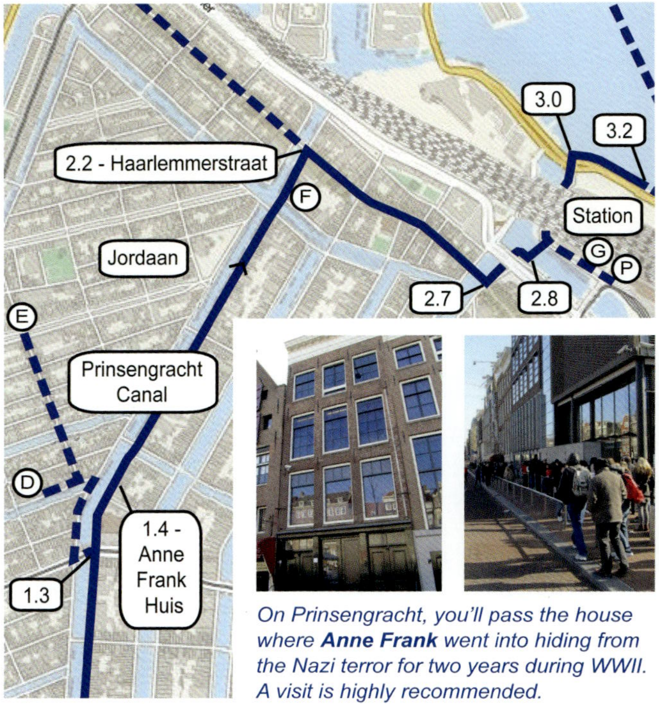

*On Prinsengracht, you'll pass the house where **Anne Frank** went into hiding from the Nazi terror for two years during WWII. A visit is highly recommended.*

Amsterdam Route A: City Centre, River Amstel, greenbelts and Schiphol Airport

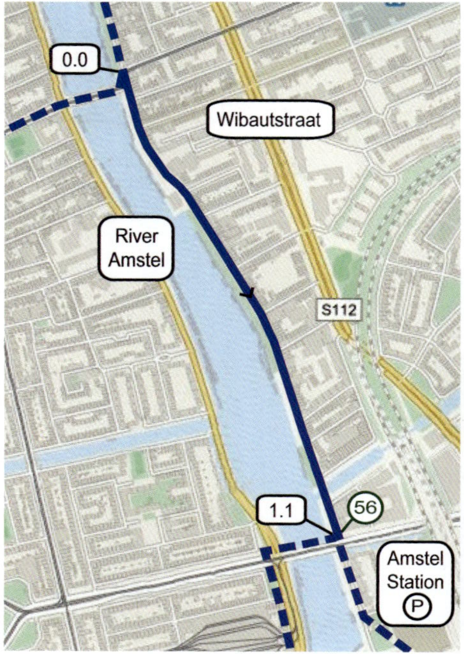

Amsterdam Route A4

0.0 (3.4) At rd crossing "Ruyschstraat", with tram tracks, cross rd ↑ onto one-way rd (Weesperzijde, *LF 2a*), keep ↑
1.1 At jct with lhts, at *KP 56*, at river bridge "Berlagebrug", end of route A4

For Route A5 (all A routes), see page 35.
For Route B1 (all B routes), see page 41.

The **River Amstel** gave Amsterdam its name. At **Dam Square** (not on our routes), this river was dammed at fishing village "Amstelredam" in the 13th century. Since then, various sections of the original river course have been filled in. The River Amstel is technically speaking not a river, but a canal, as its basin is entirely fed by pumping stations. On our route A4, the River Amstel is at its widest, with panoramic views.

Amsterdam Route A5

0.0 *(1.1)* At jct with lhts, at river bridge → via 🚴 on right side of rd (to Amstelveen)
0.1 After bridge, at lhts ← via 🚴 crossings onto 🚴 on right side of rd (Amsteldijk, to Amstelveen)
0.6 After "Riverstaete" building, at lhts, via 🚴 crossing ↖ onto quiet riverside rd (Amsteldijk, to Amstelveen), keep ↑
3.0 ⛲ 🍴 **Amstelpark** *(no cycling in park)*
3.5 At rndabt ↑ (Amsteldijk, to Amsterdamse Bos) 🚴
⛲ 🍴 **Windmill & Rembrandt statue**
3.7 At KP 60, at 🚌 🍴 **Klein Kalfje**, → (Kalfjeslaan, to A'damse Bos & KP 84)
5.3 3rd 🚴 bridge ← and imm → via 🚴, after tunnel ↗ via 🚴 bridge, then ↓ (to Amsterdamse Bos & KP 84)
6.3 At jct with lhts ↑ (to Aalsmeer)
6.5 After tracks, at 2nd jct, end of route A5:
For Route A6 (Circular route Amsterdam Forest and for Airport), see page 36.
For Route A8 (direct route back to city), see "short-cut" in blue box on this page

---

For "short-cut" to route A8 (back to city):
6.5 At 2nd jct after tram tracks → via rd (to Bezoekerscentrum), ep ↑ via "fietspad"
7.0 At jct KP 83 → via middle 🚴 (to KP 81)
7.2 Ep, at ⛲ 🛈 **Amsterdam Forest** ← via 🚴, then cross rd and → via 🚴
7.5 After ⛲ 🍴 **De Bosbaan** end of "short-cut"
For Route A8 (back to city), see page 38

Rural river scenes on Route A5; the **Rembrandt statue**, with the closest rural windmill to the city centre, is a popular coach stop (see picture).

Amsterdam Route A: City Centre, River Amstel, greenbelts and Schiphol Airport

Amsterdam Route A6 is all about the **Amsterdam Forest**. This "Amsterdamse Bos" was created in the 1930s as a labour project. It is a mosaic of wood, grass and reedlands. It features its own 50 km long cycle path network; enough to keep you going for two days!

0.0 (6.5) At 2nd jct after tram tracks ↑ (to "Amsterdamse Manege")
0.8 2nd "fietspad" → (to "Amsterdamse Manege")
1.2 At jct → via tarmac ⌀ (to "Geitenboerderij")
2.1 2nd tarmac ⌀ → (to "Geitenboerderij")
2.7 1st tarmac ⌀ → (to "Geitenboerderij"), keep ←
3.5 Jct with right turn for ⌂ **Geitenboerderij** *(city farm "goat farm")*: *For Route A - 7 (For Schiphol Airport only), see page 37. To continue Route A - 6, reset mileage and read below:*

If you cycled from Schiphol Airport, start reading from here:

0.0 (3.5 or 7.9) Go west via tarmac ⌀ (to "Boerderij Meerzicht")
0.9 At ⌀ T-jct ← via tarmac ⌀ (to "Boerderij Meerzicht")
1.1 1st tarmac ⌀ ← (to "Boerderij Meerzicht")
1.5 At ⌀ T-jct ← via tarmac ⌀ (to "Boerderij Meerzicht"),
1.6 Cross rd ↑ via tarmac ⌀ (no signs), keep ↗
1.8 Cross car park ↑, then ← via tarmac ⌀ (rowing lake on your right)
2.1 At ⌂ ☕ **Boerderij Meerzicht** *(pancake restaurant)* → via tarmac ⌀ (to "Bezoekerscentrum")
4.5 At rd crossing with ⌂ ☕ **Bosbaan cafe** on right, end of route A6
Continue with Route A8 (to city), see page 38.

Amsterdam Route A7
From Amsterdam Forest to Schiphol Airport:

- **0.0** (3.5) At jct with right turn for 🚴🍴 **Geitenboerderij** ← via 🚲 (to Amstelveense Poel)
- **0.4** In between two viaducts → via rd (to Schiphol)
- **1.0** After canal bridge imm ← via 🚲 subway (to Schiphol), keep ↑
- **2.9** At *KP 82*, at jct with lhts ← via 🚲 (see bus station, to Schiphol)
- **3.1** At next jct with lhts follow 🚲 ↑, keep following 🚲 to Schiphol
- **5.6** At 🚲 jct ← via 🚲 (to Terminal)
- **7.2** Imm after jct with lhts ← via 🚲 (to Aankomsthal)
- **7.4** At 🚲 T-jct ← via 🚲 (to Aankomsthal)
- **7.9** End of 🚲, end of route:
  For 🚴🏨🚉☕🍴🛈 **Schiphol** walk ↖

To continue with Route A7 (back to city), see top of this page on the right

Amsterdam Route A7
From Schiphol Airport to Amsterdam Forest & City Centre:

From terminal building, walk ↗, cross area with bus lanes and taxi ranks, on pavement ↗ to 🏨 Sheraton hotel:

- **0.0** (7.9) Join tarmac 🚲, go west
- **0.5** 1st 🚲 → (to Amsterdam)
- **0.7** At jct with lhts → via 🚲 (to Amsterdam)
- **2.3** After tunnel, at 🚲 jct ↗ (to Amstelveen & *KP 82*), keep following 🚲
- **4.8** At jct with lhts, follow 🚲 ↓
- **5.0** At next jct with lhts, *KP 82*, → via 🚲 on left side of rd (to Amstelveen & *KP 97*)
- **6.9** At 🚲 T-jct → onto canal bridge
- **7.5** At T-jct ← via 🚲 on right side of rd (to Amsterdam), follow 🚲
- **7.9** 🚲 jct 🚴🍴 **Geitenboerderij**, end of route A7: continue with Route A6 (see page 36)

*Even if you are not taking your bike on the plane, **Schiphol Airport** is worth a visit. It has an excellent cycle route to the terminal and great viewing areas!*

Amsterdam Route A: City Centre, River Amstel, greenbelts and Schiphol Airport

Amsterdam Route A8

Heading away from the Amsterdam Forest and its giant rowing lake ("De Bosbaan"), you'll cycle by the **Olympic Stadium**, used for the 1928 Olympic Games. From **Haarlemmermeerstation**, **museum trams** of the 1920s era operate on a heritage line into the forest.

- **0.0** *(4.5 or 7.5)* At rd crossing near 🚻 **De Bosbaan**, cross rd and go east via wide 🚲 (to Amsterdam)
- **0.1** Before tram tracks ← via 🚲 (to Amsterdam-West)
- **0.3** Ep ↑ via "fietsstraat", after bridge ↑ via 🚲, keep ↑
- **0.9** Cross motorway slip rd ↑ via 🚲 under viaducts
- **1.3** Cross rd ↑ via 🚲 (Piet Kranenbergpad), keep ↑
- **1.7** 🚻 **Olympic Stadium** *(for access, → via bridge)*
- **2.0** Ep ↑ via rd and keep to 🚲 markings
  Extreme caution: various tram tracks in road surface!
- **2.4** At 🚻 **Haarlemmermeerstation (Museum tram)**, at T-jct, ← via rd *(caution: tram tracks in surface!)*
- **2.5** 1st rd ← (Vlietstraat)
- **2.9** Cross busy rd **Zeilstraat** ↑ (Schinkelkade)
  Note: at junctions, give way to traffic from the right!
- **3.4** At end of rd ↘ to 🚲 junction, end of route A8

Continue with Route A9 (to city), see page 39.

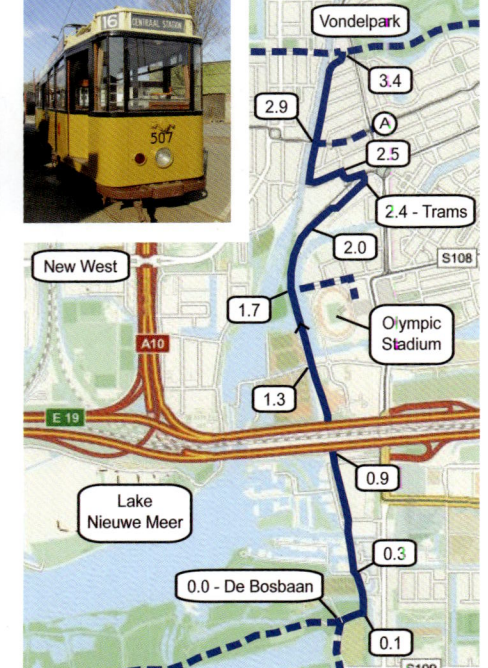

Amsterdam Route A9

The **Vondelpark** is an inner-city park, built in the late 19th century. It was part-funded by the Dutch AA, very much a cyclists' organisation at the time. There were nevertheless many debates on whether cycling should be allowed. The right to cycle in the park was secured in 1897.

0.0 (3.4 or 5.0) At 🚲 jct, go east, at lhts, cross rd ↑ via 🚲 into 🍴 **Vondelpark** (to Centrum), follow 🚲 ↑ (*LF 20a*)

Note: this path is a busy shared route; try to keep right where possible, but try to overtake pedestrians on the left

1.2 (For 🍴 ☕ 🍽 **Blauwe Theehuis** walk ↖, after 100m)

1.6 Follow 🚲 route ↗ into subway (For 🍴 ☕ 🍽 **Vertigo** ↖, after 50m)

2.1 Ep, at lhts, cross rd ↑ onto 🚲 bridge (to Centrum), follow 🚲

2.2 Ep ← via 🚲 on right side of rd (Weteringschans), imm 1st rd → (Kleine Gartmanplantsoen), end of route A9

Continue with Route A3, see page 33.

Amsterdam Route B: River Amstel, Amstelland and East Corridor

Stations: Amsterdam Centraal, Amsterdam Amstel, Abcoude, Weesp
Route options:
- *River Amstel, Rural Amstel - short (to Abcoude station):* **20 km**
  (use A1 + A4 + B1+ B2 + B4)
- *River Amstel, Rural Amstel - long (to Abcoude station):* **31 km**
  (use A1 + A4 + B1+ B3 + B4)
- *River Amstel, Rural Amstel (short) & Gein (to Weesp station):* **29 km**
  (use A1 + A4 + B1+ B2 + B4 + B5 + C4)
- *River Amstel, Rural Amstel (long) & Gein (to Weesp station):* **40 km**
  (use A1 + A4 + B1+ B3 + B4 + B5 + C4)
- *River Amstel, Rural Amstel & Gein (short) and East Corridor:* **39 km**
  (use A1 + A4 + B1+ B2 + B4 + B5 + B6)
- *River Amstel, Rural Amstel & Gein (long) and East Corridor:* **53 km**
  (use A1 + A4 + B1+ B3 + B4 + B5 + B6)

Cycling time: 3 - 5 hours (🚲 28%, 🚶 71%, ⛴ 1%)

In "peat-country" **Amstelland**, just south of Amsterdam, the **River Amstel** and tributaries such as **Waver**, **Holendrecht** and **Gein** form a patchwork of scenic waterways. Guided by leafy country lanes on old Dutch dykes, lined with dairy farms, you'll cycle via **Ouderkerk** and **Abcoude** towns. Various **one way routes** take you from Central station to Abcoude or Weesp stations (back by train). Cycle **"full circle"** via the **East Corridor** to experience the **full continuity of Dutch urban main cycle routes**.

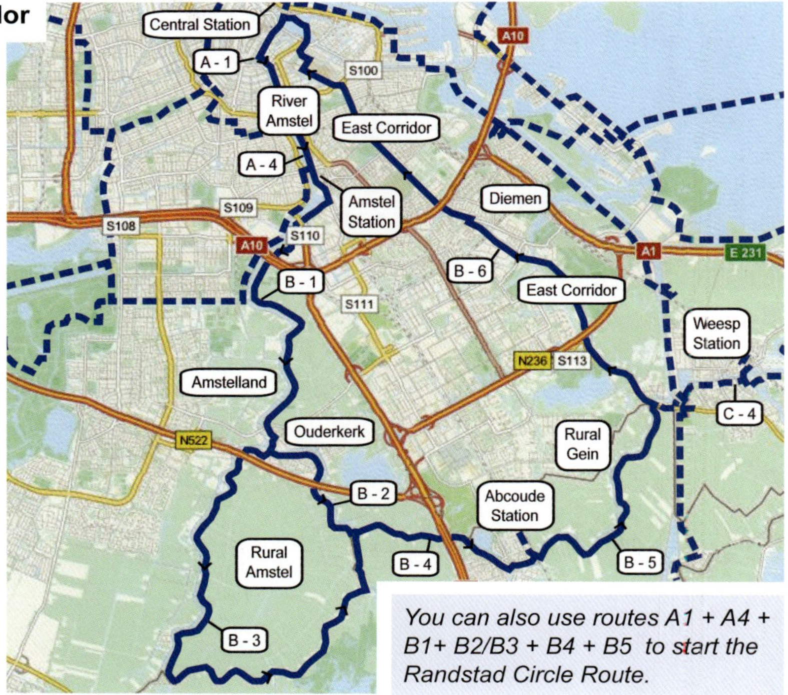

You can also use routes A1 + A4 + B1+ B2/B3 + B4 + B5 to start the Randstad Circle Route.

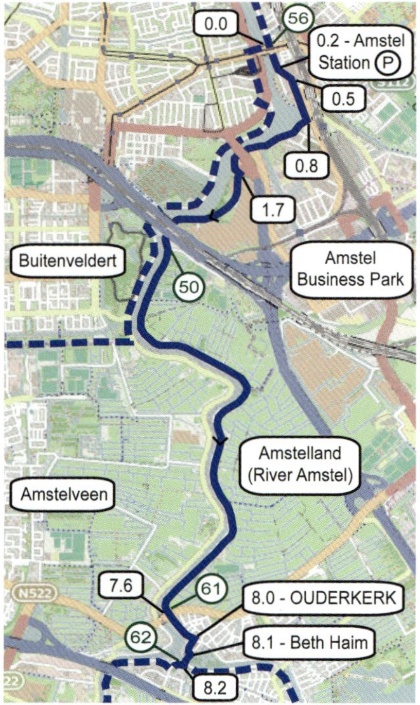

Amsterdam Route B1

To get from Central Station to the start of route B1, first cycle route A1 and A4, see pages 31 and 34. Alternatively, start route B1 directly from Amstel Station (head for Amstel river side to join the route).

- **0.0** *(1.1)* At jct with lhts, at river bridge "Berlagebrug" go south via riverside 🚲 (Weesperzijde, to Hilversum, *LF 2a*)
- **0.2** At next jct ↖ via 🚲 (to Hilversum, *ignore LF 2a*)
- **0.5** Ep, at rndabt ↑ via 🚲 on right side of rd (to Ouderkerk a/d Amstel, *LF 2a*)
- **0.8** After canal bridge, 1st 🚲 → (Korte Ouderkerkerdijk, *LF 2a*), keep ↑
- **1.7** Ep (after viaduct over rd) → via rd (to Ouderkerk a/d Amstel, *LF 2a*), at *KP 50* ↑
- **7.6** At *KP 61*, at jct with lhts ↑ via 🚲 crossing (to Ouderkerk a/d Amstel & *KP 62*)
- **8.0** In ☕ 🍴 🍺 🍽 **Ouderkerk a/d Amstel**, at pub "Heineken - De Vrije Handel", → (Kerkstraat)
- **8.1** At end of square ↗ (see ⛪ **Beth Haim Cemetery** imm on left side of rd) ⛴
- **8.2** At *KP 62*, at jct after bridge, end of route B1

For Routes B2 and B3, see page 42.

The scene of the **River Amstel** changes dramatically on this route section. The **Amstel Station** area, with its modern skyscrapers (see picture left), marks the end of the inner-city scene. Immediately after passing under the Amsterdam orbital motorway, the horizon widens. It is a pleasant ride to **Ouderkerk**. Its monumental buildings and old bridges are a reminder of the fact that this town is about 200 years older than Amsterdam. **Beth Haim** is the oldest **Jewish cemetery** of The Netherlands, established in 1614 by refugees from Portugal. This cemetery has over 28,000 graves.

Amsterdam Route B: River Amstel, Amstelland and East Corridor

Amsterdam Routes B2 and B3 take you to bridge **De Voetangel** and its cafe, but route B3 is 10.5 km longer than route B2. Both routes keep to scenic riverside routes. The **Ronde Hoep polder** perfectly shows Dutch reclamation practices of the 1100-1300s, when peat swamps were transformed into agricultural land. Farmers of the **River Waver** were known for their wealth. **Botshol Reserve** is good for bird-watching.

Route B2:

- **0.0** (8.2) Imm after river bridge, at *KP 62*, ← (Ronde Hoep Oost, to Abcoude, *LF7a*), keep ↑
- **3.1** At 🛏 🍴 **De Voetangel**, at *KP 69*, ← via bridge, end of route B2, *continue with Route B4*

Route B3:

- **0.0** (8.2) Imm after river bridge, at *KP 62*, ↑ (Ronde Hoep West, to *KP 1*)
- **0.1** 1st rd → (Achterdijk, to *KP 1*, *LF2a*), ↑
- **0.8** After motorway viaduct ↗ (to *KP 1*, *LF2a*), ↑
- **9.3** At *KP 2*, cross 1st rd bridge ↑ (Waverdijk), continue on other river bank (to *KP 50*)
- **12.4** 1st rd bridge ← to *KP 50* and imm ←, then imm ↗ via dead end rd (Dwarskade, to *KP 69*)
- **13.1** 1st 🚲 ↖ (to *KP 69*)
- **13.8** Ep, at bridge 🛏 🍴 **De Voetangel** and *KP 69*, end of route B3, *continue with Route B4*

Amsterdam Route B4

At **Voetangel Bridge** you'll leave the River Waver route and join the **River Holendrecht** route. The pleasant scenery stays much the same, although the noise of a nearby motorway-intersection can be distracting. The River Holendrecht meanders southeast though, away from the nearby Amsterdam Zuidoost developments, into scenic **Abcoude**; another town with monumental buildings and scenic church square. You cross the **Amsterdamse Straatweg** here, the first long-distance road in The Netherlands. It was commissioned by **Napoleon** and built around 1812. It was part of the "Route Imperiale 2" between Amsterdam and Paris. In Northern France, "Route Nationale 2" still exists. The motorway heading south from Amsterdam is known as "the A2"!

- **0.0** *(3.1 or 13.8)* From bridge at 🛏🍴 **De Voetangel**, at *KP 69*, go east via rd (to Abcoude & *KP 71*), keep to dyke route until you arrive in Abcoude
- **3.3** Cross rd ↑ via 🚲 crossing, after 100m, join "fietspad" ↖ (Voordijk) follow narrow path with river on your left and houses on your right
  - ← via old river bridge, then at T-jct with lhts →
  - (🎵 **Amsterdamse Straatweg**) 🚗, then imm 1st rd ←
  - (one-way street church square of 🛏🍴🛒🛍🏧🍴 **Abcoude**)
- **3.8** At T-jct ← via one-way street (see "Hubo"-shop, later sign "Kerkstraat")
- **4.2** At speed bump with 🚲 crossing over the rd, end of route
  - *For Abcoude station (for train back to Amsterdam)* → via 🚲
  - *For Route B5 (for Rural Gein, Weesp station and East Corridor to City)*
  - → via 🚲 *bridge, see page 44.*

Amsterdam Route B: River Amstel, Amstelland and East Corridor

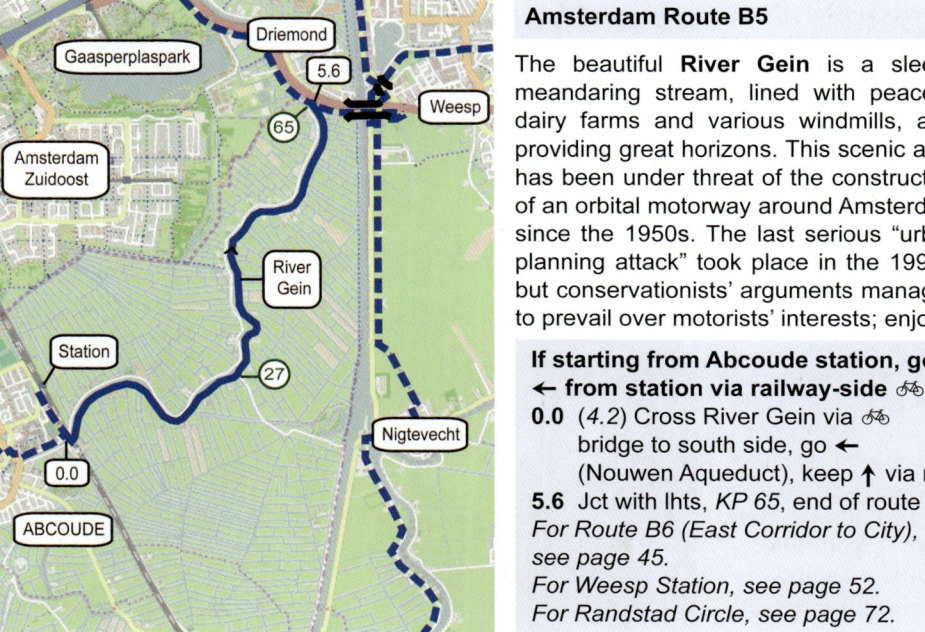

Amsterdam Route B5

The beautiful **River Gein** is a sleepy meandering stream, lined with peaceful dairy farms and various windmills, also providing great horizons. This scenic area has been under threat of the construction of an orbital motorway around Amsterdam since the 1950s. The last serious "urban planning attack" took place in the 1990s, but conservationists' arguments managed to prevail over motorists' interests; enjoy!

If starting from Abcoude station, go ← from station via railway-side 🚲

0.0 (4.2) Cross River Gein via ← bridge to south side, go ← (Nouwen Aqueduct), keep ↑ via rd
5.6 Jct with lhts, *KP 65*, end of route
For Route B6 (East Corridor to City), see page 45.
For Weesp Station, see page 52.
For Randstad Circle, see page 72.

Amsterdam Route B6

And now for something completely different! Normally we do our best to make the routes in this book as scenic as possible, keeping you away from traffic noise and main thoroughfares. On this route section we do the **opposite** and allow you to **become a Dutch cycling commuter**. We make you cycle the most direct route from **Driemond** via **Diemen** to Amsterdam's city centre. Experience how cyclists get catered for all the way on this **East Corridor**. In other countries, this may be called a "Cycling Super Highway". In The Netherlands, this is just a standard route; it doesn't even have a name! The first route section is alongside the pretty **River Gaasp**, with **Gaasperplaspark** on your left.

If starting from Weesp station, use route C4 westbound on page 52 and make your way across the high canal bridge to the "Gein" junction with traffic lights on the N236 in Driemond (using the detailed map on page 52)

- **0.0** (5.6) At jct with lhts, *KP 65*, go west via 🚲 on left side of main rd (to Amsterdam & *KP 64*), keep ↑ via 🚲
- **1.9** At jct with lhts ↑ via 🚲 on left side of rd (to Amsterdam)
- **4.6** Follow 🚲 all the way ↑, after subway ← via 🚲 on left side of rd (Weesperstraat, rd next to canal)
- **5.5** Where rd veers to left (away from canal), cross rd ↱ onto 🚲 next to canal
- **5.8** Ep → via canal bridge (use 🚲 on right side of rd), at jct with lhts via 🚲 crossings ← via 🚲 on right side of main rd (to Amsterdam), keep ↑ (☕ 🍴 **Diemen**)

Amsterdam Route B: River Amstel, Amstelland and East Corridor

Amsterdam Route B6 (continued)

So, cycling commuter; here is a game for you! According to its time table, it takes **tram 9 twelve minutes** to travel from the A10 (E35) Amsterdam orbital to the Plantage Kerklaan junction next to Artis Zoo; can you beat the tram **without jumping any red lights?**

6.4 Pass under the A10 (E35) Amsterdam orbital motorway, keeping to 🚲 on right side of rd, using 🚲 crossings at jcts with lhts (Middenweg), keep going ↑ via 🚲 all the way

9.8 At large rdnabt (with tram tracks also going around the rndabt) ↖, keep using 🚲 on right side of rndabt (to Centrum)

10.0 At next jct with lhts → via 🚲 on right side of rd (to Centrum), at next jct with lhts ↑ via 🚲 on right side of rd (Plantage Middenlaan, to Artis/Centrum)

10.7 At next jct with lhts → via 🚲 lane (Plantage Kerklaan, to Artis Zoo)

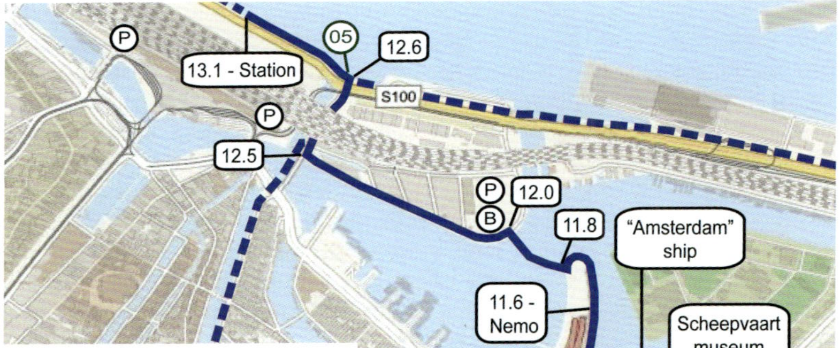

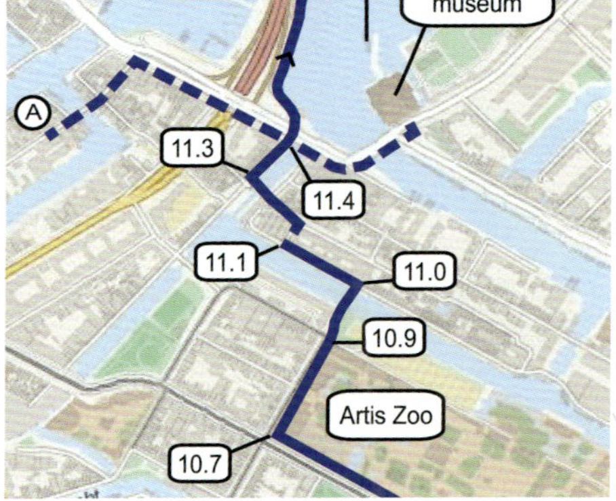

Amsterdam Route B6 (continued)

Back in the city, we resume our sightseeing activities. **Artis Zoo** is an historic city zoo, which opened in 1838. The **Scheepvaartmuseum** tells the story of Amsterdam's nautical past, with the replica trading ship **"Amsterdam"** docked at a prominent location in the harbour. Climb the steps to the roof of the science museum **Nemo** for the best city views!

10.9 After entrance ⇖ **Artis Zoo** on your right, at end of rd ↑ via 🚲 (to Windmill De Gooier)
11.0 After bridge, at ep, ← via rd (Entrepotdok)
11.1 1st rd → through building, next T-jct ← (Laagte Kadijk)
11.3 After canal bridge, imm → (Schippersgracht)
11.4 At jct with lhts ↑ cross main rd onto quiet lay-by rd, keep ↑, leading onto quayside (For ⇖ **Scheepvaartmuseum** → *at lhts*) ⇖ 🚢 **Nemo (view point)** *on left*, ⇖ **"Amsterdam" ship** *on right*
11.6
11.8 After "rounding" Nemo building imm → via 🚲 bridge (to Station)
12.0 At end of bridge ← via rd (to Station), keep ↑ onto 🚲
12.5 At jct with lhts → via 🚲 on right side of rd into tunnel
12.6 At jct with lhts ← via 🚲 on right side of rd (to A'dam Noord)
13.1 Main ferry landing at Central Station, end of route B6.

Amsterdam Route C: Rhine Canal, Weesp & Muiden, New Islands and Old Villages

Stations: Amsterdam Centraal, Weesp

Route options:
- Rhine Canal & Weesp (to Weesp station): **16 km** (use C1 + C3 + C4)
- From Weesp station to Muiden, New Islands and Old Villages: **30 km**
  (use C4 + C5 + C6 + C7 + E4)
- Rhine Canal, New Islands and Old Villages: **29 km**
  (use C1 + C2 + C6 + C7 + E4; you can also travel to Muiden by ferry)
- Rhine Canal, Weesp & Muiden, New Islands and Old Villages: **46 km**
  (use C1 + C3 + C4 + C5 + C6 + C7 + E4)

Cycling time: 3 - 5 hours (🚲 65%, 🚶 35%)

Lots of variety on this route. From the 1990s, Amsterdam revamped its rundown **eastern docklands** into a residential district with stunning **modern urban architecture**. This area keeps being extended on newly reclaimed islands (the IJburg district). Just to the south runs the dead-straight **Amsterdam-Rhine shipping canal**, where large freight barges set off for their long journeys on the River Rhine to Germany, France and Switzerland. The canal towpath provides a traffic-free super highway out of the city for those starting off on the **Randstad Circle Route**. It also takes you to the pretty towns of **Weesp** and **Muiden**, both on the **River Vecht** (see also page 72 and beyond). At Muiden, you can visit the superb **Muiderslot Castle**, dating from the 1200s. From Muiden, you'll make your way back via IJburg into **Waterland** with some very charming old villages.

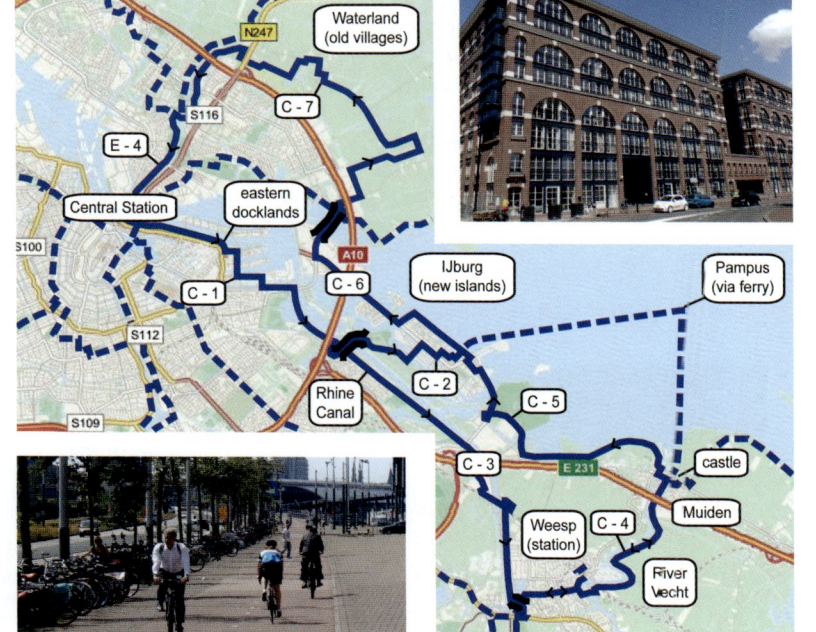

Amsterdam Route C1 starts with the **Piet Hein Kade** route. Here, modern buildings such as the **Bimhuis Concert Hall** and the **PTA Cruise Ship Terminal** stand alongside refurbished warehouses like **Willem de Zwijger**.

Don't miss the views over the stylish bridges to **Borneo Island** (see picture). The **Amsterdam-Rhine shipping canal** is 72 km long and opened in 1952, providing a direct link to the River Rhine.

0.0 From main ferry landing at Central Station, go east via 🚴 along water (to A'dam Oost), keep ↑ (to Zeeburg)

2.6 After office building "SBS" (on left side of path), cross tram tracks and imm ← via 🚴 (note: do *not* cross main rd to tunnel entrance!)

2.9 At jct with lhts → via 🚴 on right side of rd (C. van Eesterenlaan) ⇐ **Borneo island bridges** *(after 100m, on left side of rd on horizon)*

3.4 Just before T-jct ← onto cobbled one-way lay-by rd, at end ↑ via 🚴 (Cruquiusweg, see sign after 50m)

3.9 Ep ↗ onto rndabt, → via 🚴 on right side (Th K. van Lohuizenlaan)

4.2 At T-jct ← via 🚴 on left side of rd *(Caution: although this narrow path is not officially one-way, it gets mainly used by opposite flow!)*

4.3 1st rd ↖ (Flevoparkweg (to Diemen/A'dam Zuidoost)

4.9 At rndabt → via canal rd (to Diemen/A'dam Zuidoost & *KP 54*)

6.4 After motorway viaduct, stop at *KP 55*; end of route C1

For Route C2 (via New Islands & Old Villages only), see page 50.
*For Route C3 (for Rhine Canal, Weesp & Muiden, New Islands and Old Villages) and **Randstad Circle Route**, see page 51.*

Amsterdam Route C: Rhine Canal, Weesp & Muiden, New Islands and Old Villages

Amsterdam Route C2 takes you on the **Nescio Bridge**, the longest, purpose-built, cycle bridge of The Netherlands. It will bring you across the Rhine Canal to **Diemerpark** and **IJburg**. At **IJburg Harbour** you can take a pedestrian ferry to **Muiderslot Castle** via Pampus. **Fort Pampus** (see picture top right) is a **sea fort**, built in 1895. It is part of the historic Defence Line of Amsterdam, listed as World Heritage. It has a museum and cafe. From IJburg, the ferry (also carrying bikes) departs daily at 11am, return to IJburg at 3.15pm. There are also second sailings in the afternoon, see www.veerdienstamsterdam.nl and page 53.

- **0.0** (6.4) After motorway viaduct, at *KP 55*, → via ⌖ (to IJburg & *KP 15*), onto ⌖ **Nescio Bridge**
- **0.7** At end of bridge → via ⌖ (to Muiden via Park & *KP 15*), then after 100m 2nd path ↖ (to Speelweide, *cycling permitted*)
- **2.0** 2nd path ↙ via bridge (to IJburg), ep ↑ via rd (Diemerparklaan)
- **2.4** At jct with lhts at ⍰ **IJburg** (*shops*) → via ⌖ on right side of rd
- **2.8** At next jct with lhts ← (first cross side rd, then line up to ← and press button to cross main rd as required!) (Lumierestraat)
- **2.9** 1st rd → (Maria Austriastraat), at end of rd ↑ via ⌖ bridge
- **3.1** 1st rd ← (Taconiskade), imm → via quay side 🚢 🍴 **IJburg Harbour**, (⛴ **Pampus** *and* **Muiderslot ferry** *opposite NAP cafe*), ← via quay
- **3.5** At end of quay side rd, cross rd ↑ to lakeside ⌖, end of route C2

Continue with Route C6 back to City via Old Villages, see page 54.

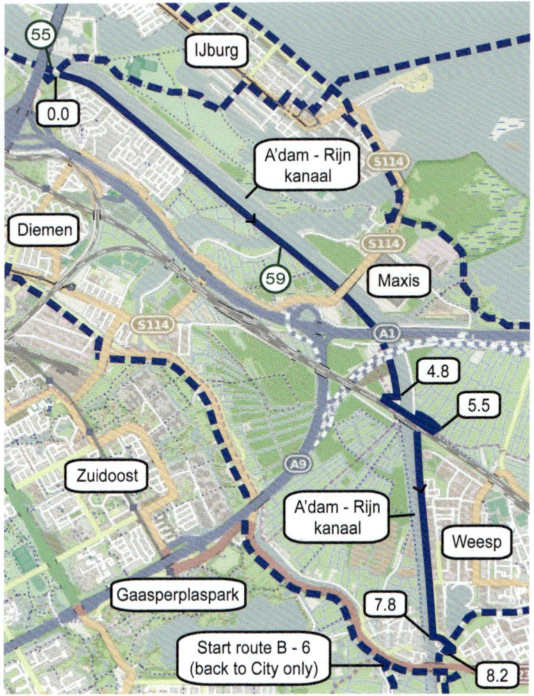

Amsterdam Route C3 on the **Rhine Canal** gives you a glimpse of the 1400 km long Dutch network of waterways, suitable for large barges. The Dutch fleet consists of approximately 7,500 barges, carrying 30% of all freight in The Netherlands. Dutch shipping companies carry out about 50% of European inland freight shipping.

0.0 (6.4) After motorway viaduct, at KP 55, ↑ via 🚲 (to Weesp & KP 59), keep ↑ via canal towpath

4.8 Just before railway bridge over canal → via zigzag 🚲 onto railway bridge with 🚲 (to Weesp/Hilversum)

5.5 At end of bridge ↙ via 🚲 (to Muiden), at T-jct ← via 🚲 under bridge (Kanaalpad)

7.8 Where 🚲 ends at private gate ↖ via 🚲 on right side of rd, after bridge → via zigzag

8.2 At 🚲 T-jct, next to bridge "De Uitkomst"; end of route C3

For Route C4 (for Weesp & Muiden, New Islands and Old Villages), see page 52.
For Route B6, see page 45.

To continue on the Randstad Circle route, see page 73!

Amsterdam Route C: Rhine Canal, Weesp & Muiden, New Islands and Old Villages

Amsterdam Route C4:
From Route C3 to Muiden and C5:
(for transfers from/to B-routes, see map)

- **0.0** (8.2) At 🚲 T-jct, next to bridge "De Uitkomst" → (to *KP 44*)
- **1.0** At jct with lhts ↑ (Buitenveer, to Centrum), keep ↑
- **1.3** In town centre ⛴ 🏠 🛒 ☕ 🍴 **Weesp**, cross bridge ↑ (Slijkstraatbrug), dismount and walk ↑ via pedestrian st
- **1.5** At end of pedestian st → to Bastions), resume cycling *(For Weesp station ←)*
- **1.8** 1st bridge ← (to 's Graveland & *KP 45*)
- **2.0** At T-jct *KP 45* ← (to Muiden & *KP 48*), keep to riverside route (river on yr left)
- **5.7** At jct ← via paved rd (into Muiden), keep ↘
- **6.2** Historic bridge ⛴ 🏠 🛒 ☕ 🍴 **Muiden**; end of route C4

For Route C5 (for New Islands, Old Villages and back to City, see page 53)
For ⛴ Muiderslot Castle ↑ (300m)

Pretty Weesp

Amsterdam Route C4: *From Muiden to Randstad Circle route (only if you have completed the full Northern route & wish to head for Weesp station or south/east):*

- **0.0** (53.2) Just before historic river bridge ⛴ 🏠 🛒 ☕ 🍴 **Muiden** go south ↓ (to "P2 Parkeerplaats")
- **0.5** At end historic town (rd "Herengracht"), ↗ via riverside route (river on yr right)
- **4.2** At *KP 45*, 1st bridge → (to Weesp)
- **4.4** After scenic river bridge at T-jct → (Hoogstraat, to Centrum)
- **4.7** Just before next bridge ↓ (Achteromstraat)
  (For Weesp station ↑, see map)
- **4.9** At end "Achteromstraat", in town centre ⛴ 🏠 🛒 ☕ 🍴 **Weesp**, ↗ via bridge (Slijkstraatbrug), at next jcts visually ↑ (Buitenveer)
- **5.2** At jct with lhts ↑ (to Nigtevecht)
- **6.2** After tunnel of bridge "De Uitkomst", at next 🚲 jct; end of route C4

For Randstad Circle route, see page 73

Amsterdam Route C5

Note: You can skip this route section by taking a ferry via Fort Pampus to IJburg Harbour; departure daily at 2.30pm. Note this service departs from the grounds of Muiderslot Castle. The service from the public quay in Muiden only offers returns to Fort Pampus (see also page 50).

Muiderslot is one of the finest medieval **castles** of The Netherlands. It stands at the mouth of the River Vecht and dates from 1280 (open daily, €14 pp). The old sea locks at pretty **Muiden** are bustling on sunny weekend days, with many holiday boats passing through the locks. Observe this typical Dutch spectacle from one of the waterside cafe terraces. A fine cycle path takes you to **IJburg**, Amsterdam's ambitious city extension project in Lake Markermeer.

0.0 *(6.2 or 53.2)* Cross historic river bridge ⛴ 🏰 ♻ 🍴 **Muiden**, go west ➡ *(For ⛴ **Muiderslot Castle and ferry** go north, 300m)*
0.1 1st rd → (Hellingstraat), 1st rd ← (Stadssteeg)
0.3 1st rd → (Zeestraat), at next jct ↖ (to Amsterdam)
1.4 At end of rd ↑ via path *(Note: path closed November - February!)*
4.0 At 🚲 jct ↗ (to Amsterdam, LF 23a)
5.1 Imm after bridge over path ← via 🚲 (to IJburg),
5.2 Ep ← via 🚲 on left side of rd (to IJburg)
6.4 Ep → (Marius Meijboomstraat)
6.6 At jct → via 🚲 on right side of rd (to Centrum), after 30m cross rd ← onto lakeside 🚲 (Haanstrakade, to Centrum)
7.0 Jct just before bridge, end of route C5, for ♻ 🍴 **IJburg Harbour** ←
Continue with Route C6 back to City via Old Villages, see page 54

Amsterdam Route C: Rhine Canal, Weesp & Muiden, New Islands and Old Villages

Amsterdam Route C6

From IJburg's lakeside cycle path, you can look across the lake to **Durgerdam**, a pretty dyke village, part of Route D2. You'll leave IJburg via its main bridge to the city. Note there are only two lanes for motorised traffic on this bridge. With hefty parking charges in place on the whole of IJburg, public transport and cycling are the ways to go!

- **0.0** *(3.5 or 7.0)* At end of quay side rd 🛏 🍴 **IJburg Harbour** (Taconiskade), go west on lakeside 🚲 (Haanstrakade)
- **1.7** At jct with lhts → via 🚲 on right side of rd (to Centrum), keep ↑
- **3.9** After petrol station "Kriterion" on right side of path, at 2nd jct with lhts → via 🚲 on right side of rd (Zuiderzeeweg, to Noord)
- **5.2** After long bridge, at rndabt → via 🚲 on right side of rd, stop at corner of next jct with quiet rd; end of route C6

For Route C7 back to City via Old Villages, see page 55

You can also transfer here to Route D2 into Durgerdam and further into Waterland; go → on quiet rd (to Durgerdam) and cycle 300m ↑ to T-jct KP 46, then turn to page 58.

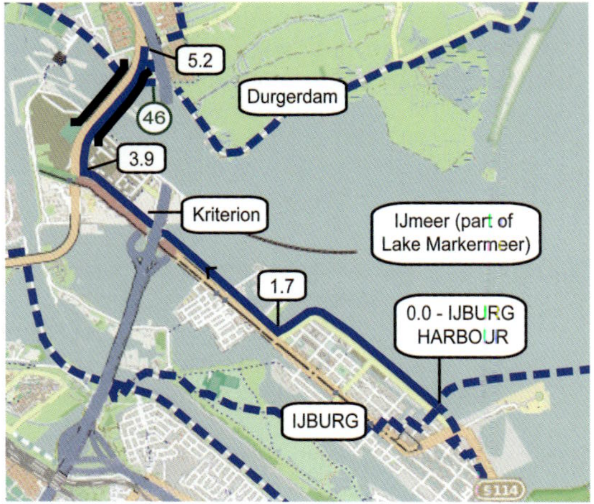

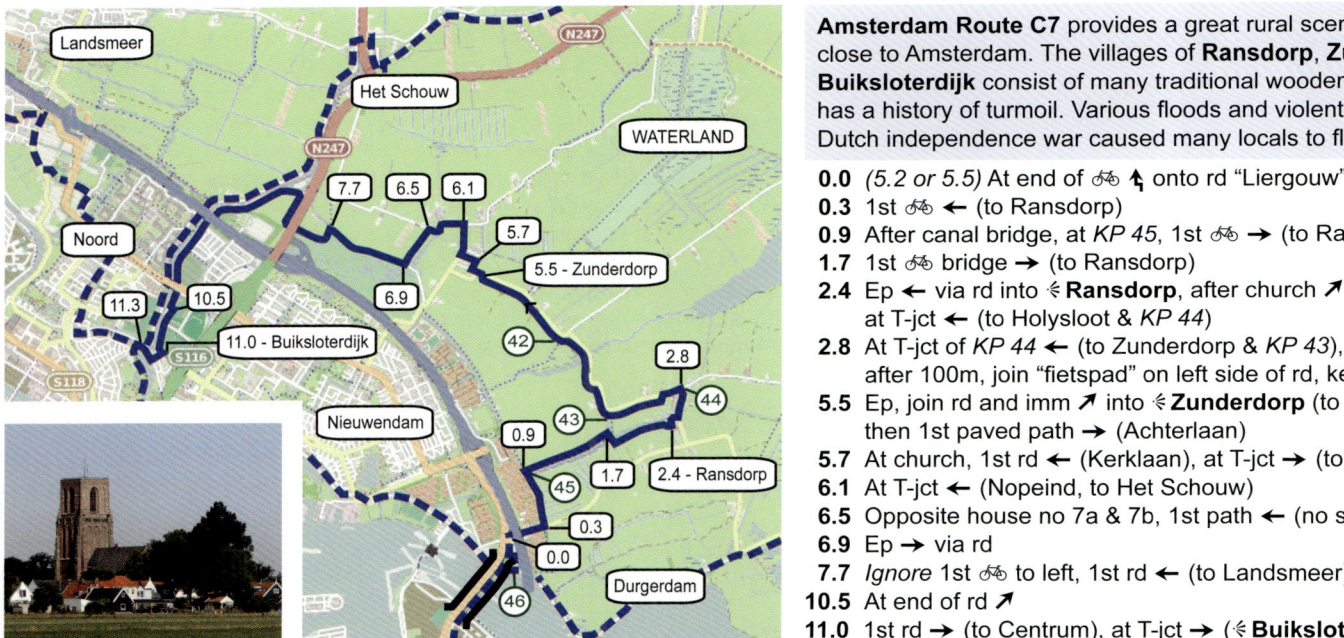

Amsterdam Route C7 provides a great rural scenic route very close to Amsterdam. The villages of **Ransdorp**, **Zunderdorp** and **Buiksloterdijk** consist of many traditional wooden houses. **Ransdorp** has a history of turmoil. Various floods and violent clashes during the Dutch independence war caused many locals to flee to Amsterdam.

- **0.0** *(5.2 or 5.5)* At end of 🚲 ↰ onto rd "Liergouw" (to Ransdorp)
- **0.3** 1st 🚲 ← (to Ransdorp)
- **0.9** After canal bridge, at *KP 45*, 1st 🚲 → (to Ransdorp & *KP 43*)
- **1.7** 1st 🚲 bridge → (to Ransdorp)
- **2.4** Ep ← via rd into ⛪ **Ransdorp**, after church ↗, at T-jct ← (to Holysloot & *KP 44*)
- **2.8** At T-jct of *KP 44* ← (to Zunderdorp & *KP 43*), after 100m, join "fietspad" on left side of rd, keep following 🚲
- **5.5** Ep, join rd and imm ↗ into ⛪ **Zunderdorp** (to *KP 40*), then 1st paved path → (Achterlaan)
- **5.7** At church, 1st rd ← (Kerklaan), at T-jct → (to *KP 41*)
- **6.1** At T-jct ← (Nopeind, to Het Schouw)
- **6.5** Opposite house no 7a & 7b, 1st path ← (no signs!)
- **6.9** Ep → via rd
- **7.7** *Ignore* 1st 🚲 to left, 1st rd ← (to Landsmeer), follow rd with bends
- **10.5** At end of rd ↗
- **11.0** 1st rd → (to Centrum), at T-jct → (⛪ **Buiksloterdijk**)
- **11.3** After bridge, at 1st ←, end of route C7

Continue with Route E4 back to City, see page 69

Views over Ransdorp

Amsterdam Route D: North Amsterdam, old seawall and Waterland

Stations: *Amsterdam Centraal*
Route options:
- *North Amsterdam and Waterland (short circuit):* **19 km**
  (use D1 + C7 + E4)
- *North Amsterdam, old seawall & Waterland (mid circuit):* **27 km**
  (use D1 + D2 + D3 + D6 + E4; **note time restrictions (ferry) on D3!**)
- *North Amsterdam, old seawall & Waterland (long circuit):* **34 km**
  (use D1 + D2 + D4 + D5 + D6 + E4)

Cycling time: *1 - 4 hours (🚲 50%, 🚶 50%)*

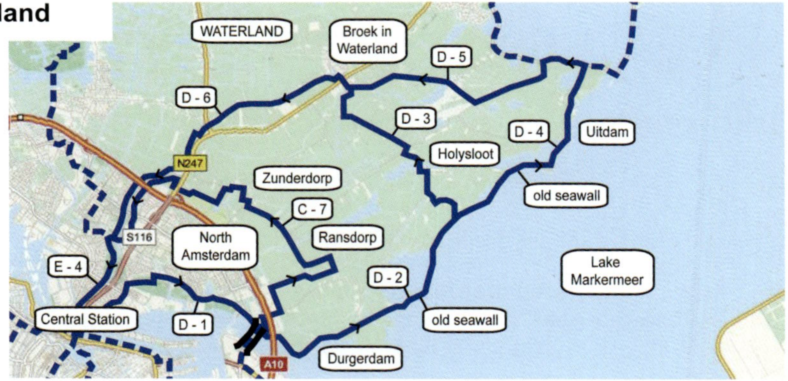

Just across the IJ-bay behind Central Station, **North Amsterdam** manages to keep its rural feel, despite modern developments. Old villages such as **Nieuwendam** and **Buiksloterdijk** remain havens of peace and quiet, just a five minutes' ferry trip away from the bustling city centre. Further north, rural **Waterland** is a very low-lying plain, with roads hardly rising 10 cms above the water level in its many canals. This area is very exposed. Away from scenic villages as **Durgerdam, Ransdorp, Holysloot, Broek in Waterland** and **Uitdam**, you won't find any shelter, so be very wary to cycle in this area on windy days! The ride on Waterland's **old seawall** is superb, providing great views over **Lake Markermeer**. With three circuits to choose from, you can make this ride as short or as long as you wish! Those starting the **Northern Route**, heading away from Amsterdam, need to use sections D1, D2 and D4 before continuing on page 118.

Amsterdam Route D1

0.0 From main ferry landing at Central Station, take ⛴ **IJ Harbour Ferry** to **IJplein** (*runs until midnight, free*), reset mileage at IJplein landing, ↑ via 🚲 (to Vliegenbos), keep ↑ via 🚲 (Meeuwenlaan)

1.6 After rndabt, at 2nd bus shelter "Merelstraat" → via 🚲 into park (via iron gate) (note: *ignore sign "Vliegenbos" at first bus shelter!*)

1.9 After entrance ▲ **Vliegenbos**, at next jct ↖ via main 🚲

2.2 1st path ←, after bridge ← via rd, at T-jct → (Nieuwendammerdijk)

2.7 At old bridge and locks ⛴ **Nieuwendam** (*cafe "'t Sluisje"*) ↑

3.6 At rd crossing ↑ via 🚲 (to Schellingwoude)

3.8 After next rd crossing imm ↗ via 🚲, continue on rd on dyke ridge, ↑ (to Schellingwoude)

4.7 Keep visually ↑ (to Durgerdam), dyke ridge on your right hand side

5.2 Jct *KP 46*, end of route D1

For Route C7 (short circuit), go ← for 300m, turn to page 55 at next jct
*For Route D2 (mid & long circuits and **Northern Route**), see page 58*

Amsterdam Route D: North Amsterdam, old seawall and Waterland

At dyke village **Durgerdam** you can enjoy panoramic lake views. On the short, fun grass path at **Holysloot** the contrast with bustling Amsterdam couldn't be greater!

Amsterdam Route D2

- **0.0** (5.2 or 5.5) At *KP 46* ↑ via 🚴 on left side of rd (to Durgerdam & *KP 45*), ↑
- **1.2** Ep ↑ via rd into ⛴ 🍴 **Durgerdam**
- **2.6** At end of village at jct of *KP 47* ↗ via 🚴 (Zuiderzeepad, to Enkhuizen & *KP 79*)
- **6.3** At *KP 79* end of route D2

For Route D4 (long circuit and **Northern Route**)*, see page 59*
For Route D3 (mid circuit), read on right:

Amsterdam Route D3 *(note ferry times!)*

- **0.0** (6.3) At *KP 79* ↖ via 🚴 down the slope, cross rd ↙ via 🚴 (to Holysloot & *KP 78*)
- **1.3** 1st rd → (to Holysloot & *KP 78*), at next jct ↑ via 🚴 on right side of rd
- **2.0** Ep to ⛴ **Holysloot**, at T-jct ← (to *KP 76*)
- **2.3** At end of rd → to ⛴ **Ferry** *(runs from mid April until Oct on Sat & Sun only, in July & Aug daily, until 5 pm, € 1 pp)*, ↑
- **2.7** End of grass path → via rd, at next jct (*KP 76*) ← via rd (to Broek in Waterland)
- **4.5** 1st rd → (into Broek in Waterland)
- **5.0** 3rd rd ↗ (Wagengouw)
- **5.2** At jct after 🚴 bridge, end of route

Continue with Route D6, see page 61

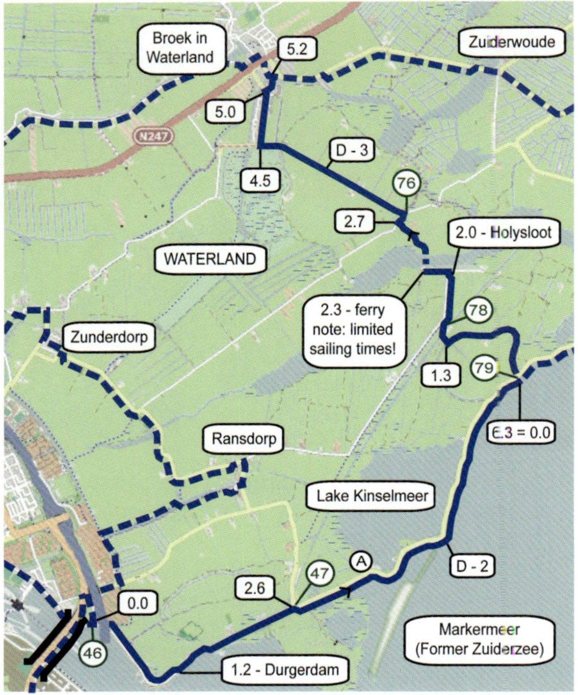

Amsterdam Route D4

Originally, the reedswamps and peat-country of **Waterland** lay well above sea level. Decaying peat resulted in subsidence of the land (and still does). This process, in combination with rising sea levels, sparked the construction of the **Waterland Seawall**. It was first commissioned way back in 1288!

The old South Sea "Zuiderzee" breached this dyke multiple times. These violent breaches created wide inland stretches of water, heading deep inland away from the seawall. The floods of 1916 initiated the construction of the Barrier Dam "Afsluitdijk" at the north end of the North Holland peninsula. The South Sea "Zuiderzee" became a lake.

- **0.0** (6.3) At *KP 79* ↑ via 🚴 (to Uitdam & *KP 77*)
- **3.2** Ep ↑ via rd into ⛬ **Uitdam**, at end of village, rejoin "fietspad" on dyke ridge ↗ (to Marken)
- **4.4** Ep ↗ via rd, after "Poort van Amsterdam" ↗ via "fietspad" (to Marken & *KP 52*)
- **5.7** Ep, cross rd to 🚴 jct of *KP 52*; end of route D4 For Route D5 (back to City), see page 60

To continue on the Northern route, see page 118!

Amsterdam Route D: North Amsterdam, old seawall and Waterland

Amsterdam Route D5

0.0 (5.7) At KP 52 ← via 🚲 on right side of rd (to Monnickendam)
1.0 At KP 53 ← down via steps, cross rd ↑ (Dijkeinde, to Zuiderwoude)
3.1 In ⇐Zuiderwoude ↑ (Zuiderwouder Dorpsstraat, to KP 57)
3.7 At church ↰ (to Broek in Waterland & KP 1), after 200m, join 🚲 on left side of rd
5.7 Ep, join rd (Peereboomweg, to Doorgaand Verkeer)
6.1 Where rd bends to the right ↱ (to Doorgaand Verkeer)
6.2 At next jct (see 🚲 to Zunderdorp heading left); end of route D5
Continue with Route D6 (back to City), see page 61

Amsterdam Route D6

Broek in Waterland is the largest village in Waterland, but the number of eateries is limited. We recommend to bring packed lunches and drinks with you on all D routes! You enter Amsterdam via the **North Holland Shipping Canal**. This canal opened in 1824 to provide an alternative route for the growing, treacherous sandbanks in the old South Sea.

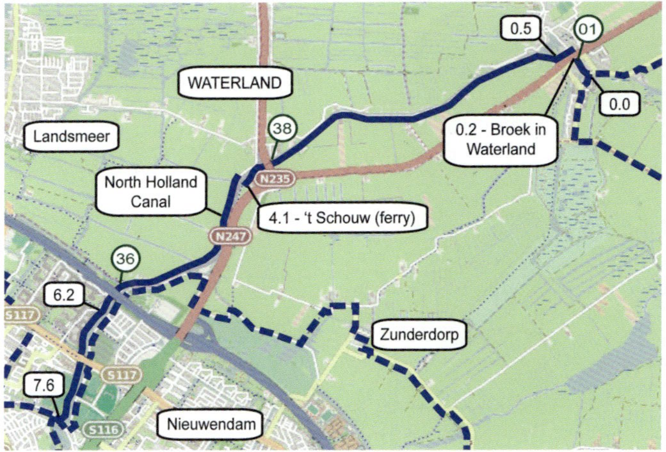

0.0 (5.2 or 6.2) At jct, go northwest (to Monnickendam & KP 1)

0.2 At T-jct of KP 1 ↑ via 🚲 bridge, after bridge ↗ into subway, after subway ↖ and imm ← via 🚲 (to Landsmeer & KP 38)
(For 🍴 **Broek in Waterland**, after subway, keep ↖ on rd, 100m)

0.5 After bridge, at ep, join rd ↗ (to Het Schouw & KP 38)

4.1 In 🍴 **'t Schouw**, at sharp bend of rd to the left → to ferry
(runs daily until 7 pm, €1 pp), after ferry ← via rd (to Amsterdam)

6.2 After viaduct of motorway orbital via 🚲 (to Centrum, LF 7a), keep ↑

7.6 At T-jct →, at 1st 🚲 ←; end of route C7

Continue with Route E4 back to City, see page 69

Amsterdam Route E: Zaandam, Zaanse Schans windmills and Twiske

Stations: Amsterdam Centraal, Amsterdam Sloterdijk, Koog-Zaandijk
Route options:
- *Zaandam and Zaanse Schans windmills (to Koog-Zaandijk): 17 km (use E1 + E2)*
- *(from Koog-Zaandijk) Zaanse Schans windmills and Twiske: 23 km (use E3 + E4)*
- *Zaandam, Zaanse Schans windmills and Twiske (circular) : 40 km (use E1 + E2 + E3 + E4)*

Cycling time: 2 - 4 hours (🚲 72%, 🛤 24%, ⛴ 4%)

This route is all about the famous **Zaanse Schans windmills reserve**, a free open air museum with the largest collection of **Dutch traditional industrial windmills**. It also features a **clog making** and a **cheese farm museum** and a **traditional village**. The tourist crowds and many souvenir shops can feel a little overwhelming, but the great number of beautiful authentic buildings in a scenic parkland setting make a visit very worthwhile. Climb the steps of at least one **running windmill** to experience the creaking sounds and majestic force of wind power! Note small charges per windmill visit do apply. The **Zaans Museum** is an on-site social history museum (open daily, €10 pp). The ride to Zaanse Schans is urban via the **Westpoort Docklands** and **Zaandam**. The ride back to the city, also to be used by **Randstad Circle Route** cyclists, is via the rural **Twiske Reserve**. Take bikes on trains to/from Koog-Zaandijk station to cycle one-way only.

On **Amsterdam Route E1** we guide you via the iconic **Fietsflat** ("Bike Flat", see picture) into one of Amsterdam's traditional shopping streets, the **Haarlemmerstraat**. **Westerpark** is a green oasis in the city. The cultural centre **Westergasfabriek** (Western Gas Works) features art-galleries, open air music performances and various cafes.

0.0 From main ferry landing at Central Station, go west via 🚲 along water (to A'dam West)

0.2 At jct with lhts ←, cross rd (to Haarlem), then imm ← via 🚲, follow bend ↗ into tunnel

0.3 After tunnel, 1st 🚲 → via 🚲 bridge (to Haarlem)
(note ⛟ **Fietsflat (Bike Flat)** on corner; *this parking is NOT guarded*)

0.5 After 🚲 bridge → via 🚲 (to Haarlem), after subway, 1st rd → into shopping street ⛟ 🚻 🍴 **Haarlemmerstraat**, keep ↑

1.4 At end of "Haarlemmerstraat" via 🚲 ↖ across square, at jct with lhts ↑ via 🚲 on left side of rd (to Haarlem)

1.6 After bridge, at next jct with lhts ↑ via 🚲 crossing, then imm ↑ via 🚲 crossing onto 🚲 on left side of rd (Houtmakade, to Haarlem)

1.7 After canal bridge 1st path ← (to Haarlem) into ⛟ **Westerpark**

2.1 1st wide 🚲 ↗ (to Haarlem)
(*For* ⛟ 🍴 **Westergasfabriek ("Western Gas Works")** *walk* ↖)

4.2 At end of park route ↑ via 🚲 (to Haarlem), ↑ under various viaducts

5.0 At jct with lhts (Radarweg); end of route E1

For Route E2 (to Zaandam, Zaanse Schans and Twiske), see page 64
For Route F1 (to Garden Cities, Vondelpark and City), see page 71

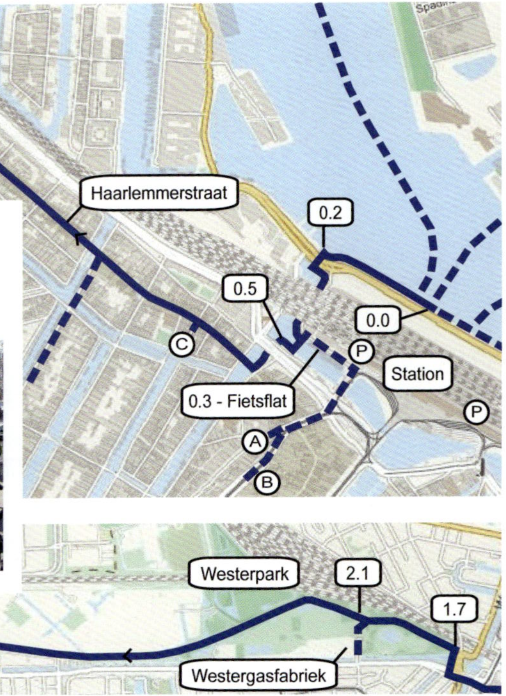

Amsterdam Route E: Zaandam, Zaanse Schans windmills and Twiske

Amsterdam Route E2

From **Sloterdijk Station** you enter the **Westpoort Docklands**. This area shows how the Dutch cycle network is completely continuous, even in places where cycling is not the obvious means of transport. You'll cross the **North Sea Canal** by ferry. This canal opened in 1876, providing a direct link between the North Sea and Amsterdam.

- **0.0** *(5.0)* At jct with lhts (Radarweg) → via 🚲 on right side of rd (to Sloterdijk), at **Sloterdijk Station** keep ↑ via 🚲
- **0.6** At jct with lhts ↑ via 🚲 on right side of rd (Radarweg, to docks "3200-3500")
- **1.1** After rd crossing "Gyroscoopweg" ⤴ via 🚲 on left side of rd (to Zaanstad), follow this 🚲 through **Westpoort Docklands**
- **4.4** Ep ← onto 🚶🚢 **Ferry Hempont** *(runs every 20 mins, day & night, free)*,
- **4.5** ↑ via 🚲 on left side of rd (to Zaandam)
- **5.9** After subway, at next jct with lhts via 🚲 crossing → (to Oude Haven), ep ← via rd

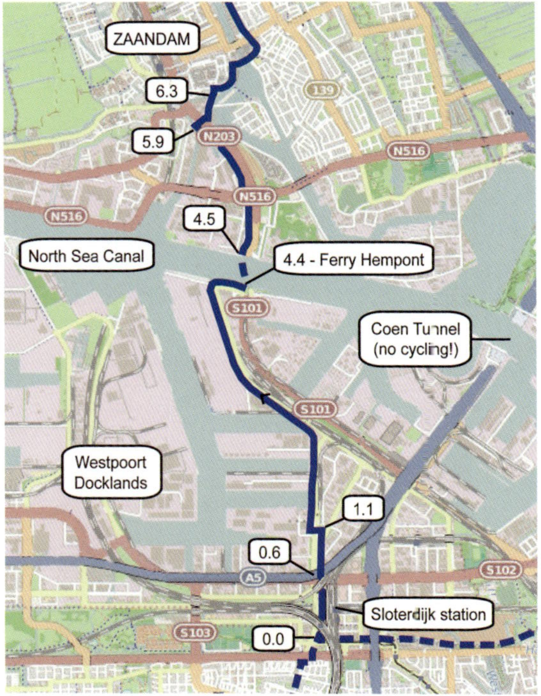

Amsterdam Route E2 (continued)

6.3 At end of rd ↑ via 🚲 bridge, at four-ways jct → (Hogendijk)
6.5 (For ⛴ **Tsar Peter House** ← down from dyke at sign, 100m)
6.7 At T-jct → (for 🚉 ☕ 🍴 **Zaandam** use bike racks across jct)
7.1 After bridge, at 3rd jct with lhts ← (to Doorgaand Verkeer)
7.2 At next jct with lhts via 🚲 crossing ↑ (Oostzijde)
9.4 At give-way jct (KP 71) ← via river bridge
(to KP 92), use 🚲 on right side of rd
9.6 After river bridge, at jct with lhts, 1st rd →
(Zuideinde, to Zaanse Schans & KP 92) 🚲
11.2 At jct with lhts → via 🚲 on left side of rd (to Zaanse Schans)
11.5 After river bridge imm ← and again ← via paved rd
11.7 Riverside square ⛴ ☕ **Zaanse Schans**, end of route E2

Continue with Route E3 via Twiske back to City, see page 66, or take the train from Koog-Zaandijk back to Amsterdam, see map

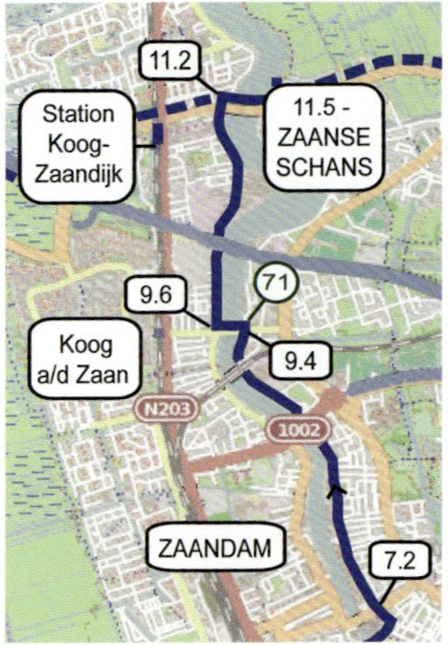

Zaandam is Amsterdam's historic "industrial estate". From the 17th century, the River Zaan got lined with over 600 industrial windmills. Well into the 19th century, many saw, paint and food-processing windmills flourished. Modern food-processing plants still provide a distinctive odour. The wooden **Tsar Peter House** dates from 1632, worth a visit (open Tue-Sun, €3 pp).

Amsterdam Route E: Zaandam, Zaanse Schans windmills and Twiske

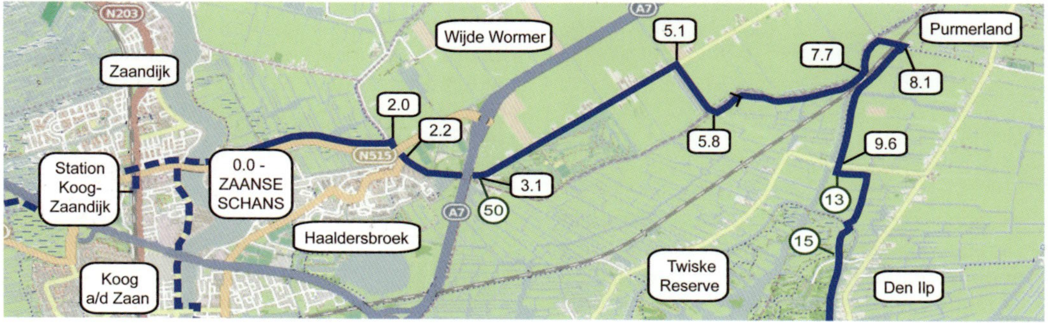

Amsterdam Route E3

Note this scenic rural route back to Amsterdam (also for those completing the **Randstad Circle Route**) is very exposed. On days with strong winds, you may prefer taking bikes on the train for a 20 minutes ride to Amsterdam Centraal.

0.0 *(11.7 or 13.5)* From Riverside square 🍴🔒 **Zaanse Schans**, return to the same way you came, back at main rd ← via 🚲 on left side of rd (to Purmerend & KP 50), at rndabt ↑
2.0 At jct with lhts → (to Purmerend & KP 50)
2.2 At 🏠🍴🍽 **Heerenhuis**, keep ↖ ("Fietsers richting Purmerend")
3.1 At KP 50 ↑ (to Neck/Purmerend & KP 33)
5.1 1st rd → (Westerdwarsweg, to KP 33)
5.8 After bridge ← via "fietspad" (to KP 33)
7.7 At jct ↗ via dyke rd (to Amsterdam), then 1st "fietspad" → (Wormerpad Nrs 5-3-2, to "Doorgaand Verkeer")
8.1 After railway crossing ↘ via "fietspad" (to Oostzaan)

Amsterdam Route E3 (continued)

9.6 At rd crossing, KP 13, ↑ via "fietspad", imm ← (to Het Twiske & KP 15)
9.8 1st 🚲 → (to Het Twiske & KP 15)
10.5 1st 🚲 ← (to Infocentrum & KP 15), at next two rd crossings ↑ via 🚲 (see signs to "Boerderij")

The **Twiske Reserve** is a designated green buffer, withdrawn from agriculture in 1972. Since then, the area has been redesigned for "nature development" and recreation. The circular cycle path around the area was also built for **rollerblading**.

12.8 At T-jct ← via 🚲 (to "Boerderij")
13.0 At jct ↑ via 🚲 (to KP 20, LF 7a)
13.4 At jct ↑ via 🚲
(note: *ignore* signs KP 20 and LF 7a)
13.9 At T-jct 🚲 → and 1st 🚲 ← (to KP 19, see also mushroom sign 25216), keep going ↑ (to KP 19)
14.7 At KP 19 🚲 ← via 🚲 (Het Luijendijkje, to Landsmeer/Amsterdam), keep ↑

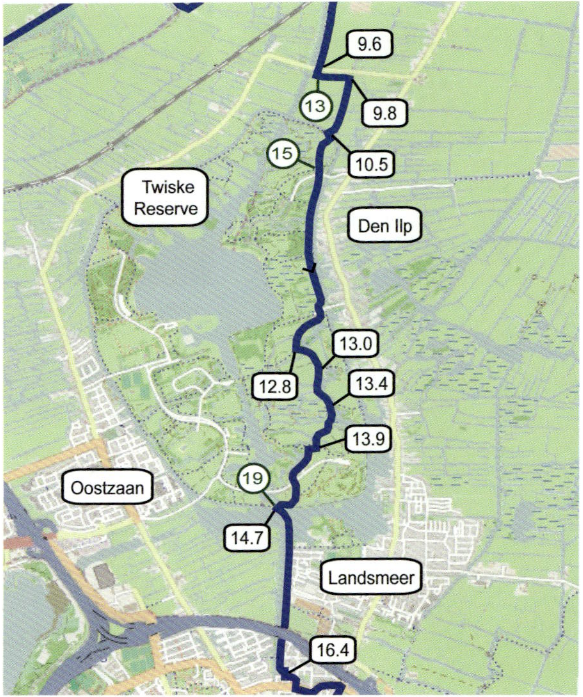

*The clog (or wooden-shoe) making museum at **Zaanse Schans** has probably the largest stock of "klompen" in the world, catering for all sizes!*

Amsterdam Route E: Zaandam, Zaanse Schans windmills and Twiske

Amsterdam Route E3 (continued)

16.4 Ep ← via residential rd (to Centrum/Buikslotermeerplein)
16.6 At T-jct ← via rd with 🚲 lanes 🚃, follow bends (Stentorstraat)
17.0 At cross rds jct → (Kadoelenweg, to Amsterdam)
17.6 1st rd ← (to Zunderdorp), at end ↑ via 🚲 (Kadoelenpad)
18.1 After traditional bridge, 1st rd → (to Centrum/Buikslotermeerplein)
18.3 After city farm buildings on left side of rd ↖ via 🚲, at next jct keep ↖ via low-level 🚲 (to Centrum/Buikslotermeerplein)
18.9 After passing through tunnel, 1st 🚲 → (takes you through another tunnel), at rd crossing ↑ via 🚲 (Koopvaardersplantsoen), keep ↑ (to Buikslotermeerplein/Schellingwoude)
19.8 At house no 176 on right hand side of path ← via 🚲
20.0 Keep ↑ via 🚲 with ⚓ **Buiksloterdijk** on left side of path
20.5 Ep ↑ via rd for 15m, then 1st 🚲 →; end of route E3
Continue with Route E4 back to City, see page 69

This route is another opportunity to experience the pleasant patchwork that makes up **North Amsterdam**. You'll cycle via various housing estates, all with different designs, according to the period in which they were built. There are also various "no man's lands", still managing to escape new developments. Last but not least, the remains of once independent villages can be very scenic, especially at **Buiksloterdijk**.

Amsterdam Route E4

- **0.0** (7.6, 11.3 or 20.5) Go south via canal-side 🚲 (to Centrum, *LF 7a*), keep ↑ via this canal-side 🚲, feeds at end onto residential rd
- **2.2** At T-jct ← via 🚲 on left side of rd (to Centrum, *LF 7a*) *Caution: busy traffic flow from opposite direction likely!*
- **2.5** Dismount at ferry landing and join ⛴ **IJ Harbour Ferry** (*runs day & night, free*), end of route E4.

This is also the end of the **Randstad Circle Route**. If you joined this route elsewhere and wish to continue this route (towards River Vecht and Utrecht), use routes C1 and C3 (see pages 49 and 51).

Amsterdam Route F: Westerpark, "Garden Cities" and Vondelpark

Stations: Amsterdam Centraal, Amsterdam Sloterdijk
Route options:
- (from Sloterdijk) "Garden Cities", Vondelpark & The City: 10 km (use F1 + A9 + A3)
- Westerpark, "Garden Cities", Vondelpark & The City: 15 km (use E1 + F1 + A9 + A3)

Cycling time: 1 - 2 hours (🚲 75%, 🚶 25%)

If you enjoy light-pedaling and urban sight-seeing by bike, you'll enjoy this **compact inner-city route**. The ride explores Amsterdam well beyond its obvious tourist attractions, to various neighbourhoods were many Amsterdammers live and work. Once again, you'll be experiencing the Dutch cycling infrastructure at its best. You'll travel the spacious "Garden Cities" of West-Amsterdam. These districts, known as **New West** were built from the 1950s. Lots of green spaces and private gardens were provided for its residents. That was a novelty at the time, as high apartment buildings with small balconies, without any parks nearby, were the design of **Old West**, developed into the 1930s. The green corridors **Westerpark**, **Rembrandtpark** and **Vondelpark** make a pleasant ride through densely populated areas. As the historic city centre is also included on this ride, you'll get a great flavour of Amsterdam's varied architecture.

The Old West architecture on the left, the New West Garden Cities on the right.

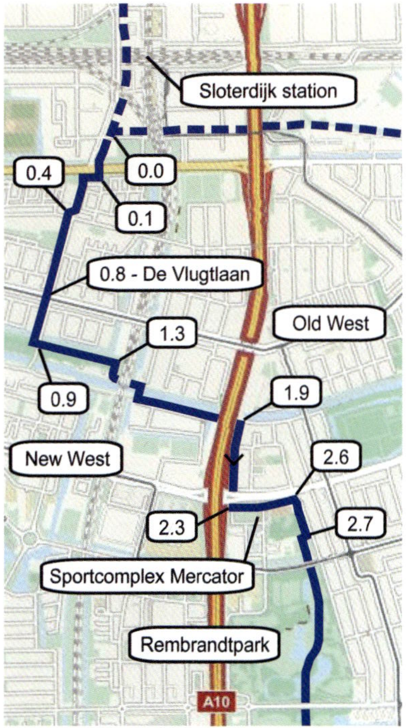

Amsterdam Route F1

To join route F1, first cycle route **E1** from Central Station (see page 63) or join directly from **Sloterdijk station**.

- 0.0 (5.0) At jct with lhts (Radarweg) ← via 🚲 on left side of rd (to Halfweg)
- 0.1 At next jct with lhts cross ↑, then → via 🚲 (to Geuzenveld), then 1st 🚲 ← (to Osdorp, *LF 20a*), ep ↑ via rd (Fockstraat)
- 0.4 At jct ↑ via 🚲 on right side of rd (to Osdorp, *LF 20a*)
- 0.8 At jct with lhts ⚊ **De Vlugtlaan** ↑ via 🚲 on right side of rd (to Osdorp, *LF 20a*)
- 0.9 After canal bridge ← via 🚲 crossing onto 🚲 (to Centrum, *LF 20a*)
- 1.3 Ep → via 🚲, after tunnel under railway cross canal ↑, continue via 🚲 route (to Centrum, *LF 20a*)
- 1.9 Imm after tunnel under orbital motorway, 1st 🚲 → (*LF 20a*), at end of 🚲 on right side of quiet rd (Rosskade), keep ↑ into subway
- 2.3 After subway, 1st rd ← (*LF 20a*, **Sportcomplex Mercator** on right)
- 2.6 At end of rd ↗, after 10m → via 🚲 on right side of rd (*LF 20a*)
- 2.7 1st "fietspad" → (Orteliuspad, *LF 20a*), imm ← via 🚲, in ⚊ **Rembrandtpark** keep ↑ via 🚲 (*LF 20a*)
- 4.5 At end of park route ↖ via 🚲 bridge, then follow sharp bend ↙ onto 🚲 on left side of rd (to Centrum, *LF 20a*), at lhts keep ↑
- 5.0 After 🚲 bridge over canal, at next 🚲 jct, end of route F1

Continue with Route A9 back to City, see page 39

Randstad Circle: Route 1: River Vecht (23 km)

Stations: Amsterdam Centraal, see route C1 & C3 (extra 15 km!) Weesp, see route C4 (extra 2 km!), Breukelen
Cycling time: 1 - 1.5 hours (🚲 13%, 🚶 87%)

To join the **Randstad Circle** route from Amsterdam Central station, first cycle **Amsterdam routes C1 and C3**. These will take you to **start** of this route section. If you cycle all Randstad Circle route sections (including routes C1/C3 and E3/E4 at the end), you'll complete a full circle from/to Amsterdam Central station, a ride of 337 km (208 miles) in total.

This **River Vecht** route section is an old-time favourite for many Dutch cyclists; try to avoid busy sunny sunday afternoons! It can hardly get more tranquil than this. The sleepy River Vecht takes you into a leafy green, Dutch landscape with dairy farms, windmills and scenic country houses. Every other hundred metres or so, another peaceful view awaits you. The **merchants** of the **Dutch Golden Age** built their country mansions and estates here. The further south you go, the bigger these get, often with large gardens and sometimes distinctive "tea houses" on the water side. Many of these mansions were built on foundations of older fortifications.

In medieval times, **forces of Holland and Utrecht** regularly clashed in this area ("vecht" means literally "fight" in Dutch). This natural north-south trading route was very important, as it still is today. Just to the west (but out of your sight) the ten-lanes wide motorway A2, a four-tracks railway and the busy Amsterdam-Rhine shipping canal take all today's through traffic!

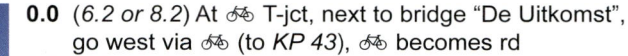

Start the Randstad Circle Route from Amsterdam Central Station by using Amsterdam Routes C1 and C3 (15 km, see pages 49 and 51). This will get you to the start of this route section. You could also use Routes A1, A4, B1, B2/B3, B4 and B5 to get here (27-38 km, see pages 31, 34 and 41-44).

For Amsterdam Route C4 (6 km), see page 52. This is the route from the end of the Northern route. Use this link if you are "transferring" from the Northern route onto the Randstad Circle route and/or if you wish to continue onto the Eastern route at the end of this River Vecht section.

0.0 *(6.2 or 8.2)* At 🚲 T-jct, next to bridge "De Uitkomst", go west via 🚲 (to *KP 43*), 🚲 becomes rd
0.2 At T-jct ↗ via 🚲 on right side of main rd, ep cross rd ←, then at *KP 43* 1st rd → (to Loenen & *KP 42*)
0.9 At bend of rd to the left, ↑ (to Loenen & *KP 42*)
3.5 In **Nigtevecht**, at ep, follow rd, opposite bus stop → (Raadhuisstraat, to Loenen)
3.9 At jct with main rd ↰ onto 🚲 on left side of rd, after bridge 1st rd ← (Vreelandse Weg), keep ↑ 🚲

From here, you cycle alongside the River Vecht.

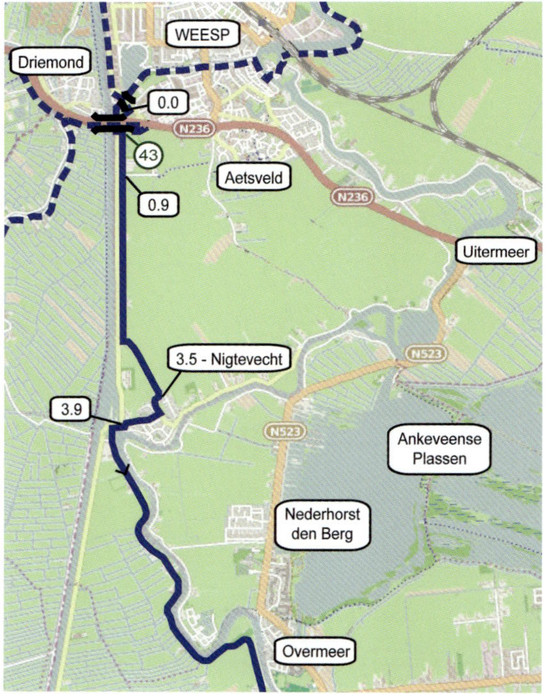

Randstad Circle: Route 1: River Vecht (23 km)

At peaceful **Vreeland** (literally "peaceful land"), you can have lunch at a pancake restaurant. Slightly off-route, there are more lunch options in **Loenen** and **Breukelen**. You may know the name Breukelen as "Brooklyn". The City of New York in the United States started as a Dutch colony, known as "New Amsterdam". The New York district "Brooklyn" was named after this Dutch town. If you wish, you could regard the bridge at Breukelen as the orginal **Brooklyn Bridge**!

- **10.7** In Vreeland, 1st rd ↖ (to Loenen)
- **11.0** At jct ↖, imm ↙ via bridge ⛽ 🏨 🛏 🛍 🍽 **Vreeland**
- **11.2** At jct with "stop"-sign → (to Loenen), rd becomes 🚲
- **11.5** After subway at ep ↗ (Boslaan, to Loenen & *KP 25*)
- **14.5** At *KP 25* cross rd ↑ (to Nieuwersluis & *KP 2*)
- **16.1** At *KP 2* and bridge ⛩ **Nieuwersluis** ↑ (to Breukelen & *KP 84*)

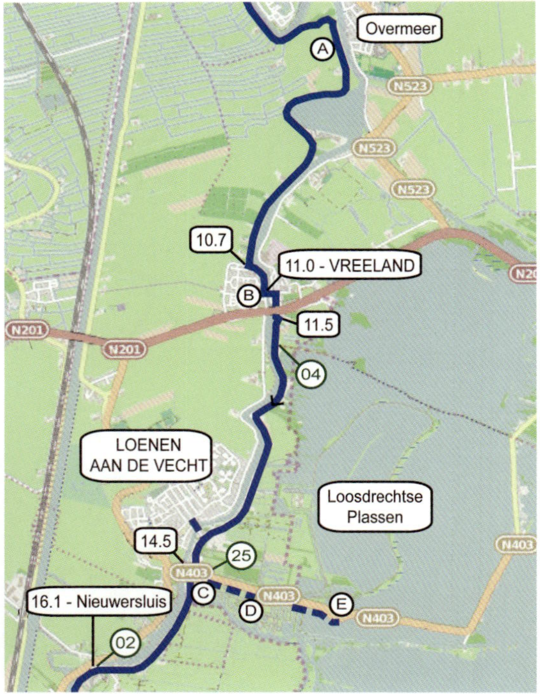

19.0 At KP 84, at 🚲 **Breukelen "Brooklyn Bridge"** ↑ (to Maarssen & KP 46)
(For 🚉 🛏 🍴 Breukelen & station, see bottom page)
20.1 🚲 **Nijenrode Castle**
(on your right, on other river bank)

The original **Nijenrode Castle** was built around 1275. After being destroyed and rebuilt several times, it became a stately home in 1675. Having lost its defensive function, it has been more or less a "folly" since then. It is the most outlandish you can find on the Vecht route. Generations of rich people lived at Nijenrode, until it was converted into a business university in 1988.

22.8 🛏 🍴 **Geesberge**, end of route
For start Eastern route to Nijmegen, see page 130.
For continued Randstad route to Utrecht, see page 77.

Route to 🚉 🛏 🍴 Breukelen & station:
19.0 At KP 84 → via 🚲 **"Brooklyn Bridge"**
19.1 1st rd ← (Dannestraat)
19.2 At T-jct ← (to Utrecht) 🚗
19.4 At rndabt → via 🚲 on right side of rd (to Utrecht)
20.6 At rndabt ← via 🚲 crossings (to Kockengen)
20.7 Breukelen station, end of route

Randstad Circle: Route 2: City of Utrecht (27 km)

Stations: Breukelen (see page 130, extra 6 km!), Utrecht Centraal, Utrecht Terwijde
Cycling time: 1.5 - 3 hours (🚲 37%, 🚶 63%)

Utrecht is the fourth largest city of The Netherlands. Its marvel is the central **Old Canal** ("Oude Gracht"), without doubt the most scenic canal of the country. It is located on the historic course of the **River Vecht** and was created by damming the river at the city boundaries. This made it possible to lower the water level by approximately four metres, creating an inner-city harbour wharf system with storage cellars below street level. Most cellars now house restaurants, art galleries, offices and even a B&B!

The 112 metre-tall **Dom Tower** is Utrecht's other distinctive landmark. It is Europe's second highest cathedral tower (the highest being Cologne's in Germany). The tower was separated from the cathedral during a fierce storm in 1674, making part of the cathedral collapse. A pavement pattern on the square in front of the tower shows the original contours of the cathedral. The 465 steps to the tower summit are the closest you can get to a climbing adventure in The Netherlands. Guided tours start every hour from the Tourist Information Centre opposite the tower (open daily, €9 pp).

With a large **student population**, Utrecht is a lively city with a great night life. It also attracts **shoppers** from across the country. At **Jaarbeursplein** you'll find the **world's largest bike park**, with spaces for 12,500 bicycles!

You'll cycle into Utrecht by following the full course of the **River Vecht**. If you start from **Breukelen station** (see page 130), you'll be able to witness a unique transformation from rural to urban environment, just by cycling the banks of a tranquil river stream. You'll leave Utrecht via the large-scale **Leidsche Rijn development**.

Our Utrecht route ends at majestic **De Haar Castle**. This stunning folly was built in 1892 on top of the foundations of old castle ruins. The building's weight is too much for the original foundations, causing cracks in walls. Restoration works are on the way to preserve the building (open daily; €4 pp gardens only, €14 pp castle and gardens).

- **0.0** (5.5 or 22.8) At 🏨 🛏 ⛽ 🍽 **Geesberge** go south ↑ via riverside rd
- **0.3** 1st rd → (to Centrum/Maarssenbroek, to KP 46)
- **1.2** In shopping street 🍴 🍽 ⛽ 🍽 ↗ **Maarssen** → (Kaatsbaan, to KP 46)
- **1.4** At KP 46, 1st rd ← (Langegracht, to Oud-Zuilen & KP 45)
- **1.7** At T-jct → (to Oud-Zuilen & KP 45), keep ↑ via riverside rd
- **5.3** In ⛽ **Oud-Zuijlen** just before river bridge ↖ (keep river on your right side), keep ↑ via riverside rd

Castle **Slot Zuylen** can be viewed via a wide gravel path on the left side of the road, just beyond the bridge junction. Gardens open Tue/Wed/Thu/Sat/Sun (€1 pp), guided castle tours Sat & Sun only (€9 pp).

- **7.2** At jct → (to Centrum & KP28), keep to riverside route
- **9.0** At T-jct → (Jagerskade) and → (Anthoniedijk, to Centrum), keep ↑
- **10.3** After passing locks in river on your right side, ↑ via 🚲 bridge

There can't be many children's book characters who have their own square. The Dutch little rabbit **Nijntje**, known in English as **Miffy**, has her own statue in her home town Utrecht: "Nijntje Pleintje", on your left!

De Haar Castle

Randstad Circle: Route 2: City of Utrecht (27 km)

10.3 Imm after 🚲 bridge (with ⬅ **Nijntje Pleintje** on your left) ↑ to other side of main canal (Oude Gracht, *LF7a*)
10.7 ***Dismount*** at main rd jct, walk ↑ via canal route (Oude Gracht)
11.1 Where the main canal disappears into a tunnel (you'll be walking on a square on top of it!), after town hall 1st rd ⬅ (Oudkerkhof)
11.2 *For Guarded Bike Park* **U-Stal Stadhuis** *on next square* ⬅ *For Route* ⬅ 🛗 🚻 ☕ 🍴 🛒 🏛 🚻 ⚑ **Utrecht** cycle ↑, at jct → (Domstraat)
11.4 At T-jct →, (to *KP 38*), ↑ via cobbled rd, follow rd ⬆ around ⬅ **Dom Tower Utrecht** (Servetstraat), keep ↑
11.7 At T-jct → via wide rd, follow bend to left, keep ↑

The city of Utrecht is **rebuilding** its historic canals around the city centre. An ugly dual carriageway, built in the 1970s on the course of the **Catharijnesingel** canal (just before the **Dutch cycling revolution** got underway), will be removed and refilled with water. Also; **Utrecht Centraal**, the busiest railway station of The Netherlands, needs to cater for 100 million travellers per year by 2030. On-going building works, diversions and inconveniences will be likely until 2019!

12.1 At bus station → via 🚲 on right side of bus/railway station area
12.5 At end of railway station area (square/green "Smakkelaarsveld") ⬅ via 🚲 (Van Sijpesteijntunnel under railway, *LF 4b*), ep ↖ via 🚲
13.0 At major jct with lhts cross main rd via crossings ↑, ↑ onto quiet rd with canal on right hand side (Leidseweg, *LF 4b*)

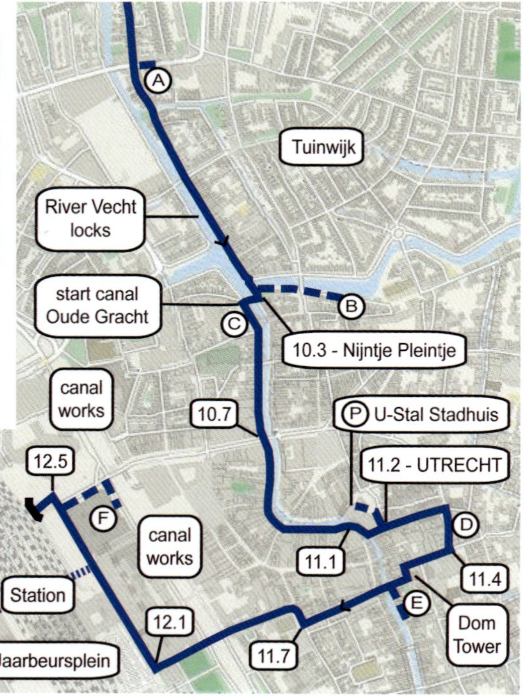

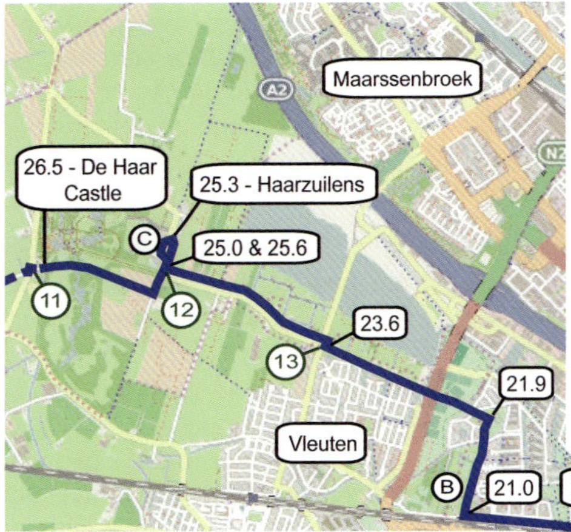

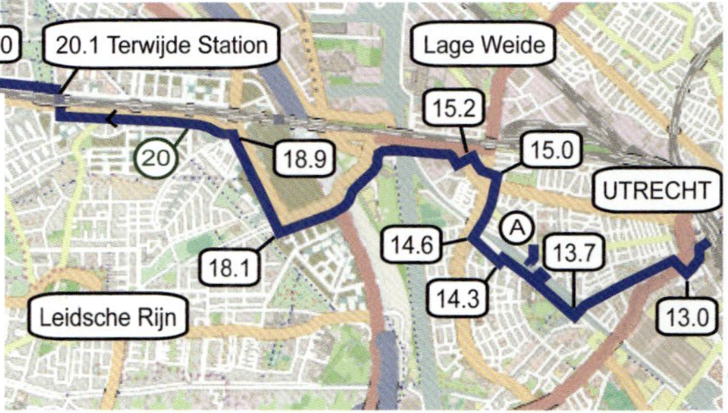

13.7	↑ via 🚲 bridge over wide canal and imm → via 🚲 (to Lage Weide/Vleuten)
14.3	At sign "dead end" ↱ onto rd (Kanaalweg)
14.6	At jct → via 🚲 on right side of main rd (to Lage Weide), at lhts ↑
15.0	At major jct with lhts ← via crossings onto 🚲 on right side of rd (to Terwijde/Vleuten)
15.2	Cross rd ↱ via lhts, keep ↑ via 🚲 on left side of rd
18.1	At rndabt "Kamilleweg" via crossings onto 🚲 on left side of main rd (to Terwijde/Vleuten)
18.9	At jct with lhts ← 🚲 on left side of rd (Hoefweg, to Terwijde/Vleuten & KP 20)
20.1	At 4th jct with lhts → to 🚉 🚲 **Terwijde Station**, after viaduct imm ← via rd (Hof ter Weydeweg)
21.0	After end estate, 1st rd → (Enghlaan, to KP 13)
21.9	At T-jct ←, keep ↑ via 🚲 (to De Haar & KP 13)
23.6	At KP 13 ↑ via on right side of main rd (to De Haar)
25.0	At jct KP 12 → (to Haarzuilens/Breukelen)
25.3	At end of 🏨🍴 **Haarzuilens Village Green** ←, loop back around green, at T-jct → (back to KP 12)
25.6	Back at jct KP 12 ↑ (to De Haar Castle & KP 11), then 1st rd → (to De Haar Castle & KP 11)
26.5	🏨 🏰 **De Haar Castle** (main gate), end of route (to continue, see page 81)

Rush hour on the cycle route to Leidsche Rijn and Terwijde developments

Haarzuilens village green, built in 1898.

Randstad Circle: Route 3: The Green Heart (32 km)

Stations: Woerden, Gouda (see page 85, extra 2 km!)
Cycling time: 2-3 hours (🚲 14%, 🚶 86%)

The **Green Heart** is the common name for the greenbelt closely surrounded by the "big four" cities of The Netherlands; Amsterdam, The Hague, Utrecht and Rotterdam. This route takes you through one of its prettiest sections. On the way to the town of Woerden, you encounter some typical country lanes through **diary farm country**. You also follow a towpath alongside the **Old Rhine**, a peaceful stream on the course of where the main flow of the River Rhine used to be during Roman times. This was the natural northern border of the Roman Empire on the continent!

From the town of Woerden, you cycle alongside the extremely pretty **Lange Linschoten** stream. If you fancy some peaceful canoeing, consider a stay at **Natuurcamping De Boerderij**. This venue features a campsite, Bed & Breakfast and a canoe rental on a working farm.

The town of **Oudewater** is home to the **Witch Weighing Museum**. Holy Roman Emperor Charles V (reign 1519-1556) was convinced that the Oudewater weighing scales were the only "fair equipment" in his European empire to determine whether or not someone was a witch. In Dutch known as **Heksenwaag**, this small museum is a recipe for fun, especially because you can check yourself and your family on "witchcraft"-worthiness on the original scales (open Tue-Sun, €5 pp).

- **0.0** (26.5) From main gate ⬅🏰 **De Haar Castle** head west, at jct *KP 11* ↖ (Lagehaarse Dijk, to *KP 10*)
- **0.7** At end of rd, at *KP 10*, → via 🚲 (Kortjakse Pad, to *KP 9*)
- **1.6** Ep, at *KP 9*, ← via rd (Gerverscop, to *KP 73*)
- **5.1** At T-jct *KP 73* ← via 🚲 on left side of rd (Leidsestraatweg, to *KP 72* & *KP 74*)
- **5.2** 1st rd →, after bridge → (Breeveld, to *KP 72*)
- **6.8** At *KP 72* ↑ (to *KP 71*)
- **7.8** Just before main rd ↗ via 🚲 under bridge (to Centrum & *KP 71*), after tunnel, cross rd ↑ and imm ↗ via narrow 🚲 (towpath)
- **10.3** Ep ← via 🚲 on left side of rd, at jct ↗ via crossing to 🚲 on right side of rd, keep ↑ (to Station & *KP 69*)

Woerden is an old market town that has been extended massively to house Utrecht commuters since the 1970s. The town centre is 300m off our route (see signs for "Centrum"). The high street has plenty of shops, cafes, etc. There are also services on the station square (directly on our route), for if you are just after some drinks and "food on the go".

- **10.5** In front of station 🏨 🍴 🏪 ⚓ ⤴ **Woerden** → via 🚲 (to Linschoten), after subway follow traffic-calmed route (to *KP 69*)
- **11.8** After cycling through two tunnels, 1st rd → (Polaner Zandweg, to *KP 69*)
- **12.2** After bridge ← (Korte Linschoten W.Z., to *KP 69*)
- **12.6** After motorway viaduct, at *KP 69*, 2nd rd → (Haardijk, to *KP 94*), keep ↑

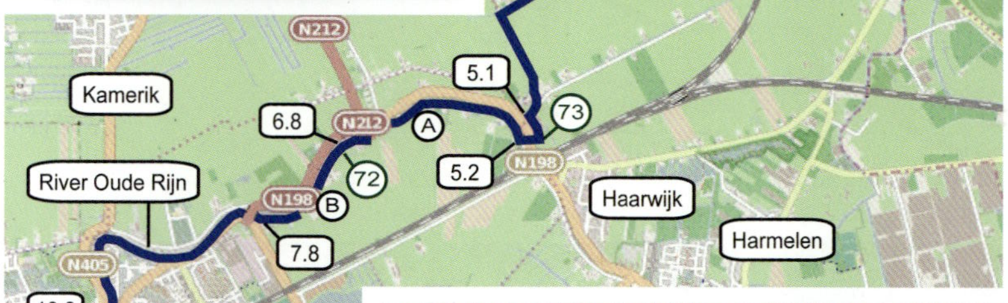

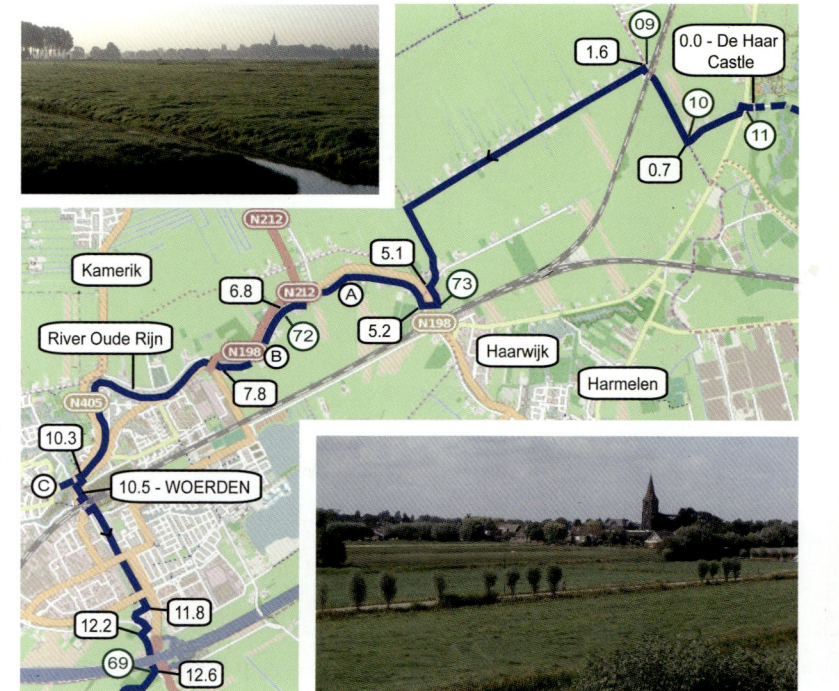

Randstad Circle: Route 3: The Green Heart (32 km)

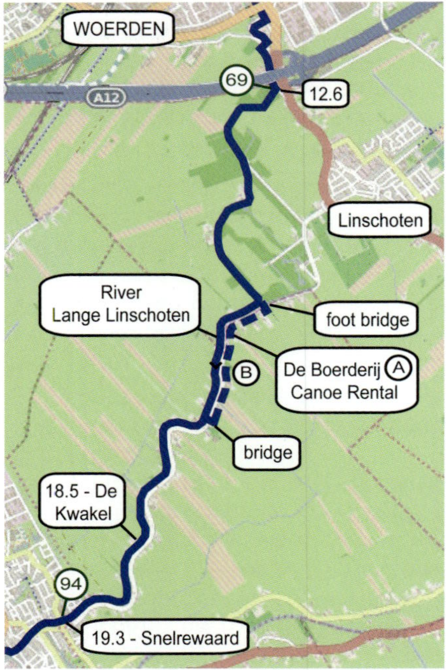

- 18.5 Theetuin De Kwakel
- 19.3 In **Snelreward**, at *KP 94*, ↑
- 19.7 At *KP 93* ↑ (Kromme Haven, to Centrum & *KP 92*)
- 20.0 In ✦ ⌂ ⚓ ☕ 🍴 ℍ ⚐ **Oudewater**, on central square ↑ (Peperstraat)
- 20.1 At next jct ↑ (Wijdstraat, to Hekendorp/Haastrecht)
- 20.2 At church ↖ via narrow rd (Helletje), at canal ↗
- 20.3 At *KP 92* ↑ via 🚲 (to Hekendorp/Haastrecht & *KP 14*)
- 20.8 At T-jct ↖ (to Hekendorp/Haastrecht & *KP 14*)

If you are lucky enough to receive a "not being a witch" certificate at the "Heksenwaag" (right), you can truly relax on Oudewater square!

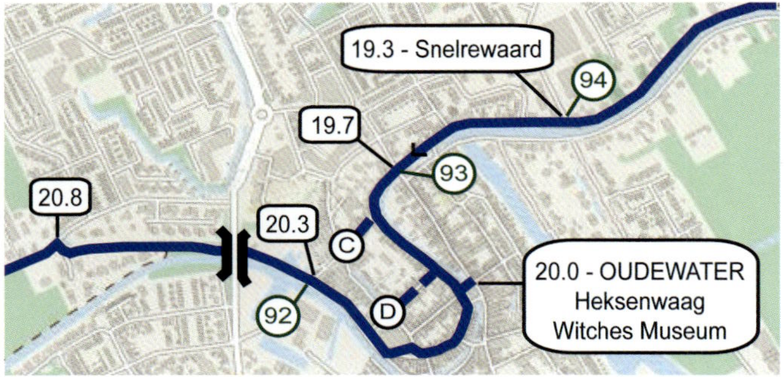

Beyond Oudewater, on the way to Gouda, you have the opportunity to stock up on **authentic Gouda cheese** directly from some Gouda cheese farms. You'll also pass the historic site of **Goejanverwellesluis** in the village of **Hekendorp**; read on the next page to find out what all the fuss was about!

The Goejanverwellesluis history:

In 1787, Dutch Republicans (referring to themselves as "patriots") gained enough power to deny their King William V the control of the army and access to his royal palace in The Hague. The King was forced to reside in the east of the country. This defeat was not taken lightly by his wife, Wilhelmina of Prussia, and she decided to head for The Hague. News about her journey spread. Gouda Republicans stopped her horse carriage and entourage at the **bridge** over the **locks of Goejanverwellesluis**.

Wilhelmina was sent back east. Wilhelmina's brother, in charge of Prussia (part of today's Germany), was not pleased. The Prussian army invaded The Netherlands and ended the Republican revolt, reinstating William V and his wife Wilhelmina in The Hague.

24.6 At jct *KP 14* in 🏠 **Hekendorp**, at bridge over locks ⇐ **Goejanverwellesluis** ↑ (to Haastrecht & *KP 12*), keep to dyke rd

26.8 ⇐ 🧀 **Kaasboerderij De Twee Hoeven**
(Buy authentic Gouda Cheese from the farm!)

27.8 At jct ↑ (Steinse Dijk, to Gouda) via dyke rd

28.3 ⇐ 🧀 **Kaasboerderij 't Klooster**
(Buy authentic Gouda Cheese from the farm!)

30.0 Cross rd ↑ (Goejanverwelledijk, to *KP 40*)

31.8 At end of rd ↑ onto 🚲 on right side of rd

31.9 Traffic lhts opposite river bridge, end of route:
For Gouda City Centre short circular route and for route to Gouda station, see page 85.
For circular route from Gouda to Kinderdijk windmills World Heritage, see pages 86-89.
For continued route to Delft, see page 91.

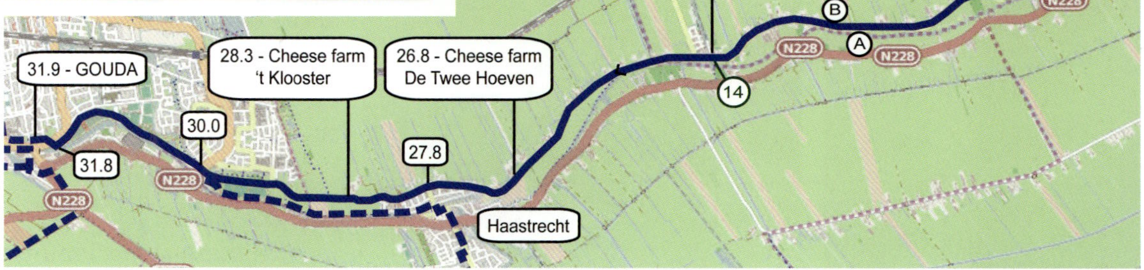

Randstad Circle: Route 4: Gouda & Kinderdijk windmills (61 km)

Stations: Gouda
Cycling time: 4-6 hours (🚲 48%, 🚶 50%, 🚂 1%, ⛴ 1%)

This is a circular route, starting and ending in **Gouda**, taking you to the **World Heritage Kinderdijk windmills**. You can cycle this route as a **day trip** from Gouda station or as an **extra route** on the main circular. Note this route is pretty exposed; the anti-clockwise direction of travel is chosen with prevailing southwesterlies in mind. Buy food and drink in Gouda before setting off, as there is not much on the way other than at Kinderdijk halfway.

The historic city of **Gouda** is famous for its **cheese**. On its large triangular market square with its prominent **town hall**, a traditional **cheese market** is held on Thursdays (April-August, 10am - 1pm, free). The **Goudse Waag Cheese Museum** is based in the historic weigh house (open daily, €5 pp). You may also want to visit the **Sint Jans Church**, reknown for its stained glass windows displaying scenes of the Bible (Mon-Sat, €4 pp). You'll leave Gouda via the bridge across the tidal **Hollandse IJssel River** and cycle into a wide expanse of low lying flats. The villages **Achterbroek** and **Berkenwoude** and the woods of **Loetbos** provide some route variety. The **City of Rotterdam** isn't included in this book, but if you would like to pay a visit to this great modern city, you could take the **watertaxi** from Kinderdijk. For more information and reservations, see www.watertaxirotterdam.nl.

For users starting at Gouda station: See the dotted line on the map to find your way from the station to "Markt" Square to join the route below at "Markt" square after 1.3 km. This is a short **circular route**, starting and ending at **KP40**, at the lights next to the river bridge. This is where the Green Heart route ends (see page 83), where the Kinderdijk circular route starts/ends (see pages 86-89) and where the route to Delft starts (see page 91). Also use the route below if you go towards Gouda station!

- 0.0 (2.7, 31.9 or 58.3) At lhts (*KP 40*), go west on 🚲 on right side
- 0.2 At next jct with lhts ↗ via 🚲 on right side of rd (to Centrum), join rd at bottom of slope (end of 🚲) 🚗
- 0.5 At jct with lhts ↙ via 🚲 bridge (Doelenbrug, to Doelenstraat)
- 0.7 1st rd → (Groeneweg), then 2nd rd → via car park (Koepoort), then imm ↙ (Geuzenstraat)
- 1.0 At T-jct ↙ (Langetiendeweg, to Markt), ↑ into pedestrian zone
- 1.2 Follow bend → (Langetiendeweg, to Markt), at "Markt" Square ⛲🏠⛲☕🍴🏨 ↑ **Gouda** ↙
(For station ↑ across square, see dotted line on map for route)
- 1.3 In south corner of "Markt" into "Wijdstraat" (to *KP 41*), at jct ↗ and ↙ onto canal bridge, imm → (to 🏨 **Hotel Keizerskroon**)
Note: one way road without contraflow; dismount and walk bikes!
- 1.6 2nd rd ↙ (Keizersstraat, to 🏨 **Keizerskroon**), *resume cycling!*
- 1.8 At T-jct ↙ (to "De Mondriaan"), keep ↑ (Korte Noodgodsstraat)
- 2.0 Before 2nd bridge → (Westhaven)
- 2.2 Use pedestrian lhts to cross rd, ↙ via 🚲 on right side (to *KP 40*)

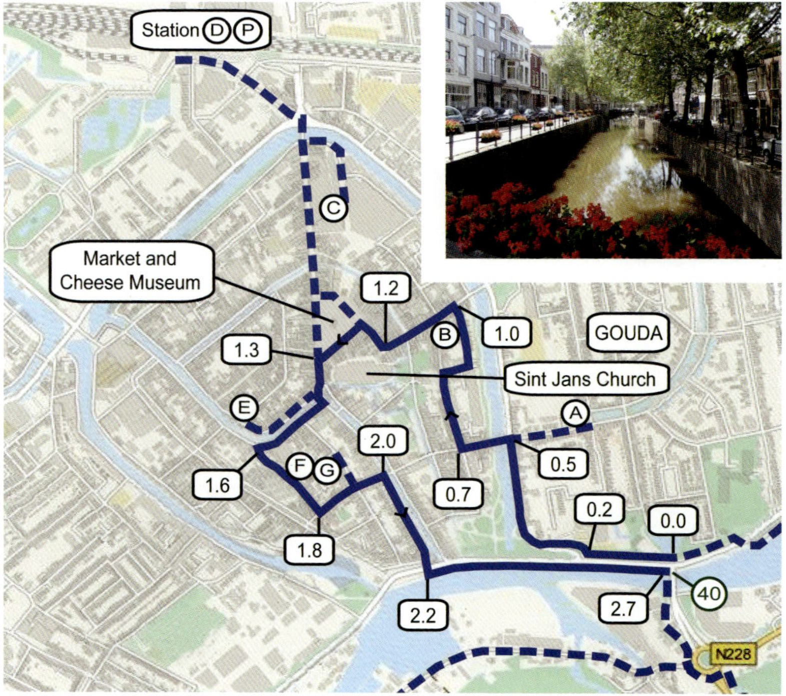

Randstad Circle: Route 4: Gouda & Kinderdijk windmills (61 km)

At **World Heritage Kinderdijk** you'll find the largest concentration of **Dutch windmills**, dating from 1740. Their only purpose is to pump water from lower lying areas into higher lying canals. The Netherlands once counted an estimated 10,000 windmills, of which just over 1,200 windmills survive today.

0.0 (2.7 or 31.9) At *KP 40*, go south on bridge via 🚲 on right side of rd
0.2 At rndabt *KP 9* ↰ via crossings to 🚲 on left side of rd
 (to Bergambacht & *KP 10*), ↑ at next rndabt via 🚲 on left side of rd
0.8 At *KP 10*, cross rd → (Gouderakse Tiendweg, to Ouderkerk & *KP 11*)
2.6 At T-jct *KP 11* ← (to *KP 13*), after 200m follow bend of road to →
5.1 At *KP 13*, ignore sign *LF2a*, 1st 🚲 ← (to Achterbroek & *KP 57*)
6.4 Ep, at *KP 57* → via rd (to Berkenwoude & *KP 19*)
8.2 At T-jct *KP 19* ← (Kerkweg, to Berkenwoude)
10.4 At T-jct *KP 21* → (Westeinde, to Lekkerkerk & *KP 20*)
12.4 At *KP 20*, 1st 🚲 ← (to *KP 25*)
13.4 At T-jct *KP 25* → (to Lekkerkerk & *KP 68*)
14.2 After ⛴ **Canoe Centre Loetbos**, at *KP 68*, ↑ (to Rotterdam & *KP 66*)

- **16.3** At pumping station "Hillekade" ↗, use rd crossings and continue via 🚲 (to *KP 66*)
- **18.0** At *KP 66* ←, cross rds and ←, then 1st 🚲 → (to Krimpen a/d Lek & *KP 63*), on right side of rd
- **19.5** *Ignore sign LF2a*, keep ↑ (to Kinderdijk)
- **19.8** Cross rd ↑ onto "Breekade", *ignore all 🚲 signs!*
- **20.2** At T-jct → (Oosterlekdijk), 1st rd ↖ via dyke rd
- **21.2** Keep ↑, at main rd jct ← to ⛴ **Kinderdijk Ferry** *(runs every 10 mins, daily until midnight, €1 pp)*
- **21.4** In ⛴ **Kinderdijk** 1st rd ← (to Nieuw Lekkerland & *KP 3*), at end "fietsstraat" ↑ via 🚲
- **21.9** At jct *KP 3* ← via rd 🚗, then → via car park to ⛴ **World Heritage Kinderdijk windmills**

Kinderdijk is truly best explored by bike. Access is free, but if you wish to view windmills from inside, you'll need to purchase tickets at the main entrance. Two windmills can be visited (open daily, €8 pp). With our route, you'll leave this world heritage site by the back entrance, so if you want to purchase food, drinks or souvenirs, it is best to do so on arrival.

- **22.2** At end car park, ↑ via "fietspad", keep ↑ (*LF2a*)
- **25.6** At *KP 19* ↑ via 🚲 (to Streefkerk & *KP 7*)
- **30.6** At T-jct *KP 7* ← (to Streefkerk & *KP 5*)
- **32.2** At *KP 5* → to ⛴ **Streefkerk windmills**

Randstad Circle: Route 4: Gouda & Kinderdijk windmills (61 km)

Streefkerk windmills

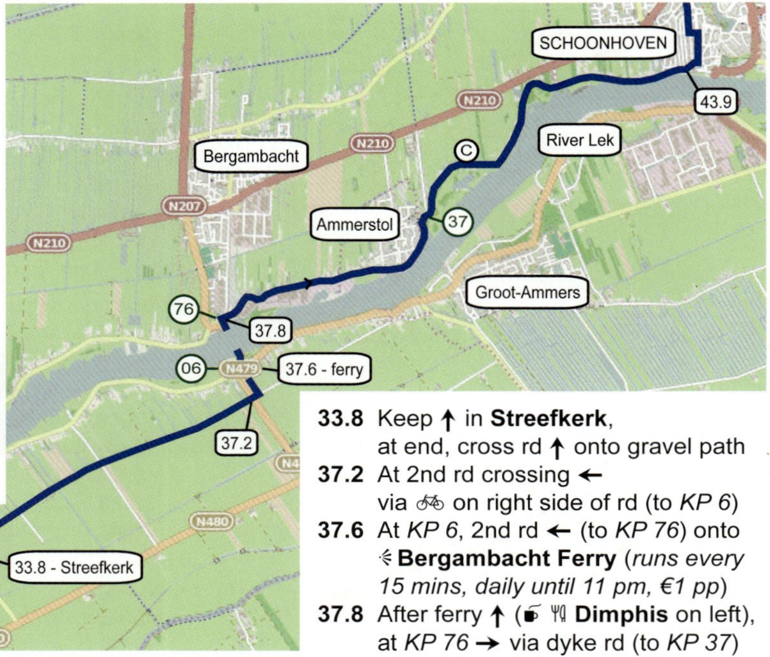

33.8 Keep ↑ in **Streefkerk**, at end, cross rd ↑ onto gravel path
37.2 At 2nd rd crossing ←, via 🚲 on right side of rd (to *KP 6*)
37.6 At *KP 6*, 2nd rd ← (to *KP 76*) onto ⛴ **Bergambacht Ferry** (*runs every 15 mins, daily until 11 pm, €1 pp*)
37.8 After ferry ↑ (☕ 🍴 **Dimphis** on left), at *KP 76* → via dyke rd (to *KP 37*)

43.9 At 🏨 **Hotel Belvedere** ↑ (to *KP 10*)
44.1 After canal bridge imm ← (Haven)
44.4 In ⛪🏨☕🍴🏛🚲 **Schoonhoven** at 2nd square (church on left side) ← (Kerkstraat, to Gouda), then 1st rd → (Koestraat, to *KP 13*)
44.9 At rndabt ↑ via 🚲 crossings (Schreuderstraat, to Vlist & *KP 13*)
45.6 At T-jct *KP 13* ←, 1st rd → (to Vlist)

Schoonhoven

Schoonhoven is a well preserved historic Dutch town, locally famous for its silver and clock making trades. The **Zilvermuseum** (open Tue-Sun, €8 pp) keeps these traditions alive. The **Vlist** is a scenic stream, with many dairy farms aligned on its banks. Rowing barges were used to get the cheese to the Gouda market!

48.1 At jct *KP 11* ↗, after bridge ↖ (to Vlist & *KP 30*), keep ↑ at *KP 30* in ⇖ **Vlist** (to *KP 27*), rd becomes "fietspad"

52.9 At *KP 27*, cross rd ↑ onto "fietspad" (to Haastrecht), ep ↑ join rd 🚲

53.7 At rndabt *KP 12* ↑ via crossings into ⇖ 🏨 🍴 🛒 🍽 ⤴ **Haastrecht**

54.0 After bend to ↙, 1st rd → (Veerstraat, to Hekendorp), after bridge imm ↙ (Jaagpad), this rd becomes "fietspad"

55.8 At very end of tarmac "fietspad", join main 🚲 ↑ on dyke ridge

56.4 Cross rd ↑ (Goejanverwelledijk, to *KP 40*)

58.2 At end of rd ↑ onto 🚲 on right side of rd

58.3 Traffic lhts opposite river bridge, end of route:

For Gouda station see page 85, to continue to Delft, see page 91

Randstad Circle: Route 5: Low lands, Delft & City of Glass (67 km)

Stations: Gouda (see page 85, extra 2 km!), Rodenrijs, Delft, Hoek van Holland-Haven
Cycling time: 4-6 hours (🚴 60%, 🚶 35%, 🚢 5%)

This route takes you across the very built-up area between **Rotterdam** and **The Hague**, taking you from **Gouda** to the **Dutch Coast** via **Delft**. Stark contrasts await you here; modern/old, busy/quiet, ugly/scenic. Whatever you encounter; it never lasts long and there is plenty to see!

From Gouda, you cycle along the tidal Hollandse IJssel river to **Gouderak**. After taking the scenic ferry to **Moordrecht** (see left picture), you'll arrive in **Holland's lowest lands**. The **Zuidplaspolder** lies **6.7 m below normal high tide sea level**. If the North Sea was ever able to flood this area, the storm waters could cover the gantry sign on the A20 motorway (see right picture) completely. In this situation, most of the Randstad, including all its cities, would be flooded too. The Netherlands is the only country in the world that has a **government policy** stating that the likelihood of such an event is limited to **once in every 10,000 years**. With rising sea levels, sea defences receive set budgets to keep this risk the same year after year...

At **Tweemanspolder** traditional windmills provide great horizons. The **Rottemeren Lakes** cycle path can get crowded with Rotterdam folks. It is the last splash of green before the suburban zone of **Berkel en Rodenrijs**. Perfect cycle paths take you in between greenhouses and housing estates.

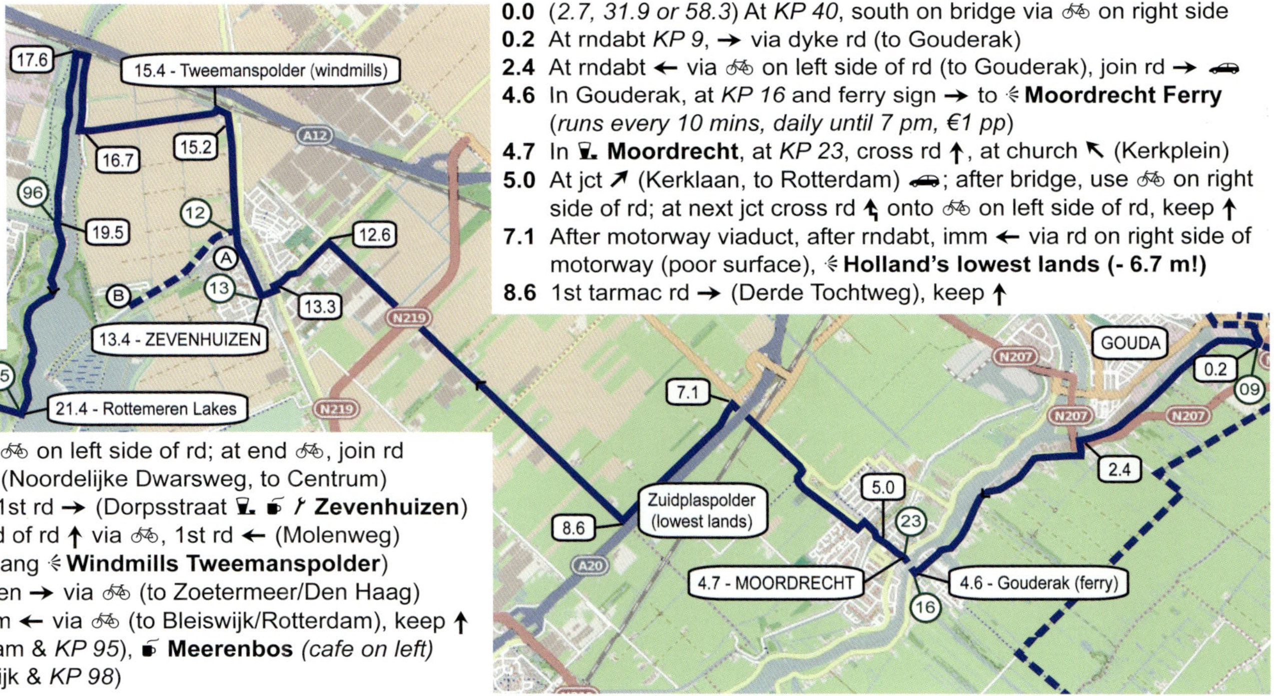

- **0.0** (2.7, 31.9 or 58.3) At KP 40, south on bridge via 🚲 on right side
- **0.2** At mdabt KP 9, → via dyke rd (to Gouderak)
- **2.4** At mdabt ← via 🚲 on left side of rd (to Gouderak)
- **4.6** In Gouderak, at KP 16 and ferry sign → to ⛴ **Moordrecht Ferry** (runs every 10 mins, daily until 7 pm, €1 pp)
- **4.7** In ⛪ **Moordrecht**, at KP 23, cross rd ↑, at church ↖ (Kerkplein)
- **5.0** At jct ↗ (Kerklaan, to Rotterdam) 🚲, after bridge, use 🚲 on right side of rd; at next jct cross rd ↱ onto 🚲 on left side of rd, keep ↑
- **7.1** After motorway viaduct, after rndabt, imm ← via rd on right side of motorway (poor surface), ⛪ **Holland's lowest lands** (- 6.7 m!)
- **8.6** 1st tarmac rd → (Derde Tochtweg), keep ↑

- **12.6** At "give way" jct ← via 🚲 on left side of rd; at end 🚲, join rd
- **13.3** At T-jct ← and imm → (Noordelijke Dwarsweg, to Centrum)
- **13.4** After bridge, at KP 13, 1st rd → (Dorpsstraat ⛪ 🍴 ↘ **Zevenhuizen**)
- **15.2** Keep ↑, just before end of rd ↑ via 🚲, 1st rd ← (Molenweg)
- **15.4** 1st rd ↖ (to Molenviergang ⛪ **Windmills Tweemanspolder**)
- **16.7** At T-jct ↱ via bridge, then → via 🚲 (to Zoetermeer/Den Haag)
- **17.6** After bridge and ⊹ imm ← via 🚲 (to Bleiswijk/Rotterdam), keep ↑
- **19.5** At KP 96 ↑ (to Rotterdam & KP 95), 🍴 **Meerenbos** (cafe on left)
- **21.4** At KP 95, → (to Bleiswijk & KP 98)

Tweemanspolder/Rottemeren

Randstad Circle: Route 5: Low lands, Delft & City of Glass (67 km)

Beyond Berkel en Rodenrijs you enter the green buffer to Delft. You may find the narrow cycle path at **Ackerdijkse Plassen Reserve** slightly below "Dutch standards".

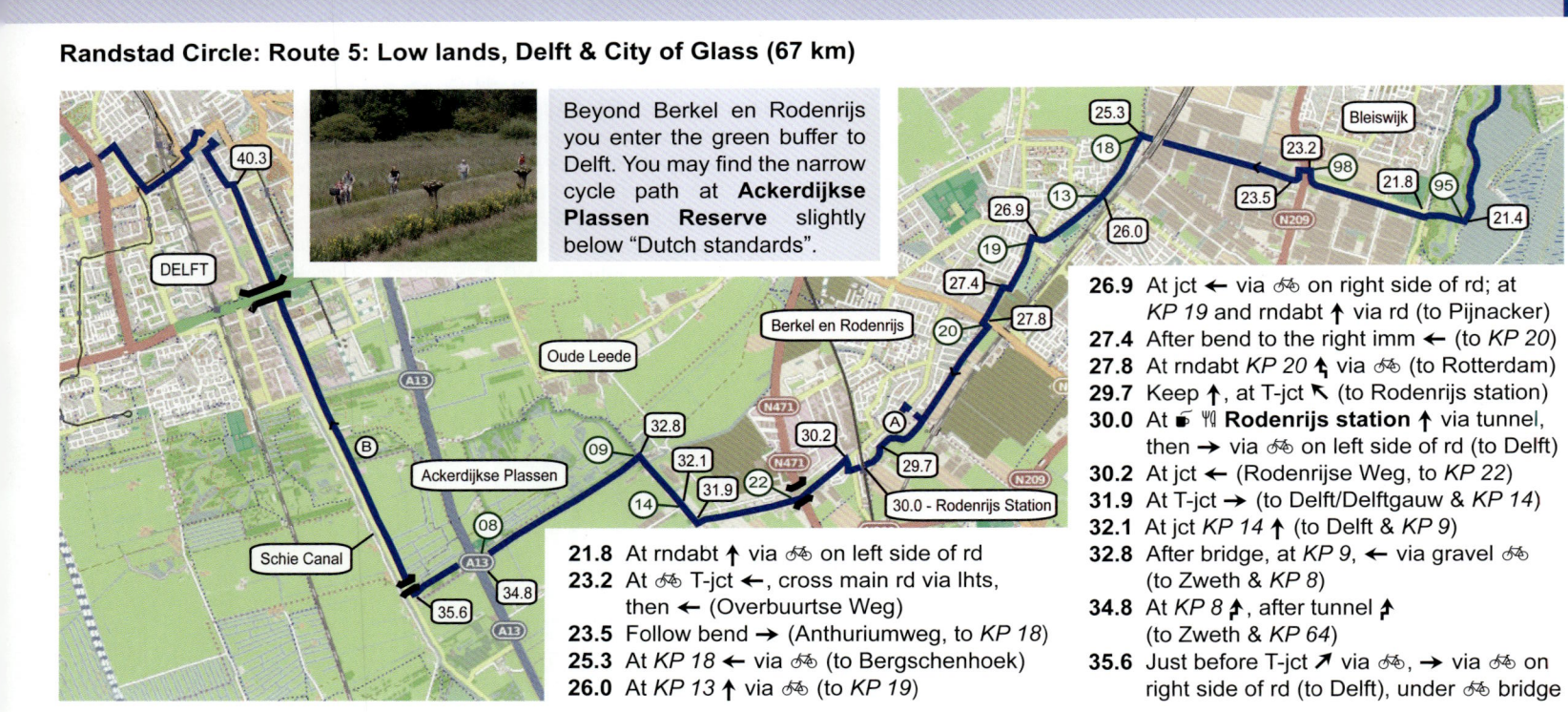

- 21.8 At rndabt ↑ via 🚲 on left side of rd
- 23.2 At 🚲 T-jct ←, cross main rd via lhts, then ← (Overbuurtse Weg)
- 23.5 Follow bend → (Anthuriumweg, to KP 18)
- 25.3 At KP 18 ← via 🚲 (to Bergschenhoek)
- 26.0 At KP 13 ↑ via 🚲 (to KP 19)
- 26.9 At jct ←, via 🚲 on right side of rd; at KP 19 and rndabt ↑ via rd (to Pijnacker)
- 27.4 After bend to the right imm ← (to KP 20)
- 27.8 At rndabt KP 20 ↱ via 🚲 (to Rotterdam)
- 29.7 Keep ↑, at T-jct ↖ (to Rodenrijs station)
- 30.0 At 🚉 ¶ **Rodenrijs station** ↑ via tunnel, then → via 🚲 on left side of rd (to Delft)
- 30.2 At jct ← (Rodenrijse Weg, to KP 22)
- 31.9 At T-jct → (to Delft/Delftgauw & KP 14)
- 32.1 At jct KP 14 ↑ (to Delft & KP 9)
- 32.8 After bridge, at KP 9, ← via gravel 🚲 (to Zweth & KP 8)
- 34.8 At KP 8 ↑, after tunnel ↗ (to Zweth & KP 64)
- 35.6 Just before T-jct ↗ via 🚲, → via 🚲 on right side of rd (to Delft), under 🚲 bridge

Delft is famous for its **pottery**. Find out about **Delftware** in Delft at **Porceleyne Fles** (open daily, €13 pp) or visit the **Candelaer shop** on Kerkstraat near Markt Square. Delft played an important role in Dutch history. **William of Orange** (also known as William the Silent), leader of the Dutch revolt against Spanish rule (see also page 152), was murdered in Delft in 1584. The **bullet holes** of this assassination can be viewed in the **Prinsenhof Museum**, as are displays about William's life, **Vermeer** paintings and **Delftware pottery** (open Tue-Sun, €10 pp). In the **Nieuwe Kerk**, on **Markt Square**, Dutch royals find their last resting place, alongside William of Orange's grave. Delft with its **canals** is very **scenic.** Use **guarded bike parks** (see P on map) and go for a stroll, as our cycle route only touches the side of the historic area. A **canal boat tour** from Koornmarkt is another great way of exploring Delft (running daily, €8 pp).

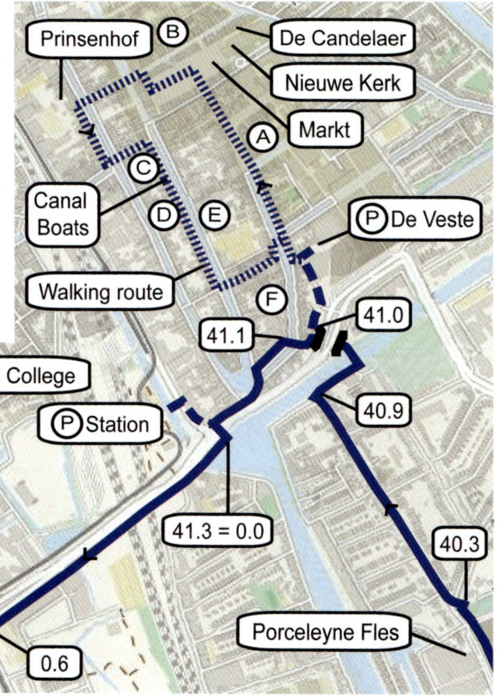

40.3 Just after ⚓ **Royal Delftware Porceleyne Fles** (on left side of rd), where rd bends to the right, cross rd ↖ (Rotterdamse Weg)
40.9 At canal → (to Centrum), 1st bridge ←, follow 🚲 into subway
41.0 (For route Delft and P De Veste, imm after subway →, see map)
41.1 Ep cross canal via 🚲 bridge, then ← (to "Doorgaand Verkeer")
41.2 ← and imm → via 🚲 on right side of main rd
41.3 At major jct with lhts ⚓ 🏠 🍴 ☕ ⛽ 🏨 🚻 **Delft** *(station on right side)*, ***reset mileage*** to **0.0**, 🚴 via crossings onto 🚲 on left side of rd
0.6 At jct with lhts → via 🚲 on right side of rd (Krakeelpolderweg)
1.1 After 🛒 *shops*, before canal bridge, on corner Stanislas College, ← via canal rd (Buitenwatersloot, to Hoek van Holland)

Randstad Circle: Route 5: Low lands, Delft & City of Glass (67 km)

Leaving Delft, you arrive in **Westland**, an area also known as "De Glazen Stad" (**The City of Glass**). Except for some parkland reserves, such as **Staalduyn** (see picture on left), greenhouses dominate the horizon. Flowers, plants, fruit and vegetables are produced here all year round for a global market. It is very likely that some produce from this area will find its way to your local garden centre or supermarket.

- **1.4** After passing under viaduct, via bridge ↑ to right side of canal (to Naaldwijk), keep ↑ via "Buitenwatersloot" and "Hoornse Kanaal"
- **2.7** In 🛏 🍴 **Den Hoorn** at "*Snackbar De Pitstop*" ↖, follow canal route (Rijksstraatweg) 🚗
- **2.9** 1st bridge ←, cross canal, than imm ↗ onto canal rd (Tramkade)
- **4.9** At split of paths ↗ via canalside 🚲, keep ↑
- **5.6** At T-jct (*KP 56*) 🛏 🍴 **Schipluiden** →, after bridge ← (to Maasland)
- **6.0** At T-jct ←, 🚲 on right side, imm ↑ via 🚲 ← (to 't Woudt & *KP 55*)
- **6.8** At *KP 55* ↑ onto canal bridge (to *KP 32*)
- **8.9** At 2nd sharp bend to the right ↑ via 🚲 (to *KP 32*)
- **9.6** At *KP 32* → via 🚲 ← (to *KP 27*), keep ↑
- **10.9** At rndabt ←, via crossings to 🚲 on right side of rd (Crezeelaan), ep ← via lay-by rd (see petrol station *Pin & Go* on right side of rd)
- **11.2** At *KP 27*, 1st rd → (Laan van Adrichem), after bridge imm → and 1st 🚲 ← (to *KP 15*)
- **12.4** Ep ← via rd (to *KP 15*), 1st rd → via 🚲 on right side (Kasteelweg)

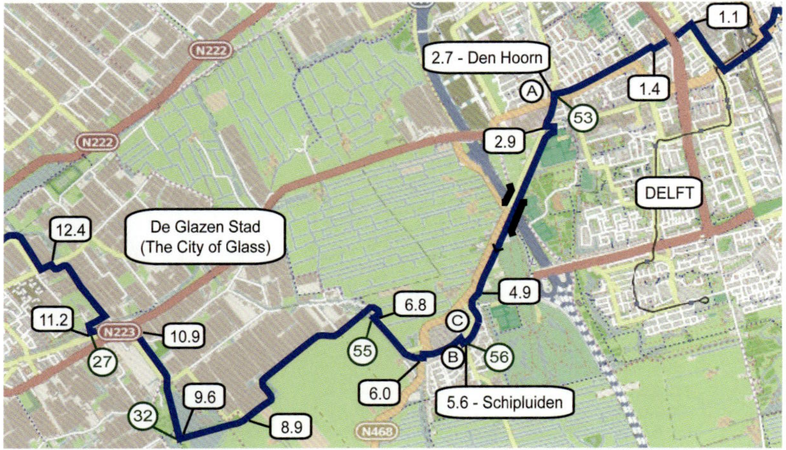

13.4	After canal bridge, join rd ↑, stay on this rd 🚗
14.9	At end "Zandheullaan" ← via 🚴 on left side
15.1	At jct with lhts ← via 🚴 on left side of rd (to Naaldwijk/Hoek van Holland) *(For 🚆 Flora Holland ↑ via 🚴 crossings)* *(For 🚆 Westlands Museum → via 🚴; 1.5 km)*
15.7	At jct with lhts ↑ via 🚴 crossings (to Naaldwijk)
16.3	Ep ↗ via lay-by rd, at KP 16 ↑ (Alicantestraat), 🚆 **Naaldwijk** *(petrol station on right after 100m)*
17.4	Keep ↑ via 🚴/lay-by rd, at 2nd rndabt → via 🚴 crossings to 🚴 on left side of rd (Galgeweg)
18.7	1st rd ← via 🚴 on right (Heenweg, to KP 18), at ep, join rd ↑, *give way to traffic from the right!*
19.6	At end ↗ up the slope (to KP 18), press button at lhts, cross ↑ (to KP 18); at next jct ↑ on dyke
20.5	At end of dyke rd, follow "Oude Hooislag" route
21.1	At KP 18 → (to Hoek van Holland & KP 19)
22.3	Ep, at KP 19, ← via 🚴 on left side of rd (Haakweg, to Hoek v. Holland & KP 22), keep ←
23.5	At KP 22 ↗ via 🚴 on dyke ridge (to Station) *(For 🚆 **Maeslantkering Barrier** ↘ via 🚴; 2 km)*
24.7	At 🚴 jct ↖ via 🚴 (to Station/Hanwich)
25.3	*Dismount at zebra*, walk ← via railway crossing, then → *resume cycling* to main railway crossing; end of route *(to continue & for ferries, page 96)*

Experience the **surreal display** of large scale flower auctioning at **Flora Holland Naaldwijk** (Mon-Wed & Fri, 7-9 am only). The **Westlands Museum** shows the history of the City of Glass (€ 4pp).

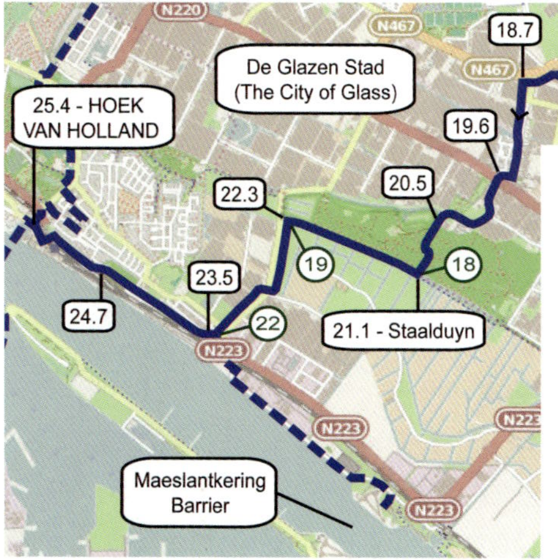

The **Maeslantkering Barrier** with two huge doors can close the Rotterdam shipping canal during storms (English tours on Sat or Sun).

Randstad Circle: Route 6: Hook of Holland & The Hague (28 km)

Stations: Hoek van Holland-Haven, Den Haag Centraal
Cycling time: 2-3 hours (🚴 78%, 🚶 20%, 🚢 2%)

Hoek van Holland (literally "Corner of Holland") marks the southern end of Holland's 118 km (73-miles) sandy beach. The local beach is a popular destination for Rotterdam folks in summer, as it is only 20 minutes by train from Rotterdam Central Station. **Hook** is also known for its **ferry to Harwich**. Ferry services have been running since 1893. If you also wish to **cycle in England** in combination with your Dutch cycle trip, have a look at our **London-Land's End Cycle Route** publication, which allows you to cycle traffic-calmed from Harwich via London, Bath and Bristol to England's western tip in Cornwall (see www.london-landsendcycleroutebook.com). Another important link from Hook is the **ferry to Maasvlakte**, from where you can cycle to the Rotterdam ferry terminal to **Hull**. If you cycle our **southern route**, you'll need to use this link as well, see pages 154-155.

0.0 (13.7 or 25.4) Cross railway and join 🚴 on right side of rd, 1st 🚴 → and imm → into 🏠 🚲 🍴 🛍 ℹ️ 🍴 ⬈ **Hoek van Holland** (Prins Hendrikstraat)
0.4 3rd rd ← (Concordiastraat)
0.5 At T-jct ← (1e Scheepvaartstraat)
0.6 At T-jct → (Rietdijkstraat), at next T-jct ← (Planciusstraat)
0.8 At T-jct → via 🚴 on left side of rd (Harwichweg)

HOEK VAN HOLLAND (HOOK OF HOLLAND)

Station Hoek van Holland Haven

Ferry terminal from/to Harwich

ferry to/from Maasvlakte

The **Dutch coastal cycle route** takes you quickly from Hook to The Hague. **Ter Heyde** is a prominent spot to enter the beach, but there are many access points. **De Zandmotor** is a man-made wide beach; the latest Dutch trick of coastal defence. It has been **built to be washed away** by the waves. Its sand crystals should strengthen the beaches further north!

- **1.5** At T-jct via 🚲 crossing → via residential street on left side of rd (Dirk van den Burgweg)
- **1.7** 2nd rd ← via residential street on left side of rd (Schelpweg)
- **2.0** At *KP 21* → cross rd, → via 🚲 and imm ← via 🚲 (to Kijkduin & *KP 5*)
- **3.0** At jct, cross rd, ← via 🚲 (to Kijkduin), keep ↑
- **3.6** At end of rd ↗ via 🚲 (to Kijkduin/Den Haag)
- **5.1** Cross rd ↑ via 🚲 (to Monster/Den Haag & *KP 9*)
- **5.8** At split of paths ↗ via 🚲 (via subway)
- **7.8** At *KP 9* ↑, after historic cannons ← via rd (Doormanweg, to Strand) into ⚓ 🏛 **Ter Heyde**
- **8.0** At steps (*beach access*) → (Evertsenstraat)
- **8.2** 2nd rd → (Kortenaerstraat), 1st rd ← (Van Speykstraat)
- **8.4** At end residential area ← via 🚲 (to Kijkduin), after 50m, 1st 🚲 ← (paved path), keep ↑

Randstad Circle: Route 6: Hook of Holland & The Hague (28 km)

Our route takes in many prominent landmarks of the city of **The Hague** (Den Haag), such as the **Peace Palace** (Vredespaleis, see left). Built to promote international dialogue, it houses the **International Court of Justice** (expo open Tue-Sun, free)

Keep cycling to the free **Buitenhof guarded bike park** and park up there to allow some time for exploring the city centre's attractions on foot. The **Binnenhof** is a medieval square with the **Knights' Hall** (Ridderzaal), home of the Dutch government. Walk across this square to visit the **Mauritshuis Museum** with paintings of Dutch masters **Rembrandt** and **Vermeer** (open daily, €14 pp). Have a drink on a cosy terrace on **Plein** (literally "Square"), next to the Mauritshuis. Walk back via the bike park to **Noordeinde street** (see picture right) to see the small **Royal Palace Noordeinde** where the **Dutch King** has his working office. Also on this street, you'll find the **Panorama Mesdag Museum**, housing a **full circle panorama painting** of the Dutch coast, painted in 1881 (open daily, €10 pp).

Back on the bike, make your way to **Madurodam**, a Legoland-style miniature park with all Dutch well-known buildings on display (open daily, €16 pp). **Scheveningen** with its stylish 19th century **Kurhaus** is truly "The Hague at the Beach", worth the detour from our main route; use the guarded bike park!

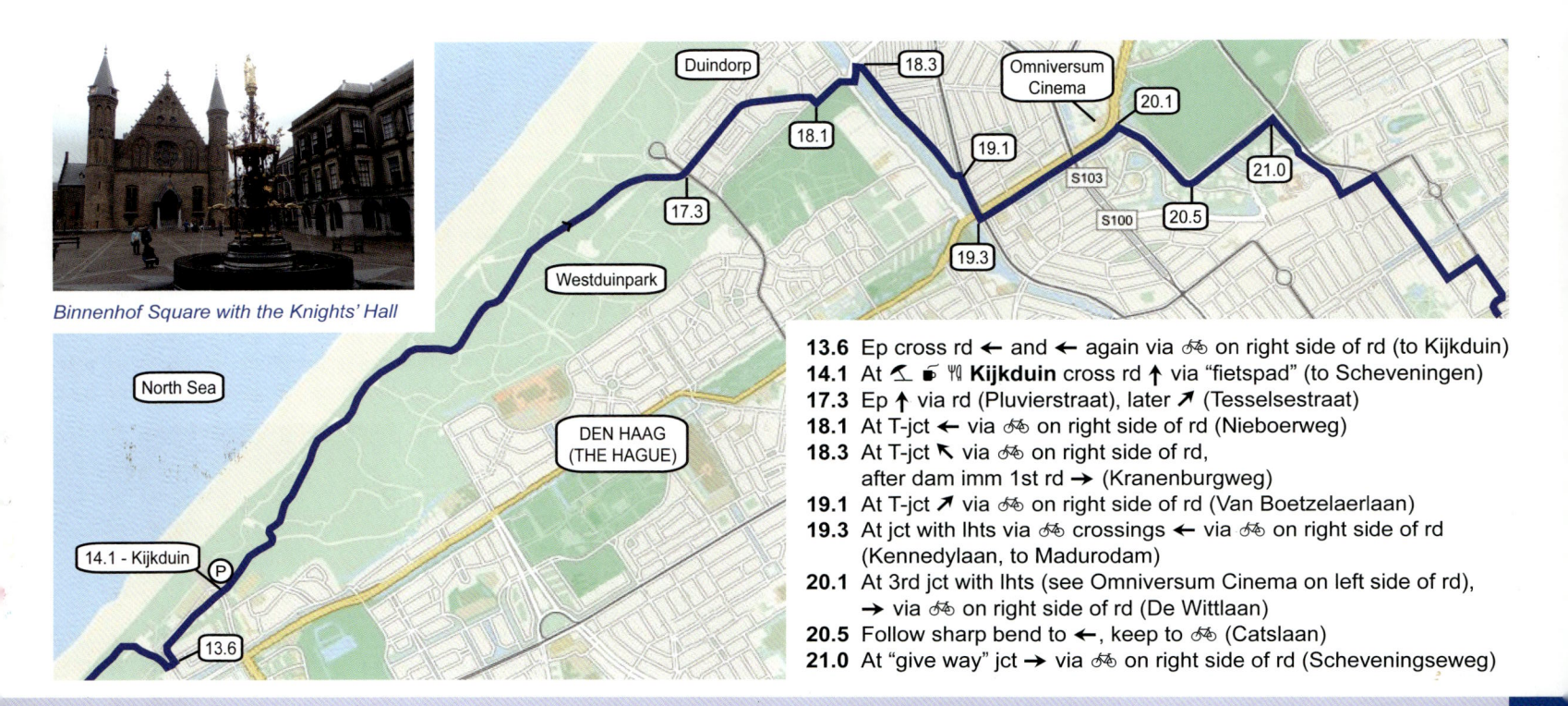

Binnenhof Square with the Knights' Hall

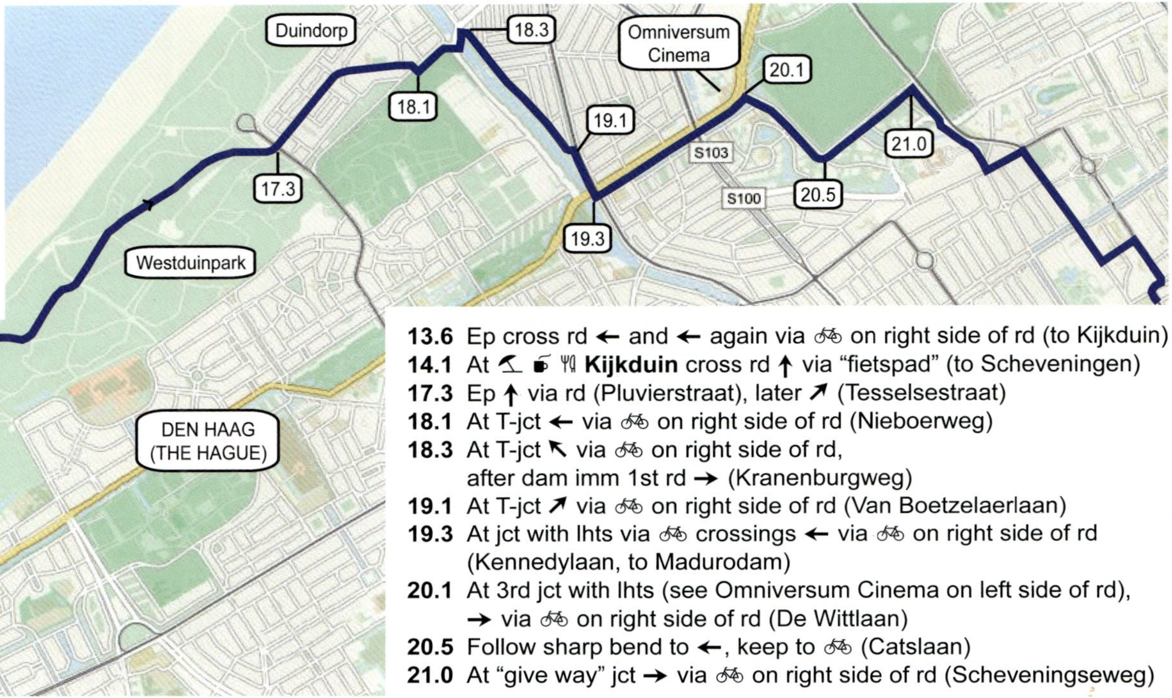

13.6 Ep cross rd ← and ← again via 🚲 on right side of rd (to Kijkduin)
14.1 At ⚓ 🛏 🍴 **Kijkduin** cross rd ↑ via "fietspad" (to Scheveningen)
17.3 Ep ↑ via rd (Pluvierstraat), later ↗ (Tesselsestraat)
18.1 At T-jct ← via 🚲 on right side of rd (Nieboerweg)
18.3 At T-jct ↖ via 🚲 on right side of rd,
      after dam imm 1st rd → (Kranenburgweg)
19.1 At T-jct ↗ via 🚲 on right side of rd (Van Boetzelaerlaan)
19.3 At jct with lhts via 🚲 crossings ← via 🚲 on right side of rd
     (Kennedylaan, to Madurodam)
20.1 At 3rd jct with lhts (see Omniversum Cinema on left side of rd),
     ↑ via 🚲 on right side of rd (De Wittlaan)
20.5 Follow sharp bend to ←, keep to 🚲 (Catslaan)
21.0 At "give way" jct via 🚲 on right side of rd (Scheveningseweg)

Randstad Circle: Route 6: Hook of Holland & The Hague (28 km)

- **21.2** At jct with lhts ↑ via 🚴 on right side of rd (Carnegieplein)
- **21.4** Follow rd ↗ alongside ⚐ **Vredespaleis** *(Peace Palace)*
- **21.6** At jct with lhts ← (to Leiden) 🚴 *(note; this can be a tricky turn!)*
- **21.7** Just at start of 🚴, 2nd rd → (Zeestraat), use 🚴 lane against flow
- **22.1** After ⚐ **Panorama Mesdag** *(on left side of rd)*, ↑ at jct (Noordeinde)
- **22.3** 1st rd ← (Oranjestraat)
- **22.5** At T-jct → (Parkstraat), use 🚴 lane, follow rd with bends
- **23.1** After lake with flag poles on left side of rd *dismount* ↗ onto square ⚐ 🏠 🍴 🍽 ℹ ↗ **Den Haag** *guarded bike park Buitenhof*
- **0.0** (23.1) Coming from guarded bike park, ← via 🚴 on right side of rd, after lake with flag poles imm → via 🚴 (Lange Vijverberg)
- **0.7** At major jct with lhts, cross ↑ via 🚴 crossings, then ← via 🚴 on right side of rd (to Scheveningen) *(For Den Haag Central Station →)*
- **1.1** At major jct with lhts, cross ↑ via 🚴 crossings (to Scheveningen), ↑

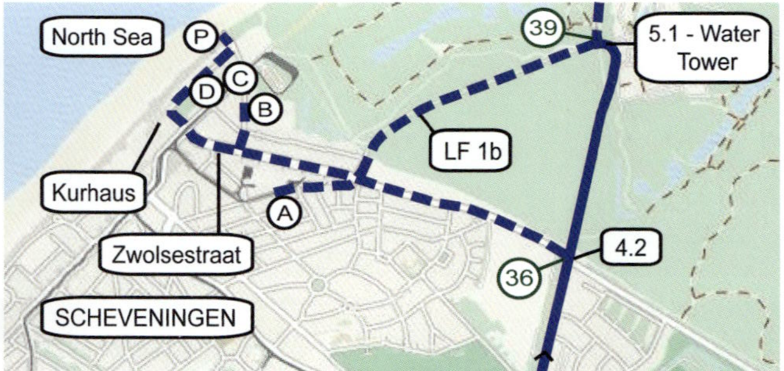

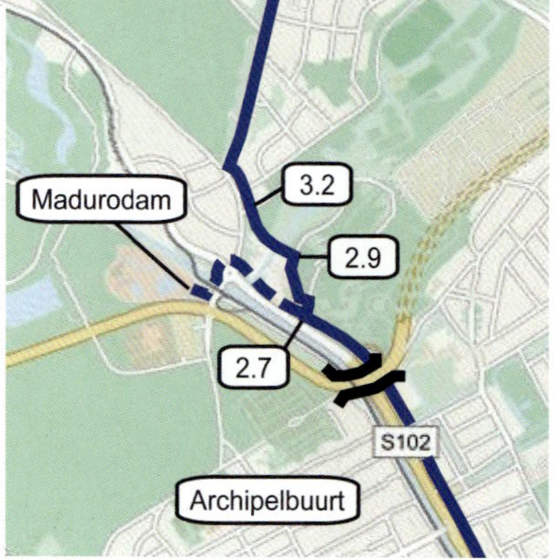

The impressive Kurhaus at Scheveningen beach and family fun in Madurodam

2.7 After cycling under viaduct and crossing slip rd, 1st rd → (St Hubertusweg) and imm ↖ (Kwekerijweg) *(For 🚲 **Madurodam** keep ↑ for 200m via 🚲 on right side of rd)*

2.9 1st 🚲 ← (imm after large office building on left side of rd)

3.2 Ep ↑ via quiet street (Badhuisweg), at T-jct ↗ (Pompstationweg)

4.2 At rd crossing KP36, *choose your route:*

For **Holland Coast Route** to Zandvoort/Haarlem ↑ via "fietspad" (to Wassenaar, *LF1b*); after **5.1** km, at water tower, see page 103.

For 🚤 🏠 🛏 🍴 **Scheveningen/Kurhaus** ← via 🚲 on right side of rd; after **5.5** km at jct with lhts ↑ via quiet rd (Zeekant), *guarded bike park Strandweg-Noordboulevard* at end of this rd on your left. After your beach visit, return inland via Zwolsestraat and take 1st 🚲 ← (to Katwijk, *LF1b*); at water tower see page 103.

Randstad Circle: Route 7: Holland Coast & Haarlem (47 km)

Stations: (Den Haag Centraal, see route 6, extra 5 km!), Zandvoort, Overveen, Haarlem
Cycling time: 3 - 5 hours (🚴 83%, 🚶 11%, 🚌 4%, 🚗 2%)

The 6,000 km long **North Sea Cycle Route** is nowhere more splendid than on its traffic-free journey across the coastal **sand dune reserves** between The Hague and Haarlem. On the Holland coast, **cycling truly comes home**, whether you are on a Dutch shopper or ride all the gears. Even when you only stay in Amsterdam, consider taking your bikes to Den Haag Central Station (one hour by train, start on page 100). Have a great day ride to Zandvoort or Haarlem (to include the tulip fields, see page 110).

You'll find yourself cycling on the smoothest **coastal highway** of your dreams, dedicated to **cycling only**! Every other mile, there is access to the **beach** for cyclists and pedestrians only, providing perfect seaside breaks. The sand dunes reserves provide **great scenery** with a certain **remote feel**, while bustling **seaside reasorts** as Katwijk, Noordwijk and Zandvoort are never far away. Although the otherwise perfect cycling conditions can briefly evaporate in these towns (even to Dutch standards), this route is without doubt one of the most special cycle routes in the world. It is an **exposed** ride though. Only cycle in reasonably fine weather and check that the prevailing southwesterlies will indeed push you forward from The Hague to Haarlem. Note our listings for this route do not feature large, expensive seaside hotels. Only B&Bs, hostels and small hotels are listed.

Seaside fun in Katwijk

- **0.0** (5.1) At water tower (*KP 39*), go north via 🚲 (to Katwijk/Wassenaar & *KP 40*), keep ↑
- **6.8** T-jct *KP 41* at 🚰 **Fresh Drinking Water Pump**:
  For 🍴 **Duinrell/Tikipool** → via 🚲 *(after 3.5 km; see blue box below)*
  For Main Route ← via 🚲 (to Strand, Katwijk a Zee & *KP 97*)
- **6.9** *For* 🍴 **Wassenaarse Slag** ↑ via 🚲 *(after 1 km)*
  For Main Route 1st 🚲 → (to Katwijk a Zee & *KP 97*)
  cross rd, ↖ follow "fietspad"

Duinrell is a theme park with various rollercoasters and fun rides. Its special attraction is the **Tikipool** with 11 worldclass slides. It is possible to purchase separate tickets for both the theme park and pool. Ticket prices for the Tikipool are based on the time you want to spend in the water, see also www.duinrell.nl (open daily). From *KP 41* and the Drinking Water pump, follow 🚲 inland, at rndabt ↗ via 🚲 (to Wassenaar), at jct with lhts → (Storm van 's Gravesandeweg, to Duinrell), use dedicated 🚲 → to enter Duinrell. Same route back to rejoin the main route.

Randstad Circle: Route 7: Holland Coast & Haarlem (47 km)

Katwijk is a relaxed seaside town, although the promenade can get very crowded in weekends and on hot summer days. Most of Katwijk's buildings are reasonably new, as the town suffered badly during WWII. The Nazis needed the Katwijk grounds for their **"Atlantik Wall"**, the coastal line of defence against the Allies. Most houses within a mile of the beach were ruthlessly cleared, except the white lighthouse. The 2014 Katwijk **coastal defence works** show a different approach. New underground car parking is integrated in new sea wall, covered up by new, man-made sand dunes!

8.2 ⛱ ☕ **Pavillion De Duinen** *(cafe only accessible by foot & bike)*
11.7 At end of 🚲 at *KP 97* ← (to Zuidboulevard/Noordwijk) 🚗
  Note: on promenade rd, give way to traffic from the right!
13.1 ⛱ 🏨 🍽 ☕ 🅿 ⛽ ► **Katwijk aan Zee**
13.7 After bend to the right, 1st rd ← onto dam
  (Buitensluis, to Noordwijk & *KP 63*)

Noordwijk was a quiet fishing village for about 800 years, until the 20th century turned it into a holiday resort. It attracts over one million visitors per year with its beach, vibrant nightlife and the nearby tulip fields.

- **14.0** After dam ↰ onto 🚲 (Rijwielpad Noordduinen, to Noordwijk)
- **16.8** At end of 🚲 ↑ via rd (Kon. Astrid Boulevard)
  Note: on promenade rd, give way to traffic from the right!
- **18.0** At T-jct ← (to Kon. Wilhelmina Boulevard) 🚗
- **18.3** Just before wide zebra crossing, 1st rd ← via 🚲 lane against main traffic flow *(tricky turn; dismount and use zebra as needed!)*
- **18.3** 🛏🍴🛍🍽 ↱ **Noordwijk** *(Palace Plein)*
- **19.0** After guarded bike park in bend to the right, at *KP 32*, 1st rd ← (Bosweg, to Zandvoort/De Zilk & *KP 43*)
- **19.5** At end of rd ↑ via "fietspad" (to Zandvoort/De Zilk & *KP 43*)

Randstad Circle: Route 7: Holland Coast & Haarlem (47 km)

Beyond Noordwijk you enter the **forests** of **Noordwijkerhout**. The pine trees are not native to the sand dunes, but were planted to stop erosion. In between the trees you'll find Dutch micro-infrastructure at its best. Paths are either dedicated to walking, cycling, horse riding or mountain biking! The **Noordwijk YHA** is perfectly located on the edge of the dunes forest. You might like to switch here to our **Tulip fields route** to Haarlem for a change of scene, see page 112. If you love the coastal scenery, keep going to **Langevelderslag**. Have a break at the eateries here as needed, because the next stretch is the most remote section of the coastal route. It is a stark contrast to arrive in **Zandvoort**. Also known as **Amsterdam at Sea**, it is full of hotels, nightlife and trendy beach cafes. The northern promenade provides continuous sea views!

Pay attention at this sign to choose the route of your choice; see directions...

20.7 At T-jct ← via 🚴 (to De Zilk/Zandvoort & KP 43), keep ↑

24.4 *Stop* at 🚴 junction with mushroom sign on right (no 21597/001; note Zandvoort is 11 km away), *choose your route to Haarlem: For the tulip fields and Keukenhof, turn to page 112, top left (note;* 🏠 *Noordwijk is featured as part of the tulip fields route) For coastal sand dunes route via Zandvoort, read below:*
  ↙ via gravel "fietspad" (to Zandvoort)

24.7 At T-jct with 🌲 ← via gravel path (to Zandvoort, LF 1b)

25.6 1st 🚴 → (to Zandvoort, LF 1b), gravel at first, later paved surface

27.1 At jct ⛺ 🍴 **Langevelderslag** ↑ via 🚴 (to Zandvoort, LF 1b)

30.4 At ⚐ **Province Border Zuid-Holland - Noord-Holland** ↑ via 🚴
34.6 At end of 🚴 → (Brederodestraat, to Haarlem, *LF 1b*)
35.4 At rndabt ↖ (Marisstraat, to Station, *LF 1b*)
35.7 At T-jct ↗ (Thorbeckestraat), at rndabt ↑ (to Station) 🚉
35.9 ⛱ 🏨 🍴 ☕ 🛒 ℹ 🚻 ⚑ **Zandvoort**
 (guarded bike park on central square on left, at Holland Casino)
36.5 Where main rd joins coast, as coastal promenade rd, join 🚴 on right side of rd
36.9 *Dismount* near "Strandhotel Zandvoort" (high building on right side), cross rd ← via crossing, → walk down via steps, join coastal 🚴

Randstad Circle: Route 7: Holland Coast & Haarlem (47 km)

At the eateries of **Bloemendaal aan Zee** the route heads inland to Haarlem's leafy suburb **Overveen**. From the **Kennemerduinen Visitor Centre** you can do various signposted walks, including the short ten minute walk to sand dune lake **Het Wed**, providing fresh water lake swimming.

39.6 Beyond eateries ⤴ ▲ 🅿 🍴 **Bloemendaal aan Zee**,
at jct "Parnassiaweg", cross main rd ↗,
join 🚲 on right side of rd (to Overveen)

43.2 After road sign "maximum speed 50 km/h", 1st "fietspad" ↗
(see yellow sign "Tetterodeweg 14 en 31")
(For ⛺ 🛏 **Kennemerduinen Visitor Centre**, keep on 🚲 next to main rd, entrance on left after 150m, see also map on page 109)

Haarlem is an historic Dutch city with many monumental buildings. In English, the place is known as "Harlem" (like the district in New York City). Being centrally located on the River Spaarne, trade and shipping brought an enormous wealth to the city during the Dutch Golden Age. Famous historic citizens are Belgium-born **painter Frans Hals** and Laurens Janszoon Coster, who invented a printing press about the same time as German Johann Gutenberg. **Mozart** is believed to have played in the St Bavo cathedral. During the 18th and 19th century beer and textiles industries were booming, as was the tulip trade. The annual **flower procession** in April is still a majestic display (http://bloemencorso-bollenstreek.nl).

A popular visitors' activity in Haarlem is the **Hofjeswandeling**, a self-guided walk via charming old streets and beautiful private inner courts, get the leaflet from the tourist information office VVV.

The **Teylers Museum** opened in 1784, well-known for its monumental building and collections (open Tue-Sun, €11 pp). Paintings of Dutch masters are shown in the **Frans Hals Museum** (open Tue-Sun, €16 pp). There is plenty of **accommodation** available in Haarlem; we have only listed those in the direct vicinity of the route. Safe overnight **bike parking** in the city centre can be found on Smedestraat, see "P" on the map. Note Haarlem's **YHA** is on the north end of town, see page 114 for its access route ("A" on the map).

- 43.9 At jct, cross main rd ↑ (Tetterodeweg)
- 44.3 On arrival in Overveen ↗ via 🚲, rejoin rd beyond jct
- 44.7 At T-jct 🏠 🚲 **Overveen →** (Bloemendaalseweg), cross railway and join narrow 🚲
- 45.0 At rndabt ← via narrow 🚲 on right side of rd (Zijlweg)
- 45.6 At jct with lhts ↑ (to Centrum)
- 46.6 At jct with lhts ↑ via 🚲 bridge, across canal ↑ via rd (Zijlstraat)
- 47.1 ⛵🏠🏨🚲🛒☕🍴ℹ️ ↗ **Haarlem** (Grote Markt), facing the St Bavo cathedral, → in front of cathedral imm ← (Spekstraat), make your way around cathedral (Lepelstraat), then
- 47.2 At next jct ↑ (Damstraat)
- 47.3 Historic building "De Waag" on river side, end of route (to continue, see page 114)

Randstad Circle: Route 8: Tulip fields & Keukenhof (33 km)

Stations: Voorhout, Haarlem
Cycling time: 1.5 - 2.5 hours (🚲 18%, 🚶 62%, 🚃 19%, 🚢 1%)

Although often displayed in pictures and paintings, the **Dutch tulip fields** only cover a small area between the cities Leiden and Haarlem, known as the **Bollenstreek** ("bulb region"). Tulips are not native to The Netherlands. Botanist Carolus Clusius brought them over from the far east and saw his first bulbs flowering on Dutch soil in 1594. The flower became quickly known for its beautiful colours. During the Dutch Golden Age, the tulip was a fashionable symbol of wealth, with prices for a single flower rocketing up to ten times the annual salary of a skilled craftsman. Dutch marketing has ensured The Netherlands is forever associated with the tulip.

Our route between **Voorhout** and **Haarlem** provides plenty of views of **commercial tulip fields**, where the bulbs are allowed to flower before being traded as Dutch bulbs on the world market. This practice provides amazing displays for an annual four-week period, shifting from **mid-March** and up to **mid-May**, depending on the spring weather. You can do this route as an **easy day ride** between Voorhout and Haarlem stations. Both stations are about 30 minutes by train from Amsterdam. The route from **Voorhout station** starts on the page below. The route is also part of the **Randstad Circle route**, offering an **alternative** for the coastal route to Haarlem. In that case you join on page 112 (see also page 106). From Haarlem, the Randstad Circle route heads for Amsterdam, see page 114.

0.0 Leave Voorhout station platform on its south end (at road crossing), ← via 🚲 on left side, after 30m cross rd ↑ via zebra and continue via 🚲 on right side of rd, at rndabt ↑ (to Noordwijkerhout & *KP 59*)
1.1 At T-jct → via 🚲 on right side of rd (Zuidelijke Randweg, to Leiden)
1.5 At rndabt ← via 🚲 crossings (Engelse Laan)
1.7 At T-jct ← (Prinsenweg, to *KP 59*)
2.9 At *KP 59*, cross main rd ↑ (Torenlaan)
4.0 After bend to the left, 1st rd → (Akervoorderlaan)
4.5 1st rd ← (Achterweg-Zuid, to *KP 55*)
5.2 At *KP 55*, 1st rd ← (to *KP 49*)
6.2 At T-jct → (Loosterweg-Zuid, to *KP 49*) 🍴
7.7 Just before start of 30 km/h zone (see signs), follow sharp bend ← (to *KP 49*) 🍴
8.9 T-jct *KP 49*:
For 🛏 🍴 Keukenhof Gardens → (entrance on left after 100m)
To continue: ← via 🚲 on left side of rd (Stationsweg, to *KP 40*)
10.5 After railway crossing, *reset mileage* to **0.0** at next jct (*KP 48*), to continue, read on page 112 on right side of the page

The **Keukenhof Gardens** are the world's most famous flower gardens. Annually, about seven million bulbs are planted to provide a glorious display in a fine parkland setting. Only open from mid-March until mid-May, the gardens attracts over 900,000 visitors per year from all over the world. Allow 2-4 hours for a worthy visit. Stay overnight in nearby **Lisse** if you wish to spend a full day in the park (open daily, €16 pp).

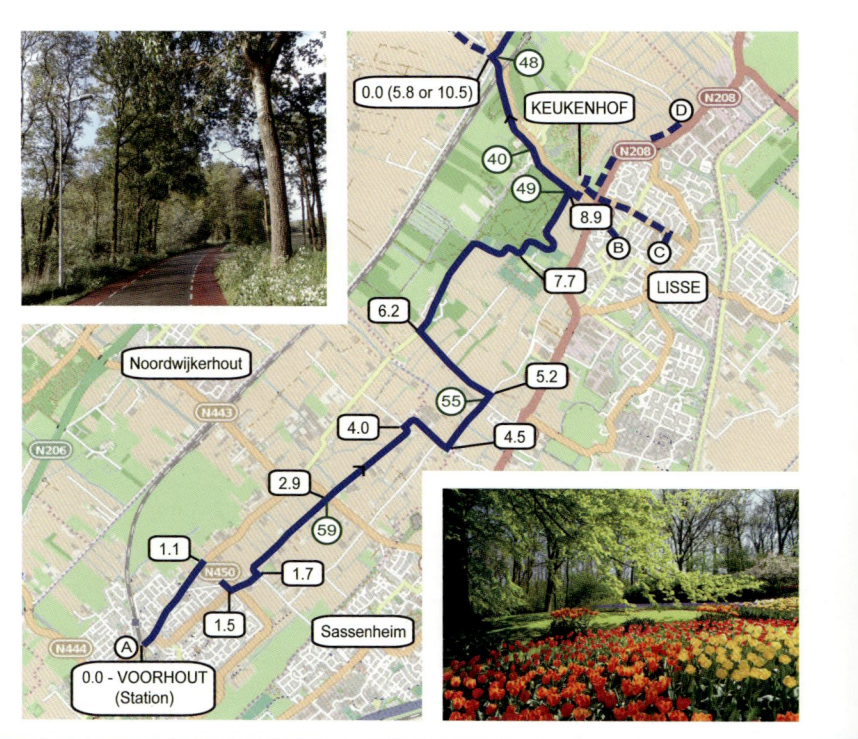

Randstad Circle: Route 8: Tulip fields & Keukenhof (33 km)

Route from Randstad Circle:

- **0.0** (24.4) At "mushroom" sign 21597/001 ↗ via tarmac 🚲 (to Noordwijkerhout), at T-jct ←
- **0.4** At KP 86, opposite 🏨 **Noordwijk**, ↑ via 🚲 on left side of rd (to De Zilk)
- **0.8** Do **not** follow bend of the cycle path to the left (leading away from rd), but join rd ↑ (see moped sign)
- **1.5** 1st rd → (Wilgendam)
- **2.5** At T-jct ← (Duinschooten, to Lisse)
- **3.1** 1st 🚲 ← (to Lisse & KP 47), at KP 47 ↑ (to KP 48)
- **3.9** Just before viaduct → up slope, ep ←, after viaduct ← down slope, cycle now under the viaduct, ↑ (Tespellaan, to Lisse & KP 48)
- **4.8** After ☕ 🍴 **Tespelduyn** (golf cafe), 1st rd ← (to KP 48), 1st 🚲 → (to KP 48)
- **5.8** At KP 48 **reset mileage** to 0.0 and read further on right side of this page

For 🎟 ☕ 🍴 **Keukenhof Gardens**
→ via 🚲 (entrance on left after 1.7 km)

Route to Haarlem:

- **0.0** (5.8 or 10.5) At KP 48 go north, cross rd (Leidse Vaart, to De Zilk & KP 11) ↗
- **2.5** At T-jct KP 11 → via 🚲 on right side of rd, after bridge imm ← (to KP 16) 🚗
- **4.5** At T-jct KP 16 → (to KP 17)
- **4.8** At KP 17, 1st rd ↖ (to KP 18)
- **6.0** At T-jct → via 🚲 on right side of rd, 1st rd ← (Bethlehemlaan)
- **6.2** 1st rd ← (Zandlaan)
- **6.9** Follow bend ↖, 1st rd → (Schoollaan)
- **7.0** 1st rd → (Harp), at next jct ↗
- **7.2** 1st "fietspad" ↗, ep ↑ (to Zwaanshoek)
- **7.9** Just before T-jct → (to Zwaanshoek)
- **8.1** 1st rd ← (to KP 56), at T-jct → 🚗 🚲

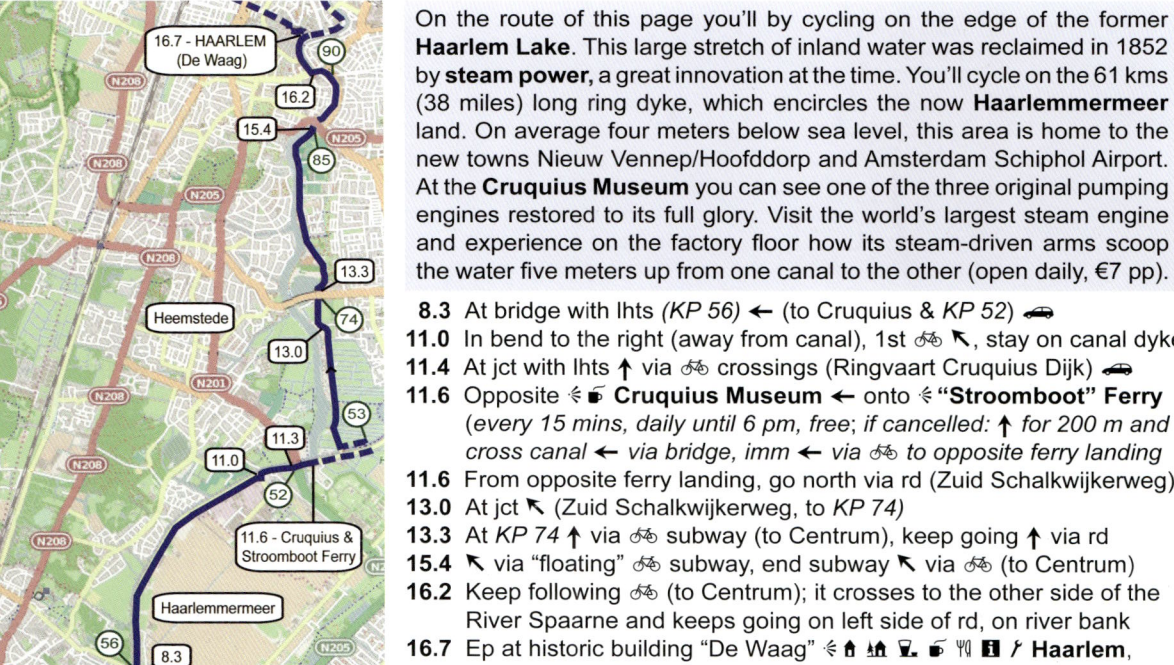

On the route of this page you'll by cycling on the edge of the former **Haarlem Lake**. This large stretch of inland water was reclaimed in 1852 by **steam power**, a great innovation at the time. You'll cycle on the 61 kms (38 miles) long ring dyke, which encircles the now **Haarlemmermeer** land. On average four meters below sea level, this area is home to the new towns Nieuw Vennep/Hoofddorp and Amsterdam Schiphol Airport. At the **Cruquius Museum** you can see one of the three original pumping engines restored to its full glory. Visit the world's largest steam engine and experience on the factory floor how its steam-driven arms scoop the water five meters up from one canal to the other (open daily, €7 pp).

8.3 At bridge with lhts (KP 56) ← (to Cruquius & KP 52) 🚲
11.0 In bend to the right (away from canal), 1st 🚲 ↖, stay on canal dyke
11.4 At jct with lhts ↑ via 🚲 crossings (Ringvaart Cruquius Dijk) 🚲
11.6 Opposite 🏛 **Cruquius Museum** ← onto ⛴ "**Stroomboot**" **Ferry** (every 15 mins, daily until 6 pm, free; if cancelled: ↑ for 200 m and cross canal ← via bridge, imm ← via 🚲 to opposite ferry landing
11.6 From opposite ferry landing, go north via rd (Zuid Schalkwijkerweg)
13.0 At jct ↖ (Zuid Schalkwijkerweg, to KP 74)
13.3 At KP 74 ↑ via 🚲 subway (to Centrum), keep going ↑ via rd
15.4 ↖ via "floating" 🚲 subway, end subway ↖ via 🚲 (to Centrum)
16.2 Keep following 🚲 (to Centrum); it crosses to the other side of the River Spaarne and keeps going on left side of rd, on river bank
16.7 Ep at historic building "De Waag" ⛴ 🏨 🚻 🛒 ☕ 🍽 ℹ ✈ **Haarlem**, end of route (for station and to continue, see pages 108-109-114)

Randstad Circle: Route 9: Spaarndam & IJmuiden (30 km)

Stations: Haarlem, Santpoort-Noord, Koog-Zaandijk
Cycling time: 1.5 - 2.5 hours (🚲 64%, 🥾 31%, ⛴ 5%))

This route section takes you from **Haarlem** via **Spaarndam** to **Zaanse Schans windmill reserve**. From there, you can continue with **Amsterdam Routes E3 and E4**, which will take you to Amsterdam Central Station. It is just 19 km from Haarlem to Zaanse Schans, but this section also contains an 11 km link to **IJmuiden**. Those travelling from/to the **Newcastle ferry** can use the route on page 116 to cycle between the IJmuiden ferry terminal and the Randstad Circle route. This link takes you via the Haarlem suburbs **Driehuis** and **Santpoort**, including the beautiful **Zandhaas windmill**.

0.0 *(16.7 or 47.3)* At junction on Spaarne River, next to historic building "De Waag", go north via 🚲 on right side of rd
0.6 At jct with lhts ↑ via 🚲 on right side of rd (to Bloemendaal)
1.2 At major jct with lhts ↑ via 🚲 on right side of rd (to Spaarndam)
3.3 At T-jct with lhts ← via 🚲 on left side of rd (to Spaarndam)
3.6 At next jct with lhts → via rd (Spaarndamse Weg, to Spaarndam)
5.5 In 🚶 **Spaarndam** *dismount* on narrow paved street and *walk* over narrow footbridge next to harbour, *keep walking* ↗ (Oostkolk)
5.6 Walk up steep slope ↗ OR make your way up dyke ridge via footpath and → on dyke ridge, both to 🚶 **Hans Brinker Statue**
For Ferry IJmuiden - Newcastle ← on dyke ridge, see page 116
For Zaanse Schans & Amsterdam → on dyke ridge, see page 117

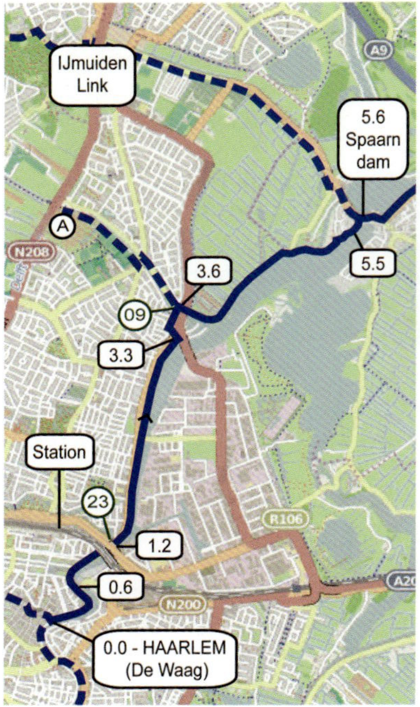

Hans Brinker is the name of a famous fictitious boy who put his finger in the dyke to prevent the land from flooding. His statue can be found on top of the old sea locks of **Spaarndam**. The tale originates from Dutch settlers in North America and became famous through the 1865 novel by American writer, Mary Mapes Dodge.

The **Haarlem - Zaanse Schans route** is very varied, given its short distance. From Haarlem, the **Spaarne River** takes you to **Spaarndam** with its Hans Brinker statue on the old sea locks (see above). From here you enter an area, only reclaimed from the sea in 1872. All what remains of this **IJ Bay** is the wide **North Sea Shipping Canal** which links the huge sea locks at IJmuiden with the inland Amsterdam Docks. The **Buitenhuizen ferry** takes you across to **Nauerna** on the north side of the former IJ Bay. Its old sea wall lies now completely inland. The **Zaanstreek** is a region well-known for its many fine traditional wooden buildings and windmills. **Westzaan** features some of these, but it is the **Zaanse Schans windmill reserve** where you want to have a longer break, see pages 62 and 66.

Zandhaas windmill in Santpoort-Noord

Randstad Circle: Route 9: Spaarndam & IJmuiden (30 km)

From IJmuiden to Spaarndam:

- 0.0 From ferry ↗ via rd ⛴
- 0.5 1st rd ← (Magadantstraat), 1st rd ↙, imm ↗ up the slope
- 0.8 At jct → (Wilhelminakade)
- 1.0 At jct →, at rndabt ↖ via ⚲ (Kennemerlaan), ep join rd ↗
- 2.2 ← via ⚲ on left side of rd, see shops 🚻 ⛽ 🍴 ➤ IJmuiden
- 2.5 2nd rd → (Velserduinweg)
- 3.0 At lhts ← via ⚲ on right side
- 4.3 After disused railway crossing, at rndabt → (to Crematorium)
- 4.8 → (to Crematorium & KP 5)
- 5.3 1st "fietspad" ← (to KP 5)
- 6.1 Ep ↖, at T-jct → (to KP 5)
- 6.9 At next jct ↖ (Middenduinweg), ↑ at railway crossing & rndabt
- 7.7 1st rd → (Velserhooftlaan)
- 8.1 At jct ← (Wustelaan)
- 8.3 At rndabt ↱ via ⚲, at subway ↑ (Slaperdijk, to KP 38), keep ↑
- 11.3 ⚜ Hans Brinker Statue

From Spaarndam to IJmuiden:

- 0.0 (5.6) At ⚜ Brinker Statue ←
- 0.4 ↑ via ⚲ on left side of rd, ↑
- 3.0 Ep via rndabt ↱ (Wustelaan)
- 3.2 3rd rd → (Velserhooftlaan)
- 3.6 At jct ← (Middenduinenweg)
- 4.1 After rndabt & railway ↑ via rd
- 4.4 ↗ (Duin en Kruidbergerweg)
- 5.0 Just before station ← (to KP 4)
- 5.2 1st "fietspad" ↗ (to KP 4)
- 6.0 Ep → via rd (to KP 4)
- 6.5 ← (Driehuizerkerkweg, to KP 4)
- 7.0 At rndabt KP 4 ← via ⚲ on right side of rd (to IJmuiden), ↖
- 8.3 At lhts → (Velserduinweg)
- 8.8 ← via ⚲ on right side of rd, see shops 🚻 ⛽ 🍴 ➤ IJmuiden
- 9.1 1st rd → (Marktplein), in bend to ↖, join ⚲ (Kennemerlaan)
- 10.2 At rndabt ↗, after bridge imm imm ← (Wilhelminakade)
- 10.5 1st rd ↙ walk down slope
- 10.8 At T-jct ↙, T-jct →, T-jct ⛴
- 11.3 ⛴ Newcastle Ferry Terminal

Ferry travellers with time on their hands should make their way to the attractive beach and sand dunes of "IJmuiden aan Zee" on the west end of town (not on this map).

From Spaarndam to Zaanse Schans:

- **0.0** *(5.6 or 11.3)* At ⛲ **Hans Brinker Statue**, go east via dyke ridge rd 🚲
- **0.3** After bridge at *KP 35* ↖ via 🚲 on left side of rd (to Amsterdam & *KP 11/17*)
- **3.9** At *KP 11* ↑ to ⛴ **Ferry Buitenhuizen** *(runs every 20 mins, day & night, free)*
- **4.1** After ferry onto 🚲 on right side of rd, at *KP 10* ↑ via 🚲 on right side of rd
- **4.3** 1st rd → via 🚲 (to Nauerna & *KP 67*)
- **5.8** Ep ↗ via dyke ridge rd (to Nauerna)
- **6.3** After 🍺 **De Vlonder** (pub) and bridge imm ← via dead end rd, becomes 🚲 (Watermolenstraat)
- **8.9** 1st rd → (Watermolenstraat)
- **9.2** After bridge, 1st rd ← (Oranjeboomstraat)
- **9.4** At T-jct ← (Torenstraat)
- **9.6** 1st rd → (Kerkstraat), cross main rd 🏠🚉 **Westzaan** ↑ (Raadhuisstraat), then 2nd rd ↖ (Raadhuisstraat, becomes Teunis Slagterstraat)
- **10.0** At T-jct ← (Van Waertstraat)
- **10.1** After short 🚲 ← (Prinsenhofstraat), at bend ↑ via 🚲, cross rd, → via 🚲
- **10.6** Where rd makes bend to the right, ↑ via 🚲 (to Zaandijk/Zaanse Schans)
- **11.7** At T-jct ← via 🚲 (to Zaandijk)
- **12.0** At jct with lhts → via 🚲 crossings onto lay-by rd on left side of main rd (Jan Mulderstraat, to Koog a/d Zaan)
- **12.5** At railway and jct with lhts ↑ via 🚲 on left side of rd (to Zaanse Schans), ↑
- **13.3** After river bridge imm ← and again ↓ via paved rd into 🏠 **Zaanse Schans**
- **13.5** Riverside square, end of route

For Amsterdam City Centre; see routes E3 and E4 (23 km), page 66

117

Northern: Route 10: Marken, Volendam & Edam (41 km)

Stations: Amsterdam Centraal, see route D1 (extra 17 km!)
Cycling time: 2.5 - 5 hours (🚲 22%, 🚶 78%)

Coastal scenery and historic towns await you on the **Northern** route. It starts with **Amsterdam Routes D1, D2** and **D4**, ending at the **start** of this route section. There are two choices for your journey to Volendam.

For Amsterdam Routes D from Central Station, see pages 56-59.
Route via Marken island and ferry (see www.markenexpress.nl)
0.0 (5.7) At KP 52 → via 🚲 on left side of rd (to Marken & KP 51)
2.4 At end of causeway, imm ← via "fietspad" (paved path on dyke)
3.6 Ep → follow path around historic harbour 🍴🛏️☕🍽️ **Marken**
3.7 Opposite "Seitje Boes Souvenirs" ← to ⛴️ **Marken Express Ferry**
(runs approx every 30 mins until 5 pm, €8 pp see website above)

Route via Monnickendam on mainland:
0.0 (5.7) At KP 52 ← via 🚲 on right side of rd (to Monnickendam)
4.5 At mdabt → via 🚲 crossing (Zuideinde, to Volendam), keep ↑
4.9 At bridge over old locks 🛏️🍴🛒🍽️☕🍽️ ✟ **Monnickendam** ↑, at next jct ↗ (Noordeinde, to "Alle richtingen", LF 21a)
5.4 At KP 56 ↑ (to Katwoude & KP 99), after 100m, join 🚲
5.9 At lhts → via rd (to Katwoude & KP 99)
11.1 At jct → via 🚲 on right side of rd (to Volendam & KP 99), ep ↑ via rd onto dyke ridge, keep to dyke ridge route (LF 21a)
12.5 🍴🛏️🛒☕🍽️ ℹ️ **Volendam** (opposite "Marken Express Ferry")

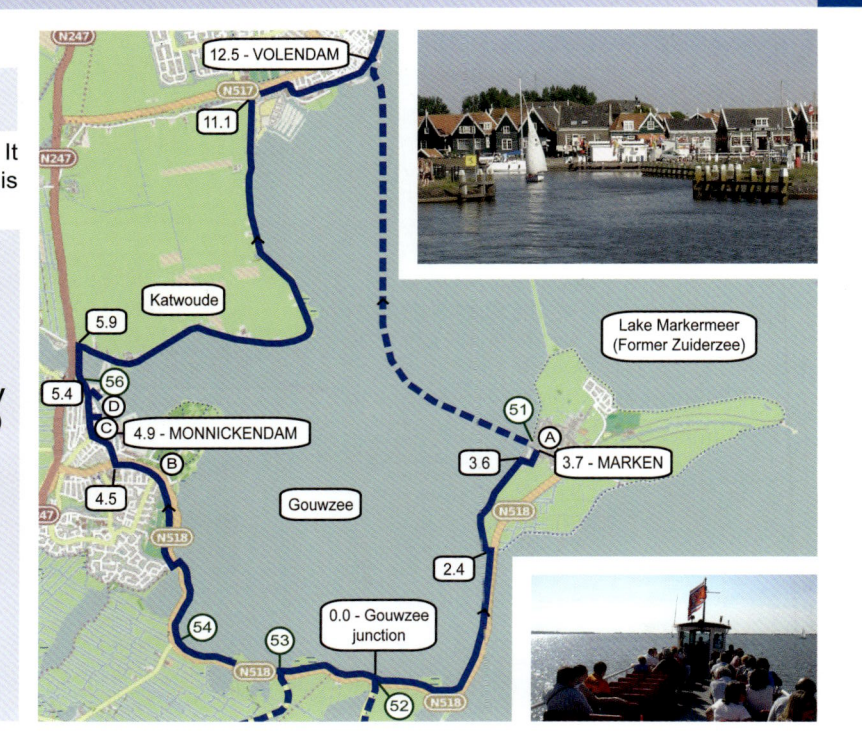

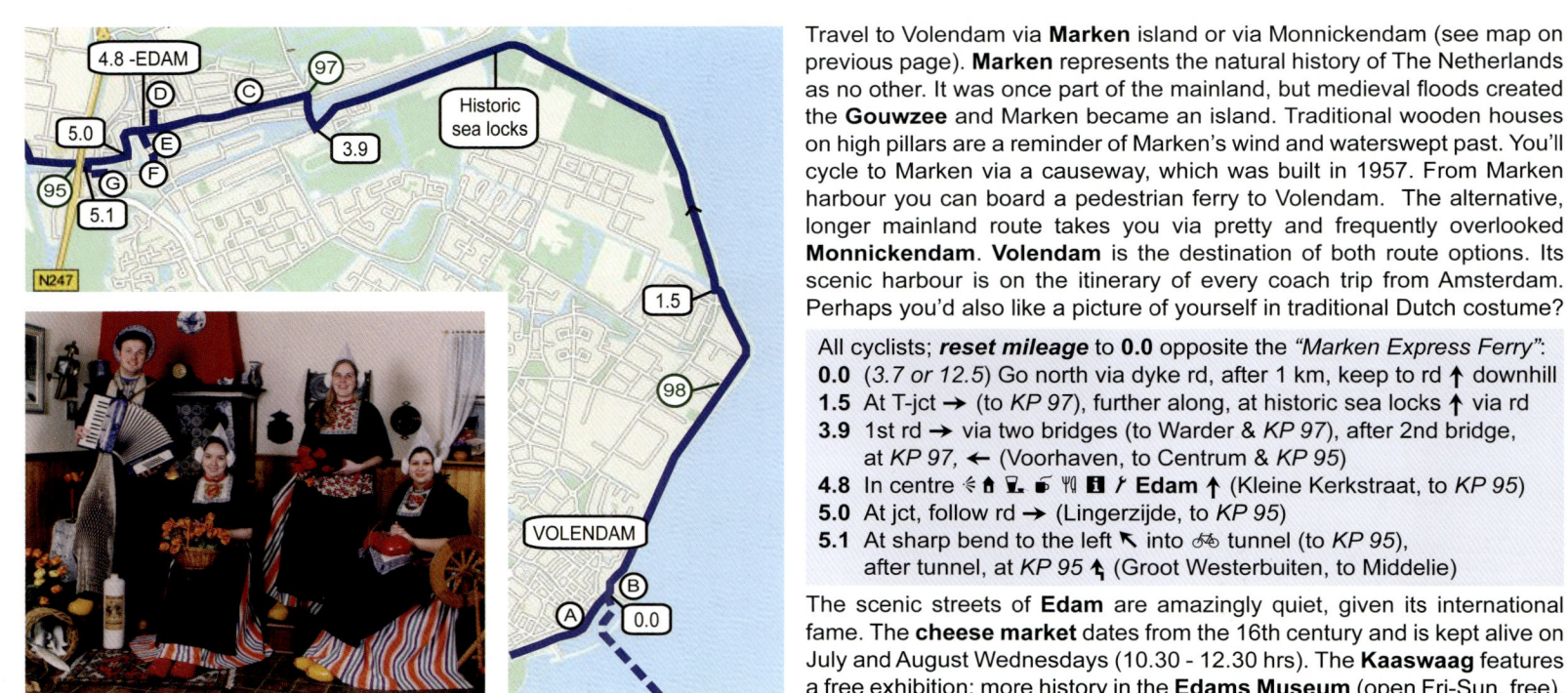

Travel to Volendam via **Marken** island or via Monnickendam (see map on previous page). **Marken** represents the natural history of The Netherlands as no other. It was once part of the mainland, but medieval floods created the **Gouwzee** and Marken became an island. Traditional wooden houses on high pillars are a reminder of Marken's wind and waterswept past. You'll cycle to Marken via a causeway, which was built in 1957. From Marken harbour you can board a pedestrian ferry to Volendam. The alternative, longer mainland route takes you via pretty and frequently overlooked **Monnickendam**. **Volendam** is the destination of both route options. Its scenic harbour is on the itinerary of every coach trip from Amsterdam. Perhaps you'd also like a picture of yourself in traditional Dutch costume?

All cyclists; *reset mileage* to **0.0** opposite the *"Marken Express Ferry".*
- **0.0** (3.7 or 12.5) Go north via dyke rd, after 1 km, keep to rd ← downhill
- **1.5** At T-jct → (to *KP 97*), further along, at historic sea locks ← via rd
- **3.9** 1st rd → via two bridges (to Warder & *KP 97*), after 2nd bridge, at *KP 97*, ← (Voorhaven, to Centrum & *KP 95*)
- **4.8** In centre 🍴🏨🛒🍽️ℹ️🅿️ **Edam** ← (Kleine Kerkstraat, to *KP 95*)
- **5.0** At jct, follow rd → (Lingerzijde, to *KP 95*)
- **5.1** At sharp bend to the left ← into 🚲 tunnel (to *KP 95*), after tunnel, at *KP 95* ↙ (Groot Westerbuiten, to Middelie)

The scenic streets of **Edam** are amazingly quiet, given its international fame. The **cheese market** dates from the 16th century and is kept alive on July and August Wednesdays (10.30 - 12.30 hrs). The **Kaaswaag** features a free exhibition; more history in the **Edams Museum** (open Fri-Sun, free).

Northern: Route 10: Marken, Volendam & Edam (41 km)

From Edam with its picturesque townhall (see picture below), the route heads north. For reasons of variety and to provide some relief from possible headwinds, we cycle inland via **Middelie** and **Oosthuizen** villages. At **Schardam** you'll have once again panoramic views over Lake Markermeer, with **Hoorn** appearing on the horizon.

5.4 Just before bridge → (Zeevangsdijkje, to Middelie)
7.0 1st rd ↗ (Buitengouwweg, road lined with trees)
8.0 At jct in 🏠 ☕ 🍴 **Middelie** ↑ (Middelie, to Oosthuizen)
9.7 At jct with ⚌ ↑ (Middelie, to Oosthuizen & *KP 11*)
13.3 At T-jct in 🛒 ☕ **Oosthuizen** → (to *KP 10*), keep ↑
14.0 At *KP 10* cross main rd ↑ (Oosteinde, to Warder)
14.3 ☕ 🍴 **Ans en Piet** *(cafe restaurant at railway crossing)*
16.0 At T-jct ← (IJsselmeerdijk, to Hoorn & *KP 83*)
17.4 ⛺ **Schardam**

*Dutch winters are generally mild, but when serious frost hits the lowlands, the Dutch go crazy with their **ice skating**. Schools, offices and factories close, as those icy flats have to be conquered! These pictures were taken near Hoorn in December 2010.*

18.5 At KP 37, 1st rd → (to Hoorn & KP 36)
20.4 🛏 🍽 **Ootje Kronkel** *(pancake restaurant)*
21.0 At KP 36 ↑ (to Hoorn & KP 58)
22.4 At KP 58 ↑ (to Hoorn & KP 59)
24.8 At next jct, KP 59, ← down from dyke ridge, then imm → into ⛺ 🏠 🛏 🍽 **Hoorn**
24.9 At 1st rd to the right (Achterom) end of route
(to continue see page 122)

Northern: Route 11: Hoorn & Enkhuizen (27 km)

Stations: Hoorn, Bovenkarspel Flora, Enkhuizen
Cycling time: 1.5 - 3 hours (🚴 9%, 🚶 82%, 🚂 9%)

The port of **Hoorn** equalled Amsterdam's in importance during the Dutch Golden Age. The city has many historic buildings. Its landmark is the **tower** overlooking the harbour, built in 1532. At its base, the statue of the **Bontekoe Boys** honours a traditional children's book, based on the journals of a 17th century skipper. The **Westfries Museum** features paintings and local artifacts, such as a display about Willem Corneliszoon Schouten, who named **Cape Horn** on the southern tip of South America after his home town (open Tue-Sun, €7 pp). Also cool is the **Museum of the 20th century** (open daily, €8 pp). If you are into **steam trains**, join the longest steam train ride in the country to **Medemblik** (open Tue-Sun).

- 0.0 (24.9) In street with shops near *KP 59 (see previous page)*, 1st rd → (Achterom, *LF 21a*)
- 0.5 In bend to the right ↘ via "fietspad" (Proostensteeg, *LF 21a*)
- 0.6 At main square ↗ (Grote Oost, to *KP 62, LF 21a*)
- 0.8 1st rd → (Wijdebrugsteeg, *LF 21a*)
- 1.0 At T-jct with harbour and landmark tower on right hand side ↓ (Oude Doelenkade, to *KP 62, LF 21a*)
- 1.3 At jct → via bridge (to "Alle richtingen" & *KP 62*)
- 1.6 At jct ↑ via 🚲 on right side of rd, leading onto dyke ridge (Schellinkhoutdijk, *LF 21a*), keep to dyke ridge route (*LF 21a*)

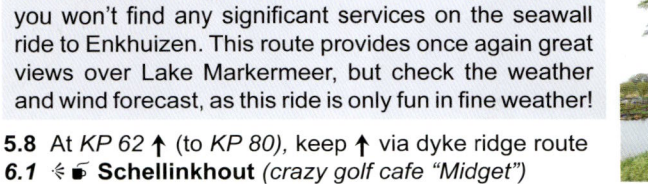

Stock up on some provisions before leaving Hoorn, as you won't find any significant services on the seawall ride to Enkhuizen. This route provides once again great views over Lake Markermeer, but check the weather and wind forecast, as this ride is only fun in fine weather!

5.8 At *KP 62* ↑ (to *KP 80*), keep ↑ via dyke ridge route
6.1 🍴 **Schellinkhout** (*crazy golf cafe "Midget"*)

Northern: Route 11: Hoorn & Enkhuizen (27 km)

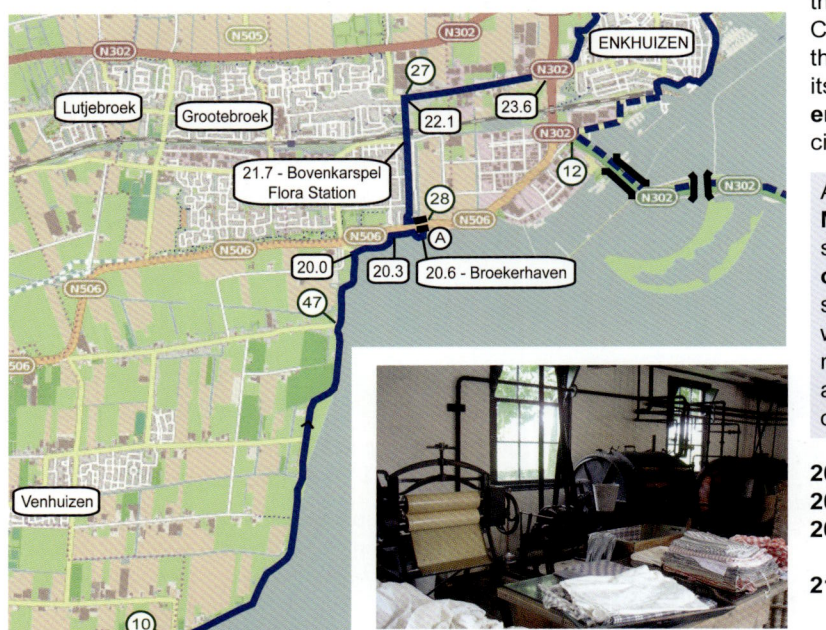

Enkhuizen has a similar history to Hoorn. It was an important port during the **Dutch Golden Age**; a stronghold for the Dutch East India Trading Company. **Fishing** also brought the city wealth. Enkhuizen used to have the largest herring fleet of the country. Enkhuizen is unique in the way that its **full medieval street and canal pattern** has survived, including the **embankments and city walls** (see pictures page 123). This is why we circumnavigate the town before making our way to the town centre.

A visit to Enkhuizen is not complete without visiting the **Zuiderzee Museum**. This is the place to find out about life on the shores of the former sea bay that brought both wealth and misery (floods) for centuries. The **open air museum** has a fine collection of historic buildings (such as a steam-powered laundrette) and interactive workshops about traditional ways of smoking fish and making sails, etc. The **indoor section** of the museum has a great collection of **historic ships** and excellent displays about the **Zuiderzee works**. This is a full day out, including a **boat tour** on the Zuiderzee, renamed as Lake IJsselmeer (open daily, €15 pp).

- 20.0 At near end of dyke rd (see main rd rndabt ahead) ↗ (to KP 28)
- 20.3 At end of rd → via 🚲 on right side of rd (to KP 28)
- 20.6 At KP 28 1st 🚲 → (to KP 27), after tunnel → (Kleine Kaai path), dismount and cross locks 🔒, 🍴 **Broekerhaven** ↑ onto paved rd
- 21.7 At jct with windmill on left corner ↑ via railway crossing (Broekerhavenweg, to Enkhuizen & KP 27) ⛴
- 22.1 At T-jct of KP 27 → (Hoofdstraat, to Enkhuizen & KP 30) ⛴

Steam-powered laundrette

26.4 - Zuiderzee Museum (indoor)

Lake IJsselmeer

Zuiderzee Museum (ferry to open air area)

27.4 - Station

ENKHUIZEN

Please note: The next route is **NOT** suitable for everyone. Take the **train** back to Amsterdam as needed!

23.6 At jct with lhts ↑ via 🚲 crossings (to Centrum & *KP 30*) 🚢
23.9 Imm after historic gate ← (Nassaustraat) and imm ↖ via "fietspad" onto historic embankment (Drechterlandroute 🚲)
25.4 At end of embankment route ↑ via rd (to *KP 30*), after bend to the right imm ← via 🚲 (Donkere Laantje), follow main path ↗ onto town wall embankment, keep going ↑
26.1 Just before playground "Speeltuin Kindervreugde" → (to Centrum), then 2nd rd ← (Van Linschotenstraat, to *KP 30*)
26.4 🚲 🍴 **Zuiderzeemuseum** *(indoor section; for open air section, buy your tickets here, access via boat ride "veerdienst" from station)*
26.8 After Zuiderzeemuseum, 1st rd →, after bridge imm ↖ (to *KP 30*)
26.9 1st rd ← (to Station & *KP 30*), dismount at bridge to walk through historic gate, ep ↗ via rd next to harbour (Drechterlandroute 🚲)
27.2 At jct ↑ (to Station) 🚢 *(For 🚲 🏨 ⛺ 🏛 ☕ 🍴 🍽 🚻 ♿ Enkhuizen →)*
27.4 Station, end of route *(to continue see page 126)*

Northern: Route 12: Dyke challenge & Flevoland (87 km)

Stations: Enkhuizen, Lelystad-Centrum, Almere Poort
Cycling time: 5 - 10 hours (🚲 86%, 🚶 14%)

This route is all about **empty, straight stretches**; only for those after a **challenge** and some **serious mileage**. Check the **weather** forecast before setting off and pay special attention to **wind directions**! The **Enkhuizen-Lelystad Dyke** provides the unique experience of cycling across a former sea. It takes you to **Flevoland**, the largest reclaimed island of the world. **Lelystad** lies in the middle of the former Zuiderzee and is named after the engineer who envisioned this surreal world, four metres below sea level.

0.0 (27.4) Next to Enkhuizen station ↑, join 🚲 on left side of rd (to KP 12) *(if you leave the station, turn →)*, keep ↑ via 🚲
1.2 At lhts (KP 12) ← via 🚲 on left side of rd (to Lelystad & KP 34)
13.0 🍴 **Trintelhaven** *(cafe at harbour, some shelter available)*

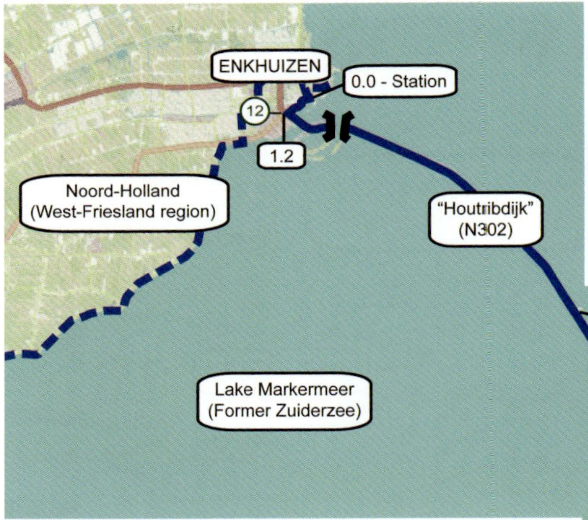

In **Lelystad**, you can choose to take the **train back to Amsterdam** or to cycle south on the **former seabed** in empty Flevoland with its many wind turbines. **Batavia Stad** is home to a replica of the 17th century trading ship **Batavia** (open daily, €11 pp), the **New Land Museum** (open Tue-Sun, €9 pp) and the **Batavia Stad Shopping Outlet**.

28.5 Ep at KP 34 ← (to Almere Stad/Centrum & KP 33)
28.9 At KP 33 on arrival in ⛽🛏🛍🍴 **Batavia Stad** choose your route:

Route to Lelystad Station:
0.0 (28.9) At KP 33 ← (to Batavia Stad Outlet/Dronten & KP 35)
0.2 After bend to the right, at entrance 🛍 **Outlet**, ← via 🚲 (to KP 35)
0.9 Follow 🚲 ↑ (to Centrum, *ignore 🚲 route signs!*), at ep ↑ via rd
1.1 At T-jct → via tarmac rd, after bend to left ⬆ onto 🚲
1.6 After bridge over main rd ↑ via 🚲 (to Almere Stad)
2.0 In bend to the right ↖ via 🚲, see bridge over canal, ↑ via 🚲
2.4 At square with shops ↑ via 🚲, at next jct ← via 🚲 (to Centrum), 🛍 **"Jol" Shopping Centre** on your left, keep ↑ via 🚲
2.7 At KP 31 ↑ via 🚲 *(to KP 37)*, ↑ via 🚲 bridge "Jolbrug"
3.4 At T-jct ← via 🚲 (to Centrum & KP 37), keep ↑ via 🚲
4.4 Ep, at rndabt, → via 🚲 on left side of rd (Stationslaan)
4.6 🚉 **Lelystad-Centrum station**, end of route

Flevoland Route south towards Amsterdam:
0.0 (28.9) At KP 33 ↑ (to Almere Stad & KP 32)
0.5 At ⛽🛏🍴 **Batavia Harbour** keep ↑ via dyke rd (Oostvaardersdijk)

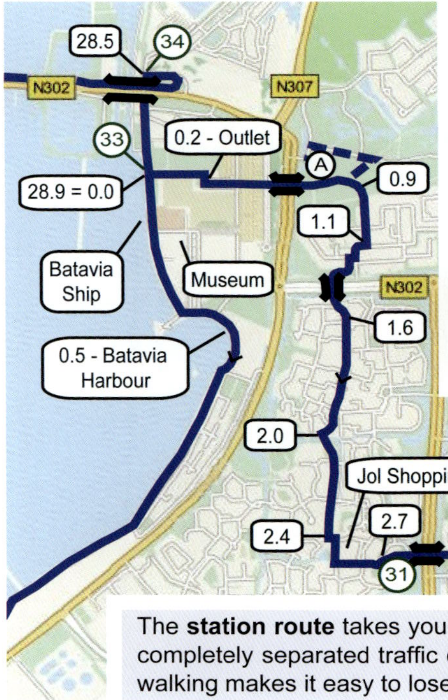

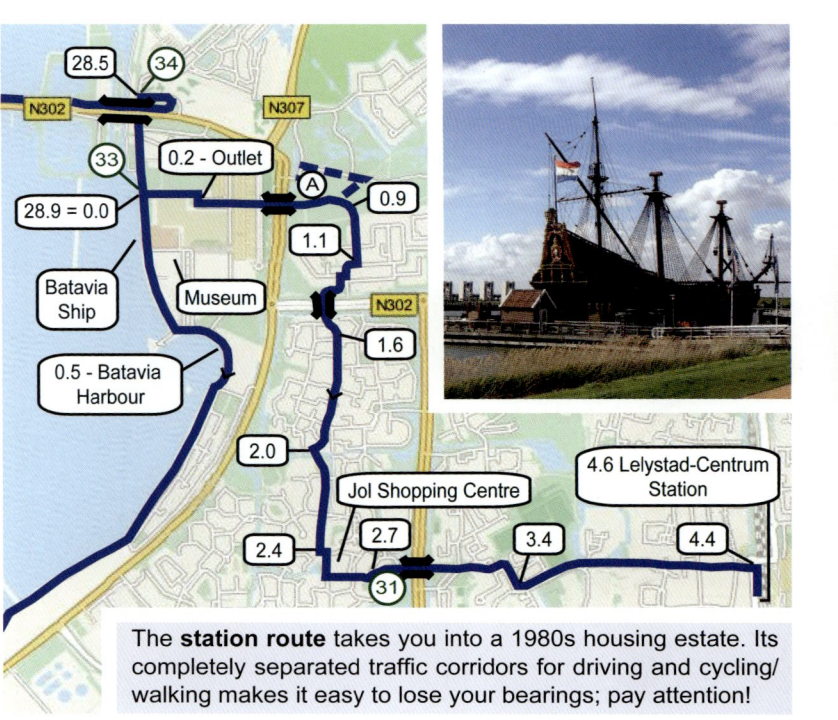

The **station route** takes you into a 1980s housing estate. Its completely separated traffic corridors for driving and cycling/walking makes it easy to lose your bearings; pay attention!

Northern: Route 12: Dyke challenge & Flevoland (87 km)

Lelystad Haven started as a **construction island** where land-reclaiming labourers lived and worked under harsh conditions between 1950 and 1968. The **Oostvaardersplassen** is one of Europe's major wetland reserves. Alongside many bird species, its inhabited by red deer, wild ponies and Heck cattle. Access is via the **Buitencentrum** only (open Tue-Sun). Cycling in Flevoland may well be at its best on the **Vogelweg** (see picture), where **horizons** and **skies** can play with your mind. It is a long, empty, super-smooth cycle path to **Almere Haven**.

- 3.0 At T-jct → via narrow 🚲 on left side of rd (Houtribweg)
- 3.3 Imm after bridge, 1st rd → (Oostvaardersdijk, ⚓ **Lelystad Haven**)
- 3.8 At T-jct → via narrow 🚲 on right side of rd
- 4.5 At rndabt via 🚲 crossings ↑ via 🚲 on left side of rd
- 5.1 At rndabt KP 24 ← via 🚲 on right side of rd (Knardijk, to Harderwijk & KP 23), keep ↑ via 🚲
- 9.3 🚲 🅿 🚻 **Buitencentrum Oostvaardersplassen**
- 10.7 At KP 8 ↖ stay on dyke ridge (to Dronten & KP 45), after high locks, go down ↗ from dyke ridge, pass under motorway
- 12.5 At KP 45 ↑ via 🚲 (to Zeewolde & KP 47)
- 16.8 At KP 47 → via 🚲 on left side of rd (Vogelweg, to Almere & KP 10)
- 27.5 At KP 31 ↑ onto 🚲 on right side of rd (Vogelweg, to Amsterdam)
- 33.1 At 🚲 ⛽ 🍴 **De Dobbe** (petrol station), at jct with lhts ↑ (Merelweg)
- 33.8 At T-jct → (to Amsterdam), after 300m 1st rd ← (to Amsterdam)

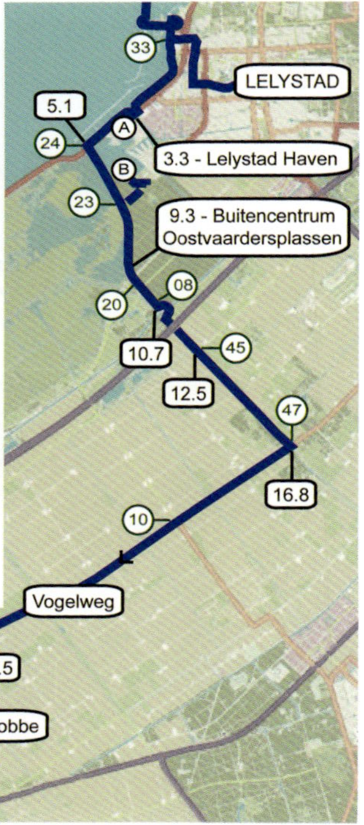

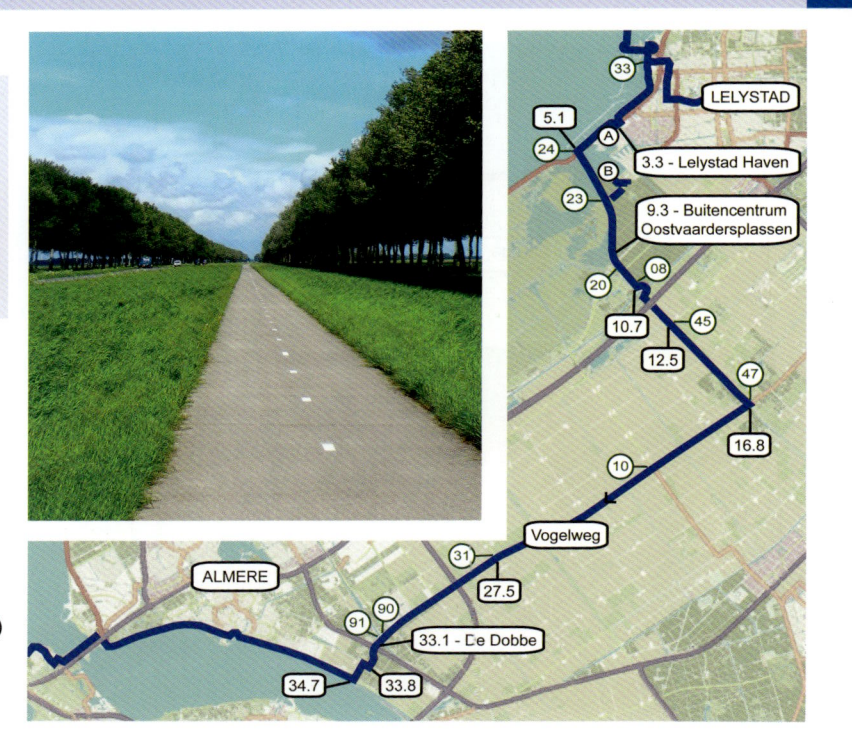

34.7 At T-jct → (to Amsterdam), on top of dyke ↗ via 🚲 on left side of rd (to Amsterdam)

39.3 At end of route ↑ via 🚲 on right side of rd (to Amsterdam & *KP 79*), at next jct ↑ via rd into ⛺ 🍴 🍽 **Almere Haven** (to Almere Poort)

In 1976, the first "Almere" citizens settled here. Today, Almere has more than 200,000 residents!

39.8 At end of harbour, 1st rd → (Deltastraat), at next jct ↑ via 🚲 (to Amsterdam & *KP 32*)

44.4 At near end of route "Gooimeerdijk-West" (see driveway to the left), ↗ over dyke ridge onto rd into polder, pass under motorway

45.0 At T-jct → (Oude Landweg, to Amsterdam)

47.2 At T-jct ←, at T-jct *KP 18* ← via 🚲 on right side of rd (to Muiderberg), follow bend to ←

47.7 1st rd → (Nienhuis Ruijskade, to *KP 17*)

48.5 In ⛺ 🏨 🍴 🍽 **Muiderberg** ↑ (see pavillion), at end lakeside rd, follow bend (Flevolaan)

49.0 At T-jct → (Brink), at *KP 17* 1st rd → (to *KP 16*), imm ↖ (Dijkweg), follow rd to end

53.1 In ⛺ 🏨 🚉 🍴 🍽 **Muiden** at T-jct → 🚢

53.2 Historic river bridge, end of route

For Amsterdam City; see route C5 (26 km) page 53
For Randstad Circle; see route C4 (6 km) page 52

At **Muiderberg** you rejoin the old mainland to **Muiden**.
For Amsterdam City Centre, see **Amsterdam route C5**.
For Randstad Circle and/or Eastern routes, see **route C4**.

The panoramic Gooimeer cycle path has been hosting the annual Holland Triathlon since 1983

Eastern: Route 13: Utrecht Ridge National Park (69 km)

Stations: Breukelen, Hollandsche Rading, Maarn, Rhenen
Cycling time: 4 - 7 hours (🚴 39%, 🚶 56%, 🚗 4%, 🚌 1%)

Join the **Eastern route** either from **Breukelen station** halfway between Amsterdam and Utrecht or join in directly by bike at the end of the **Vecht River** section on the Randstad Circle (see pages 72-75). This route section takes you onto the **Utrecht Ridge** ("Utrechtse Heuvelrug"), an area of sandy moorlands pushed up during the last ice age. It is heavily **forested** and protected by **National Park** status. The start from the Breukelen area is chosen to allow you to travel across Utrecht Ridge with a maximum exposure to its forests, its best cycle routes and most fun places to visit. Allow one or two days for this great route section!

Route from Breukelen Station:
- **0.0** Go east via 🚴 (to Breukelen-Dorp)
- **0.1** At rndabt → via 🚴 on right side of rd (to Breukelen-Dorp)
- **1.3** At rndabt ← via 🚴 crossings (to Loenen), ep join rd
- **1.5** After car park on right side of rd imm → (Markt), follow bend (Dannestraat, to Scheendijk) into ↙, 🍴 **Breukelen**
- **1.7** After canal bridge, 1st rd → (Brugstraat)
- **1.8** Imm after river bridge at KP 84 → (to Maarssen & KP 46)
- **2.8** 🏰 **Nijenrode Castle** (on right on other river bank, see page 75)
- **5.5** At ↑ 🍴 **Geesberge** end of route from Breukelen station

(Cyclists for Randstad Circle (to City of Utrecht), turn to page 77)

Cyclists from Randstad Circle (River Vecht), start reading here:
- **0.0** (5.5 or 22.8) At ↑ 🍴 **Geesberge** in front of canal bridge imm 1st rd ↙ (Machinekade), keep ↑ (Middenweg) to end

From Breukelen, you'll gradually climb above sea level and see the Dutch flat world slowly changing. The **Tienhovense Plassen** are wetlands, fed by water descending from higher ground. The Dutch have never been able to reclaim this area fully. The area is a great for bird-watching. At **Hollandsche Rading** you'll enter the forests of the Utrecht Ridge.

It is only a short ride to **Lage Vuursche**, a village that almost entirely consists of **pancake restaurants**, attracting legions of walkers and cyclists at weekends. If **crazy golf** was ever to be taken seriously, it is here. The **"Midgetgolftuinen"** features three 18-hole crazy golf courses in a parkland setting (open daily, from €8 pp per course).

Lage Vuursche mid-week...

3.7 At T-jct ←, (Laan van Nifterlake, to KP 49) 🍴 into 🛏 🍽 **Tienhoven**
4.4 At KP 49 1st rd →, (Dwarsdijk, to KP 29)
5.7 At end of rd →, via 🚴 (to KP 29), ep ↑
11.5 At jct with lhts 🛏 **Hollandsche Rading** ↑ (Vuurse Dreef, to Lage Vuursche)
13.0 At T-jct KP 98 ← (Vuurse Dreef, to Lage Vuursche)
13.4 After 🛏 🍽 **De Paddestoel** at T-jct ← via "fietspad" (to Lage Vuursche)
14.7 Ep "Loosdrechts Spoor" ↑ via car park, at jct → (to Maartensdijk) 🍴 into 🍦 🏠 ⛺ 🛏 🍽 **Lage Vuursche**
15.0 At end of village, cross rd ↖ onto gravel "fietspad" (Vuurse Steeg)
15.2 1st narrow "fietspad" ← (to Soest)
16.3 At sharp bend to the left, at jct → into "Landgoed Pijnenburg" via gravel rd, then imm ← via gravel rd (to Soest)
16.8 1st gravel rd → (Emilialaan, to Soest)
17.4 At sharp bend to the right, ↑ "fietspad"
17.6 At KP 62 cross rd, ↑ via "fietspad" on right side of rd (to Soestduinen), keep ↑ *(At side rd "Bosstraat" ← for 🛏 **Soest**)*
20.6 At KP 57 ↑ via railway crossing, join "fietspad" (to Soestduinen & KP 56)
20.9

131

Eastern: Route 13: Utrecht Ridge National Park (69 km)

The **YHA** in **Soest** is conveniently located for those who'd like to cycle this route over two days. Just further south, don't miss the views over the **Soester Duinen** on the left side of the path. These **sand dunes** are one of the few in Europe where sand deposits are left to be moved around freely by the elements. The **military** used to be a prominent "occupier" of the Utrecht Ridge, most notably at the **NATO Airbase Soesterberg**. The base is now closed and the grounds are home to the **National Military Museum** (open Tue-Sun, €10 pp). Our route crosses the former runway. At the **Soesterberg** shops we reset our mileage; a good place to refuel!

- **22.2** Ep → (to Den Dolder & *KP 56*), after 50m at *KP 56* ← via railway crossing, ↑ via rd (Paltzerweg, to *KP 55*)
- **24.2** At entrance ⬅🚶🍴 **National Military Museum** ↖ via concrete rd (Verlengde Paltzerweg)
- **24.6** At *KP 55* 1st 🚴 ➘ (Lemmenpad, "Fietsroute Soesterberg", to *KP 53*), follow 🚴 route across ⬅ **Runway NATO Airbase**
- **25.4** Ep ↖ via rd (Montgomeryweg, to *KP 53*)
- **25.7** At jct with lhts ↑ via 🚴 crossings (to Soesterberg & *KP 53*)
- **25.9** At *KP 53* (30 km/h zone 🅿 🛒🍴 **Soesterberg** on right side), **reset mileage** to 0.0, keep ↑ (Kampweg, to Austerlitz & *KP 54*)
- **1.0** After motorway viaduct, 1st rd → (Kampdwarsweg, to Austerlitz)
- **1.4** At sharp bend to the right ↑ via "fietspad" (to Austerlitz & *KP 83*)
- **3.0** At *KP 83* ↖ via "fietspad" (to Austerlitz & *KP 1*)

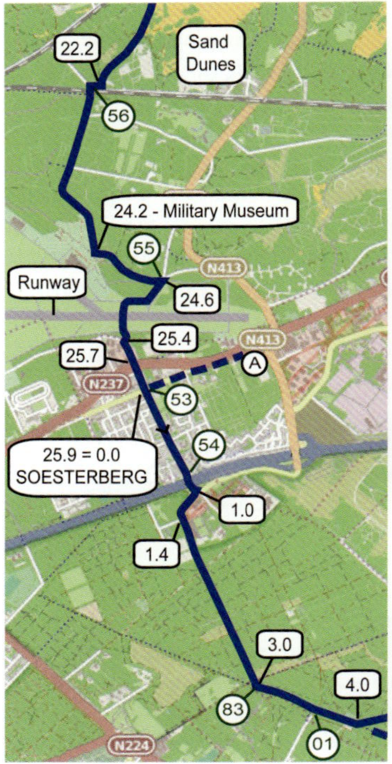

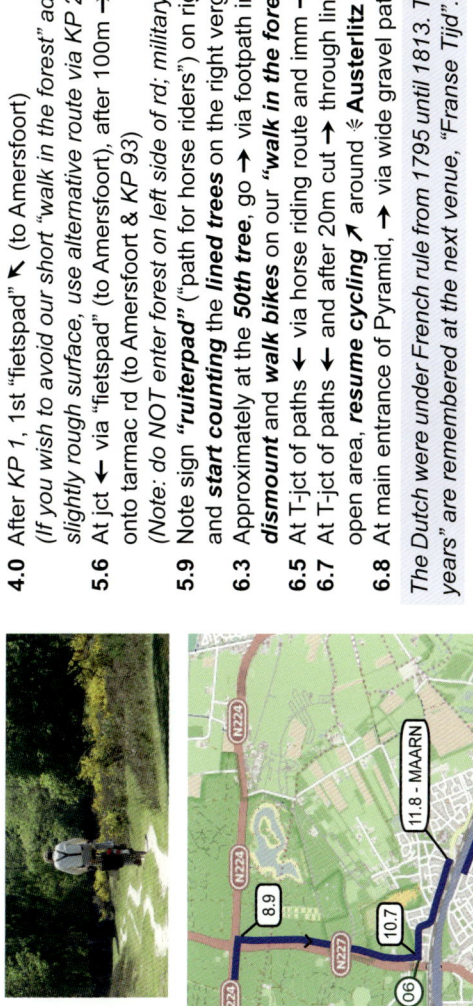

4.0 After *KP 1*, 1st "fietspad" ↖ (to Amersfoort)
(If you wish to avoid our short "walk in the forest" adventure with slightly rough surface, use alternative route via KP 2, see map)

5.6 At jct ←, via "fietspad" (to Amersfoort), after 100m → onto tarmac rd (to Amersfoort & *KP 93*)
(Note: do NOT enter forest on left side of rd; military zone!)

5.9 Note sign *"ruiterpad"* ("path for horse riders") on right side of rd and **start counting** the **lined trees** on the right verge of the road

6.3 Approximately at the **50th tree**, go → via footpath into the forest; **dismount** and **walk bikes** on our **"walk in the forest"** adventure:

6.5 At T-jct of paths ←, via horse riding route and imm → via footpath

6.7 At T-jct of paths ←, and after 20m cut → through line of bushes to open area, **resume cycling** ↗ around ☙ **Austerlitz Pyramid**

6.8 At main entrance of Pyramid, → via wide gravel path down hill

The Dutch were under French rule from 1795 until 1813. These "French years" are remembered at the next venue, "Franse Tijd".

7.2 ↗ via ☕🍴🛝 **Franse Tijd** *(restaurant & fun fair playground)* to main rd, ← via 🚲 on right side of main rd (to Woudenberg)

8.9 At jct with lhts → via 🚲 on left side of main rd (to Maarn, N227)

10.7 At jct *KP 6* ← (Poortse Bos, to Maarn & *KP 89*) 🚂

11.8 In 🍴🚂 **Maarn**, at square with clock tower ("5 Mei Plein"), → via rd into tunnel (**Maarn station** on right hand side of rd after 30m), after tunnel ← (Kapelweg, to *KP 7*), keep ↑, becomes "fietspad"

14.7 Ep (*KP 7*) ↗ via 🚲 on left side of rd, imm 1st rd ← (Wijkerweg)

Deep in the woods, we embark on a short "walk in the forest" adventure to make our way to the **Austerlitz Pyramid**, erected by French troops in 1804 to celebrate French supremacy in continental Europe. You can climb the pyramid and enjoy great forest views (€3 pp).

133

Eastern: Route 13: Utrecht Ridge National Park (69 km)

From **Maarn** the Utrecht Ridge narrows, but gains more height. A modest climb takes you over the summit to **Landgoed Broekhuizen**, a beautiful historic stately home on the edge of the forest (see picture). **Leersum** provides your first serious shopping opportunity since Soesterberg. **Amerongen** features an impressive **castle**, built on a strategic location next to the Nederrijn River. Visual displays in the castle are designed by British artist Peter Greenaway (open Tue-Sun, €10 pp). From here, we take some distance from the Utrecht Ridge, enjoying a ride with panoramic views on the **Nederrijn River dyke** to **Rhenen**. The Nederrijn is one of three branches of the River Rhine; "Waal" and "IJssel" are the other two.

17.5 Cross main rd ↑ (Darthuizerweg, to Darthuizen)
19.4 At T-jct *KP 10* ← (Broekhuizerlaan, to *KP 11*)
20.2 At *KP 11* and ⚜ **Landgoed Broekhuizen** ↑ (to Leersum & *KP 18*)
20.8 On arrival in Leersum at jct ↖ (Middelweg, *ignore 🚲 routes*)
21.5 At T-jct ←, at jct with lhts → via 🚲 on right side of rd (Rijksstraatweg) to shops 🏠 ⛽ 🍴 🍽 ⚐ **Leersum**, keep ↑
23.7 On arrival in Amerongen at mdabt ↗ (to *KP 17*), at next jct ↑ (Utrechtse Straatweg, *ignore 🚲 routes*)
24.1 At jct with start one-way flow of ⚜ 🏠 ⛽ 🍴 🍽 **Amerongen** →
24.3 At T-jct ← (Kersweg)
24.5 At T-jct →, at next T-jct ← (*For* ⚜ **Amerongen Castle** *now* ↑), for continued route, at *KP 17* 1st rd → (to Eck en Wiel & *KP 76*)

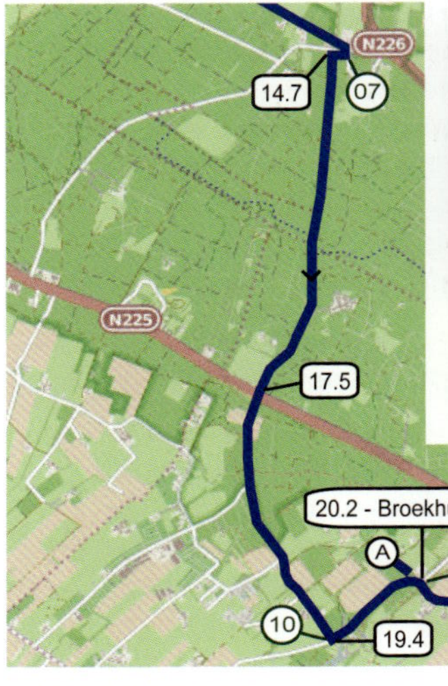

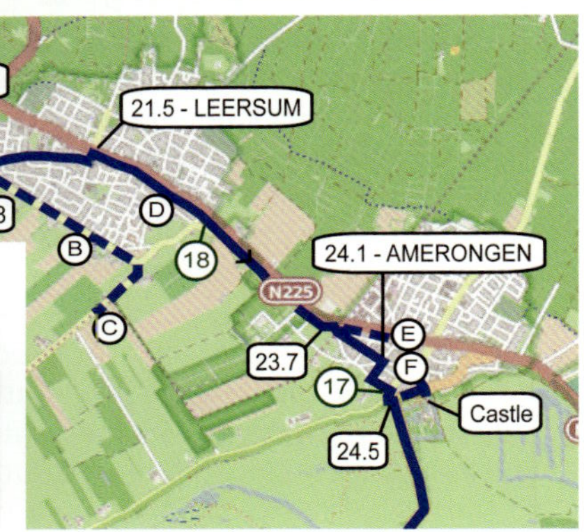

26.0 ⛴ **Nederrijn River Ferry** (see picture previous page, runs every 15 mins, daily until midnight, €1 pp)
26.3 At T-jct ←, via 🚲 on left side of rd, at next jct ↑ via dyke ridge rd (Rijnbandijk, to Rhenen & KP 77)
31.5 At KP 9, 1st rd ← (Marsdijk, to Rhenen & KP 92)
35.6 At end of dyke rd ↖ via footpath up the slope, ep ←, via 🚲 on left side of rd (N233 river bridge)
36.3 At end of bridge imm ↖ via 🚲 and imm ↖ via rd (Trambaanweg)
36.6 Imm after side rd "Duistere Weg" ↗ via "fietspad"
36.9 Ep ↑ via rd, at rndabt → (Herenstraat) (For Town Centre 🍴 🛏 🍽 ℹ **Rhenen** ←, for ↱ ↑)
37.4 Major jct with lhts, end of route (Station on left side) (to continue see page 136)

To the south, you look out over the **Betuwe** region, well-known for its fruit-produce. In 1995, 250,000 people were ordered to evacuate, as dykes were expected to collapse under the pressure of high water levels in all Rhine branches. "Space for rivers" schemes now allow controlled flooding in some areas to reduce threats.

Eastern: Route 14: Grebbeberg & River Waal (29 km)

Stations: Rhenen, Opheusden, Hemmen-Dodewaard, Nijmegen
Cycling time: 2 - 3 hours (🚲 13%, 🚶 77%, 🚗 10%)

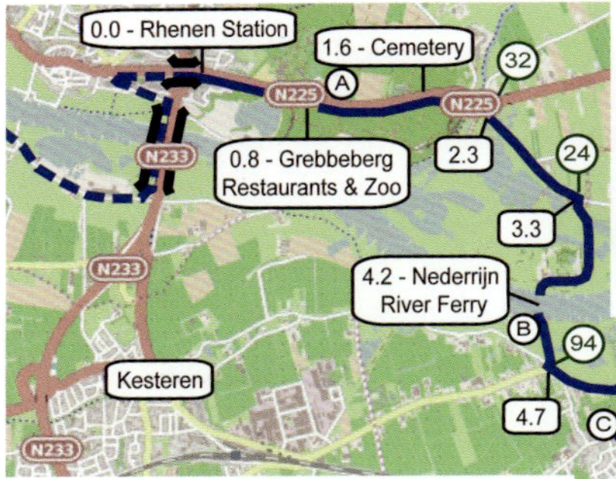

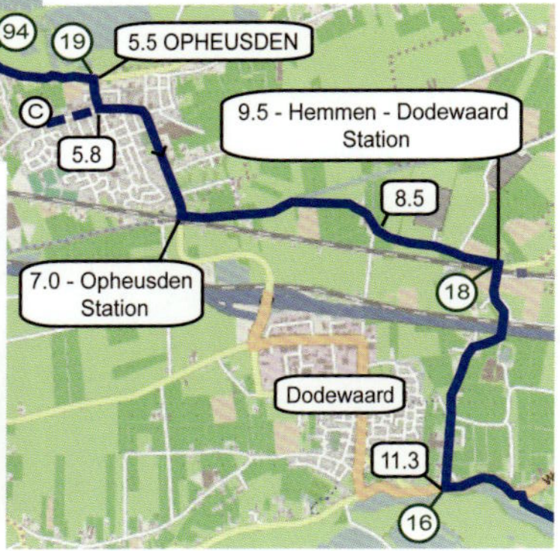

This **river route** starts with a ride on the **Grebbeberg**. This most eastern hill of the Utrecht Ridge has had military significance since the construction of the **Grebbelinie** in 1745. This defensive line would flood the lands east of the Utrecht Ridge, with military protecting the new shores. During the 1940 Nazi invasion, the Dutch returned to this old line of defence. The Nazi approach over land was stopped for three days at the Grebbeberg, with **Rhenen** suffering badly. On the Grebbeberg you'll find various restaurants, a **war cemetery** and **Ouwehand Zoo** (open daily, €21 pp).

- **0.0** (37.4) At major jct with lhts *(station on northeast side of jct)* ↑, go east via 🚲 on right side of rd (Grebbeweg, N225 to Arnhem)
- **0.8** 🏨 🛏 🍴 **Grebbeberg & Ouwehand Zoo** *(Hotel, restaurants, zoo)*
- **1.6** ⚰ **Militair Ereveld Grebbeberg** *(War Cemetery)*
- **2.3** At end of steep descent, at KP 32, ↗ via dyke ridge rd (Grebbedijk, to Opheusden & KP 24)
- **3.3** At KP 24, 1st rd → (to Opheusden & KP 94)
- **4.2** ⛴ **Nederrijn River Ferry** *(every 15 mins, daily until 9 pm, €1 pp)*
- **4.4** 🛏 🍴 **Fietsstop 't Veerhuis** *(B&B & restaurant with river views)* 🚲
- **4.7** At next jct ↖ (Rijnbandijk, to Centrum & KP 19)
- **5.5** At KP 19 → down into ⛽ ↗ **Opheusden** (to Centrum & KP 18) 🚲
- **5.8** After shops ← at jct (Lodderstraat, to Dodewaard & KP 18) 🚲
- **7.0** In front of railway crossing and station ← (Dalwagen, to KP 18)
- **8.5** 1st rd ← (De Zandvoort, to Hemmen & KP 18)
- **9.5** At KP 18 in front of station → via railway crossing (Kerkstraat, to Dodewaard & KP 16), keep going ↑

Via the **Nederrijn River Ferry** of **Opheusden** you'll make your way to the **Waal River Dyke**. Providing you don't have strong headwinds from the east, this should be a great ride. You'll have panoramic views over Europe's busiest inland shipping route all the way to **Nijmegen**. The **Snelbinder Cycle Bridge** is a special way to cycle entirely traffic-free into a city!

11.3 At T-jct *KP 16* ← (Waalbandijk, to Nijmegen & *KP 17*)
11.8 At 🛌🍴 **De Engel** & *KP 17* ↗ (Waalbandijk, to Nijmegen)
20.0 🛒 **Landwinkel** *(Farm Shop)*
20.9 ⛪🎋🏛 **Slijk Ewijk** *(Picnic table at scenic church with river views)*
22.7 ▲ 🛌🍴 **De Altena** *(Pub/cafe and campsite)*
27.4 Keep going ↑ until *KP 36* (1mm after narrow tunnel under railway, dismount and walk up steps →, ← via 🚲 (Snelbinder, to *KP 19*) *(see map for alternative, step-free route onto bridge via KP 37)*
28.7 Ep, at *KP 19*, end of route
 For Nijmegen station → via 🚲 (300m)
 For Nijmegen & Hills - Round Trip ←; see page 139

Eastern: Route 15: Nijmegen & Hills - Round Trip (25 km)

Stations: Nijmegen, Nijmegen-Heyendaal
Cycling time: 2 - 3 hours (⚲ 55%, ⚹ 37%, ⚞ 8%)

The city of **Nijmegen**, attractively located on the banks of the River Waal, was founded by the Romans. In the **Valkhof Museum** you'll find various Roman artifacts on display, alongside plenty of modern art (open Tue-Sun, €9 pp). The **Dutch Cycling Museum Velorama** has a collection of 250 historic bicycles, including the 1817 "hobby horse" (open daily, €5 pp). Nijmegen is internationally known for its **Four Days Walking Marches**.

This annual event in **July** attracts over 40,000 walkers from around the world. It is very popular with the military, as the event also commemorates **Operation Market Garden** during WWII. In 1944, the Allied forces intended to bypass Nazi defence lines in an ambitious northern advance. The bridge of Nijmegen (see picture top left on next page) was successfully taken, but the aim of the campaign, the city of Arnhem (north of Nijmegen) turned out to be "a bridge too far". To find out the full story, cycle our Round Trip from Nijmegen and visit the **National Liberation Museum** (open daily, €10 pp). This ride includes some modest climbing on **real Dutch hills**!

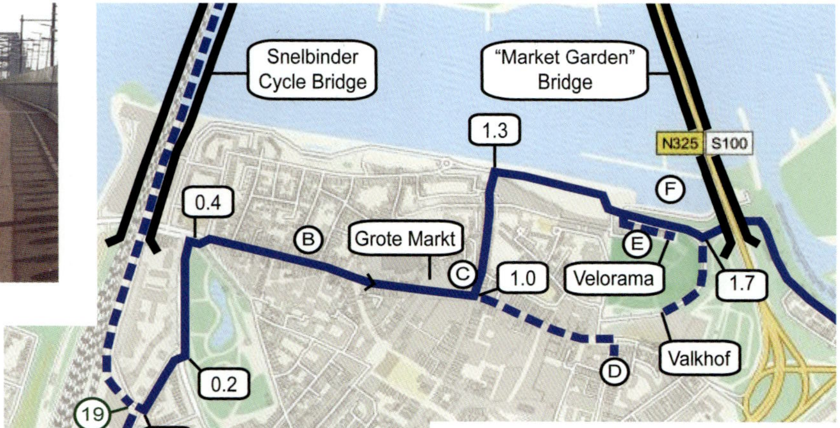

"Grote Markt"

If you start from Nijmegen station, leave the station by keeping ← for 300m (KP 19 is the south end of Snelbinder Bridge, see right picture)

0.0 (28.7) At KP 19, coming from Snelbinder Bridge ←, go north via 🚲 on right side of rd (to Weurt & KP 20)
0.2 At T-jct ← via 🚲 on right side of rd (to Weurt & KP 20)
0.4 At T-jct → via 🚲 on right side of rd, then imm via zebra ↱ into cobbled pedestrian rd (Lange Hezelstraat), 🚲 allowed, keep ↑
1.0 At far end of market square ☕🍴🛏🛒🍽🛈 ⓘ ↱ **Nijmegen** "Grote Markt" 1st rd ← (to Waalkade), keep ↑ down the hill through pedestrian zone (🚲 allowed)
1.3 Ep → via riverside promenade rd 🚢
1.7 At next main jct ↖ (Ubbergseweg, to "Doorgaand Verkeer"), pass under historic river bridge, keep ↑ 🚢
Continue reading on next page top right ("to Liberation Museum")

Eastern: Route 15: Nijmegen & Hills - Round Trip (25 km)

For route to the Liberation Museum, read on the right!

Route back to Nijmegen:
(continued from page 141)

- **6.4** At KP 9 ← via 🚲 on right side of rd (to Malden & KP 10)
- **7.0** 1st rd → (Driehuizerweg)
- **7.8** At rd crossing ↑
- **8.2** 1st rd ← (Platolaan), use 🚲 lane on one-way section
- **8.4** At T-jct → via 🚲 on right side
- **8.8** At jct with lhts ↑ via 1st 🚲 crossing, then imm cross main rd ↖ via 🚲 crossing, continue on left side of main rd (to Heyendaal station & KP 5)
- **9.0** At KP 5 ← (to Nijmegen CS & KP 17), keep going ↑
- **9.9** At KP 17 → via 🚲 on right side of rd, at lhts imm ← via 🚲 crossing (to Nijmegen CS)
- **11.2** Ep ↖ to station, end of route

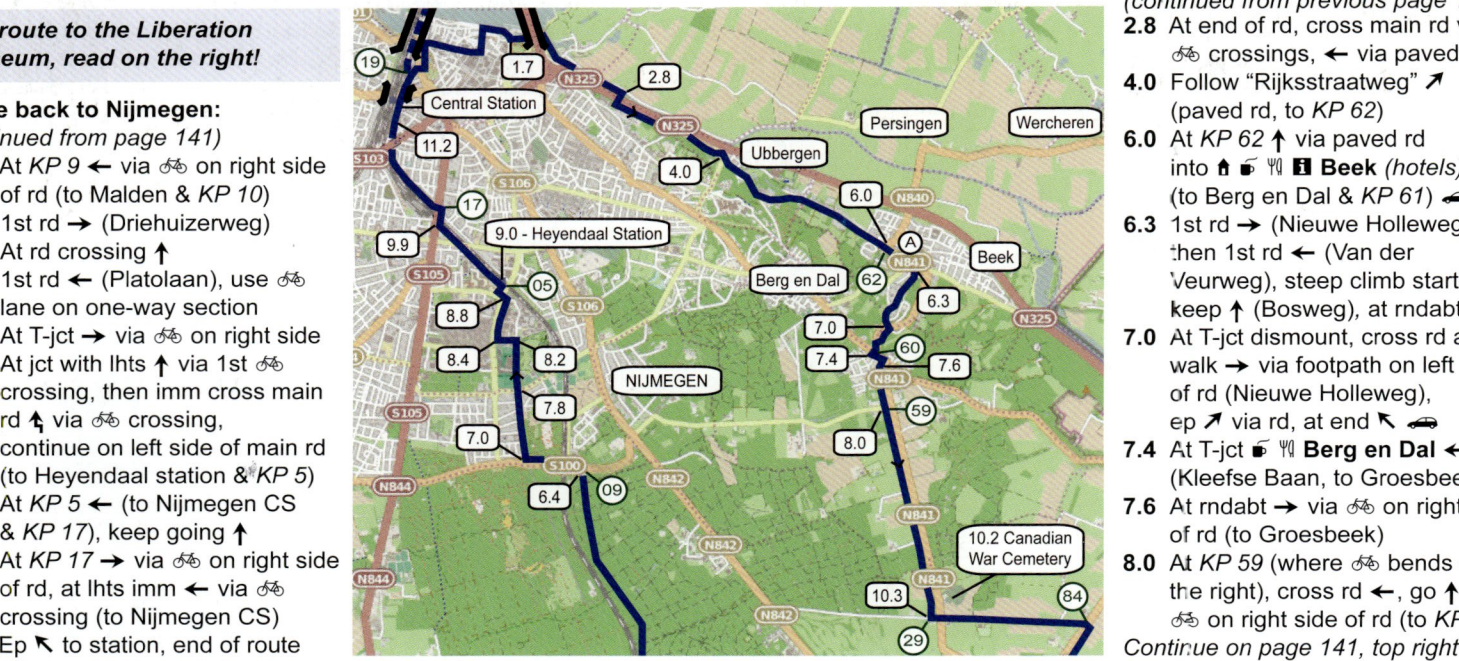

Route to the Liberation Museum:
(continued from previous page 139)

- **2.8** At end of rd, cross main rd via 🚲 crossings, ← via paved rd Follow "Rijksstraatweg" ↗ (paved rd, to KP 62)
- **4.0** At KP 62 ↑ via paved rd into 🏨 🛏 🍴 **Beek** *(hotels)* (to Berg en Dal & KP 61) 🚲
- **6.0** 1st rd → (Nieuwe Holleweg), then 1st rd ← (Van der Veurweg), steep climb starts, keep ↑ (Bosweg), at rndabt ↖
- **6.3** At T-jct dismount, cross rd and walk → via footpath on left side of rd (Nieuwe Holleweg), ep ↗ via rd, at end ↖ 🚲
- **7.4** At T-jct 🛏 🍴 **Berg en Dal** ← (Kleefse Baan, to Groesbeek)
- **7.6** At rndabt → via 🚲 on right side of rd (to Groesbeek)
- **8.0** At KP 59 (where 🚲 bends off to the right), cross rd ←, go ↑ via 🚲 on right side of rd (to KP 29)

Continue on page 141, top right

For route to the Liberation Museum, read on the right!

Route back to Nijmegen:
- **0.0** *(13.1)* From Liberation Museum, ← via 🚲 on left side of rd (to Groesbeek)
- **0.1** At T-jct ▲ 🅿 🍽 **Groesbeek** → via 🚲 on right side of rd (Nieuweweg, to Nijmegen)
- **1.4** At KP 31 cross main rd ←, then ↗ via 🚲 (Maldensebaan, to Malden & KP 32)
- **3.5** At KP 32 → via 🚲 *(to KP 9)*

Continue on page 140, top left

Route to the Liberation Museum:
(continued from previous page 140)

10.2 ⚔ **Canadian War Cemetery**
- **10.3** After cemetery, at KP 29, ← (Derde Baan, to KP 84)
- **11.8** At KP 84 → via 🚲 on left side of rd (Wylerbaan, to KP 28)
- **13.3** ⚔ 🏛 **Liberation Museum**

For return route to Nijmegen, read on left side of this page

Southern: Route 16: Vlissingen & Walcheren (36 km)

Stations: Vlissingen ("Flushing" in English)
Cycling time: 2 - 3.5 hours (🚴 65%, 🚶 30%, ⛴ 5%)

To cycle the **Southern route**, you'll need to take bicycles on the **train** to Vlissingen. Note the next railway station is 135 km away (Hoek van Holland), so once you are on your way, you are kind of committed to cycle the full Southern route (although some **backtracking** is possible from **Domburg**). The full route can easily be cycled in two to four days, depending on how many breaks you'll allow to make the most of the pleasant **coast** of the **Zeeland** province. The Port of **Vlissingen** controls the **Westerschelde** estuary. Pilot ships move in and out from the harbour to provide container ships safe passages to and from **Antwerp** in Belgium. On the promenade, the **Michiel de Ruyter statue** looks proudly over the waves. This famous admiral was responsible for the biggest defeat of the British Navy, the 1667 Medway raid. The spirit of piracy is kept high in the former armoury **Het Arsenaal**, an indoors pirate theme park with sea aquarium and tower (open daily, €13 pp). The **Muzeeum** explores Zeeland's maritime past more seriously (open daily, €9 pp).

0.0 From exit station, ↑ via zebra pattern (to Centrum), walk ↳ over locks, then ↖ via 🚴 (to Arsenaal, *LF 1b*) ← over locks (*For* ⛴ **Arsenaal →**)
2.0 At end of sea wall promenade, walk
2.1 Ep in ⛴ 🏠 🚻 ☕ 🍴 🏛 **Vlissingen** ↓ (to *KP 81*), follow bendy rd ↖ via ⛴ **Michiel de Ruyter statue**

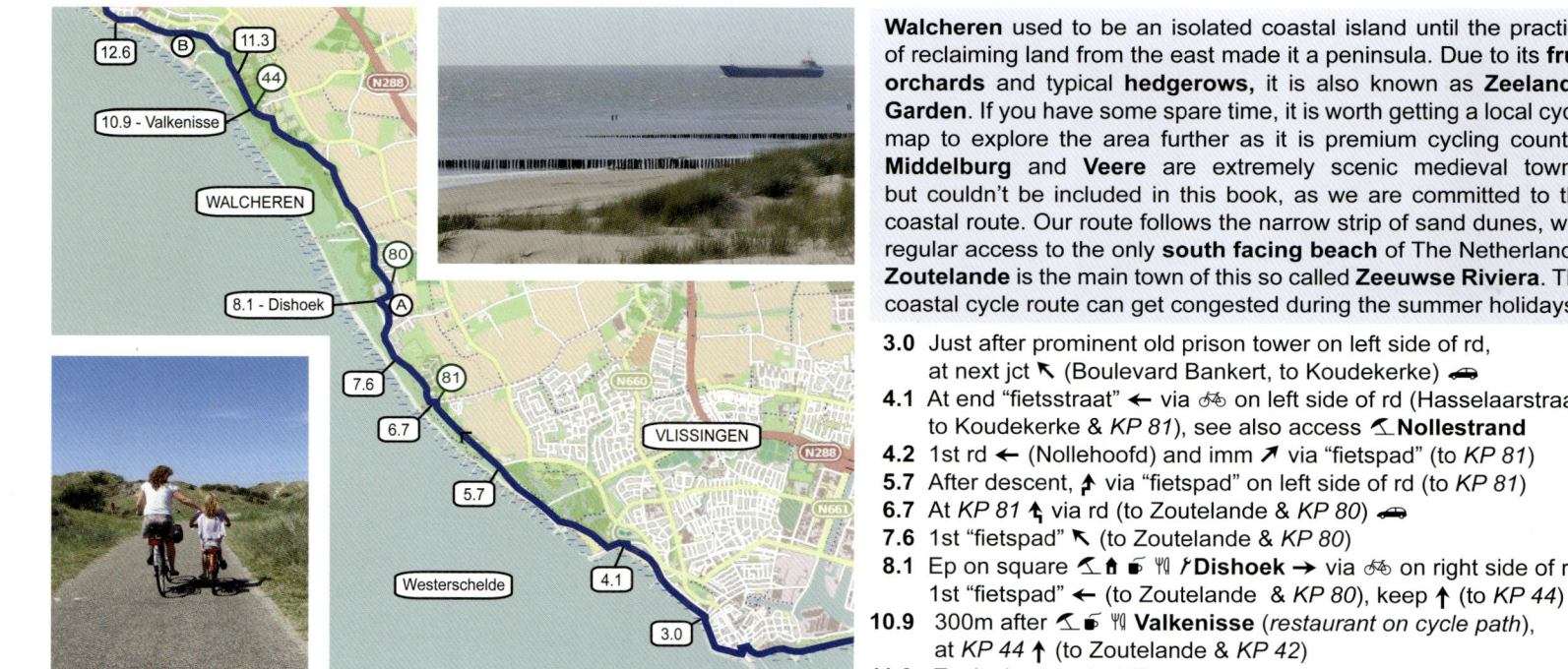

Walcheren used to be an isolated coastal island until the practice of reclaiming land from the east made it a peninsula. Due to its **fruit orchards** and typical **hedgerows**, it is also known as **Zeeland's Garden**. If you have some spare time, it is worth getting a local cycle map to explore the area further as it is premium cycling country. **Middelburg** and **Veere** are extremely scenic medieval towns, but couldn't be included in this book, as we are committed to the coastal route. Our route follows the narrow strip of sand dunes, with regular access to the only **south facing beach** of The Netherlands. **Zoutelande** is the main town of this so called **Zeeuwse Riviera**. The coastal cycle route can get congested during the summer holidays!

- **3.0** Just after prominent old prison tower on left side of rd, at next jct ↖ (Boulevard Bankert, to Koudekerke) 🚗
- **4.1** At end "fietsstraat" ↙ via 🚲 on left side of rd (Hasselaarstraat, to Koudekerke & *KP 81*), see also access ⇗ **Nollestrand**
- **4.2** 1st rd ↙ (Nollehoofd) and imm ↗ via "fietspad" (to *KP 81*)
- **5.7** After descent, ↑ via "fietspad" on left side of rd (to *KP 81*)
- **6.7** At *KP 81* ↑ via rd (to Zoutelande & *KP 80*) 🚗
- **7.6** 1st "fietspad" ↖ (to Zoutelande & *KP 80*)
- **8.1** Ep on square ⇗ 🏨 ☕ 🍴 ↗**Dishoek** → via 🚲 on right side of rd, 1st "fietspad" ↙ (to Zoutelande & *KP 80*), keep ↑ (to *KP 44*)
- **10.9** 300m after ⇗ 🍴 **Valkenisse** (*restaurant on cycle path*), at *KP 44* ↑ (to Zoutelande & *KP 42*)
- **11.3** Ep ↑ via paved rd (Duinweg), keep going ↑ (to *KP 42*)

Southern: Route 16: Vlissingen & Walcheren (36 km)

Westkapelle is the West Cape of The Netherlands, surrounded by the North Sea on three sides. Its prominent seawall was bombed in 1944 to literally drown the Nazi defences, causing flooding of the whole Walcheren island. This Allied bombing was followed by a D-Day style amphibian landing, as the **Antwerp docks** were much needed as a northern bridgehead for the advancing Allied troops. At the **Liberty Bridge**, at the **Polderhuis, dijk en oorlogsmuseum**, you'll find some great displays (open daily, €6 pp).

Cycling the Westkapelle sea wall is a popular activity

12.6 In 🛏🍴🛒☕🍽 ℹ ↗ **Zoutelande** ↑ (Langstraat, to Westkapelle)

13.0 After church on right side of rd, at jct ↖ via 🚲 on right side of rd, after 50m cross ↙ onto 🚲 on left side of rd (to Westkapelle)

13.6 After sign "leaving Zoutelande", at *KP 40*, 1st "fietspad" ↖ (to Westkapelle & *KP 10*)

15.9 Ep at access ⛵ **Scheldezicht** ↗ via rd, then imm ↖ and after 50m → via "fietspad" (to *KP 10*)

16.1 At jct ↖ via 🚲 through forest (to *KP 10*)

17.0 Ep ↑ via rd, at T-jct ← via 🚲 on left side of rd (D'Arke, to Domburg & *KP 10*), keep ↑

17.5 At ⛵🍴🛒☕🍽 ↗ **Westkapelle** ↑ *(For ⛵🍴🛒☕🍽 ↗ Westkapelle →)*

18.5 At ⛵🍴🍽 **De Westkaap** *(Coastal Restaurant)*

19.0 1st rd ← (Noorderhoofdweg, to *KP 10*)

21.0 At end of seawall rd at *KP 10* ← via 🚲 on left side of rd (to *KP 14*)

22.0 1st rd → (Trommelweg)

22.5 1st rd ↖ (Babelweg)

23.5 At T-jct → (Kromme Weg)

23.9 1st rd ← (Schansweg), ↑ (Prinsenpark) *(For return route to Zoutelande, see map)*

Domburg developed into a **seaside resort** from the 1830s. Being well away from Dutch cities, the town remained relatively small. Even now, with the bucket and spade brigade and German tourists taking over during the summer holidays, it is easy to escape from the hustle and bustle in the high street. In the forests of **De Mantelingen** you'll be cycling very much on your own. If you like budget accommodation, don't miss the **YHA**; it is beautifully located in an **historic castle** (see picture).

24.6 At T-jct ← (Brouwerijweg), keep ↑, *give way to traffic from the right!*
25.2 At T-jct → via 🚲 on right side of rd, then 2nd rd ← (Zuidstraat, to Oostkapelle)
(for 🛒 **supermarket** ↑, 50m)
25.5 At jct → into 🏠🛏🍴☕🍽🛈 ⚑ **Domburg** ⚓, at next jct ↑ via 🚲 on right side of rd (Domburgseweg, to Oostkapelle & KP 16)
26.0 At jct ↖ via 🚲 on right side of rd (to Oostkapelle)
26.9 At house "Wijde Landen" cross rd ↘ to 🚲 on left side of rd (to KP 16), after 200m 1st rd ← (Duinvlietweg, to Vrouwenpolder)
27.5 End rd → via "fietspad" to Vrouwenpolder & KP 16), ↑ (to KP 27)
29.7 Cross ↙🍴☕🍽 **Oostkapelle Beach Rd** ↑ via "fietspad" (to Vrouwenpolder)
30.3 Ep ↗ via rd (to Vrouwenpolder & KP 27), keep ↑ 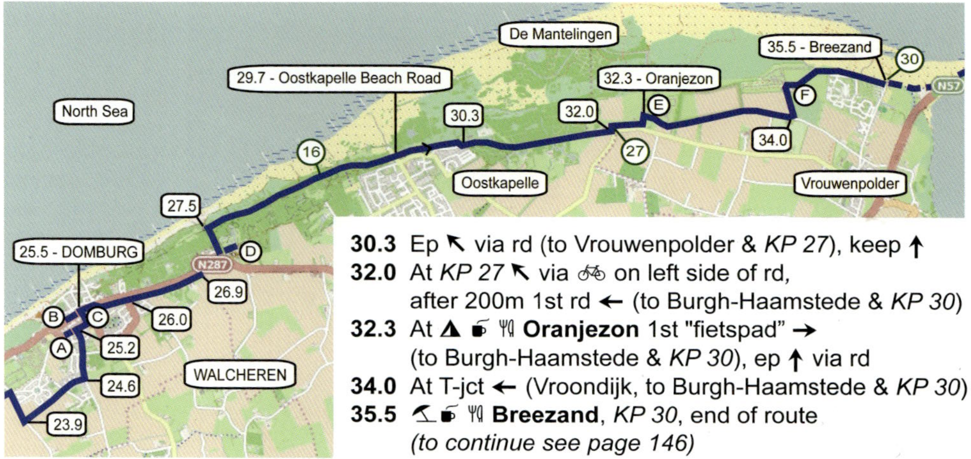
32.0 At KP 27 ↘ via 🚲 on left side of rd, after 200m 1st rd ← (to Burgh-Haamstede & KP 30)
32.3 At 🏠🛏🍴☕🍽 ⚑ **Oranjezon** 1st "fietspad" → (to Burgh-Haamstede & KP 30), ep ↑ via rd
34.0 At T-jct ← (Vroondijk, to Burgh-Haamstede & KP 30)
35.5 ↙🍴☕🍽 **Breezand**, KP 30, end of route *(to continue see page 146)*

Southern: Route 17: The Delta Dams & Schouwen (42 km)

Stations: *None (Vlissingen, route 16 or Hoek van Holland, route 19)*
Cycling time: *2.5 - 4 hours* (🚲 70%, 🚶 24%, 🚗 6%)

This route takes you across three major Delta Dams, of which the **Oosterscheldebarrier** is the largest. You'll cycle above three series of floodgates, together with a total length of two miles (three kms). This extraordinary engineering makes the first dam, the **Veerse Gat Dam**, just look like a sandcastle on the beach. At **Delta Park Neeltje Jans** you'll find excellent exhibitions about the **1953 floods**, the Delta Plan and its construction works. A visit to a **seal centre** is also included (€16 pp). On the formal coastal island of Schouwen you can join **cruises** on the **Oosterschelde National Park Estuary** from **Burghsluis**, advanced bookings advised (phone 0111 414309, www.ms-onrust.nl).

0.0 (35.5) In bend at 🏨 🍴 **Duinoord** and *KP 30* ← via closed rd (to Burgh-Haamstede & *KP 3*) onto ⇐ **Veerse Gat Dam**
3.0 At *KP 3* ↑ (to *KP 4*), at end of dam ↗ via narrow "fietspad", keep ↑
4.6 At *KP 4* ← (to *KP 70*) onto ⇐ **Oosterscheldebarrier - Roompot**
6.9 On ⇐ **Neeltje Jans island** ↑ across locks (🏨 🍴 **De Helling** (snackbar) on left side), after locks ↖ (*LF 1b*), keep going ↑ via wide tarmac dam with sand dunes on left side
9.6 At jct ↑ (Hoogh Plaetweg, to *KP 70*), leads onto ⇐ **Schaar** (*For* ⇐ 🍴 **Delta Park Neeltje Jans** exhibition centre → at jct)

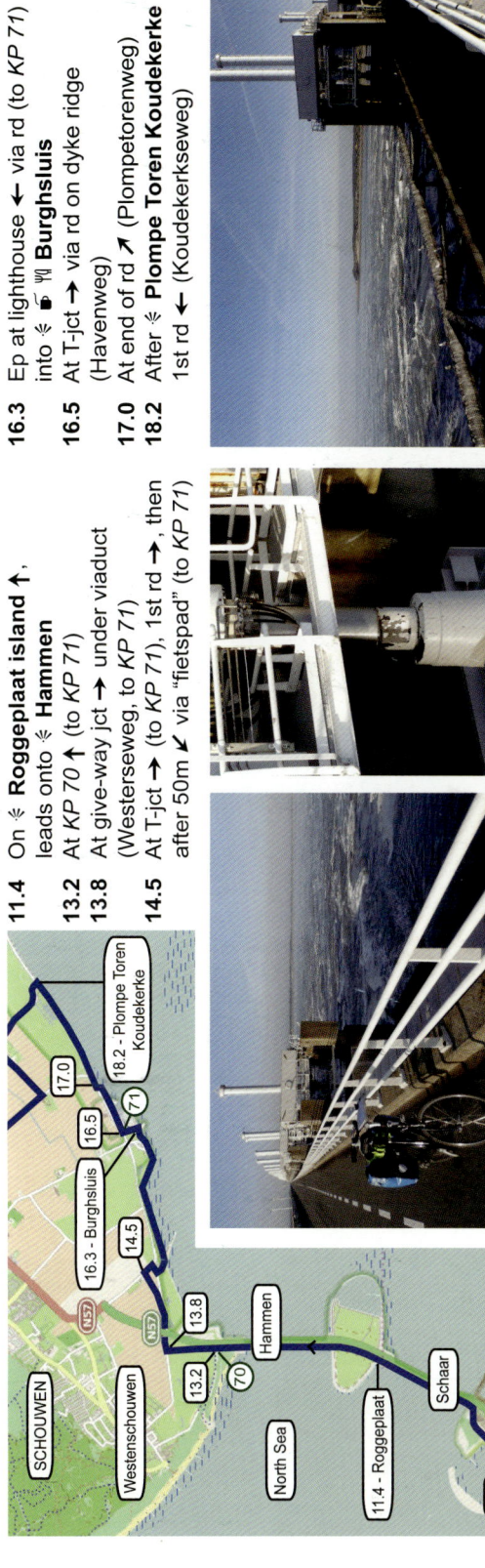

- 11.4 On ⬅ **Roggeplaat island** ↑, leads onto ⬅ **Hammen**
- 13.2 At *KP 70* ↑ (to *KP 71*)
- 13.8 At give-way jct → under viaduct (Westerseweg, to *KP 71*)
- 14.5 At T-jct → (to *KP 71*), 1st rd →, then after 50m ↙ via "fietspad" (to *KP 71*)
- 16.3 Ep at lighthouse ⬅ via rd (to *KP 71*) into ⬅ 🛏 🍴 **Burghsluis**
- 16.5 At T-jct → via rd on dyke ridge (Havenweg)
- 17.0 At end of rd ↗ (Plompetorenweg)
- 18.2 After ⬅ **Plompe Toren Koudekerke** 1st rd ⬅ (Koudekerkseweg)

The **Oosterscheldebarrier** (1986) consists of 62 flood gates, which get closed if water levels in the North Sea are expected to be higher than 3 metres above "normal high tide level". This happens about once per year. Each **floodgate** spans 42 meters. Metal **doors** weigh up to 480 tons each.

The **pillars** are 30-40 meters high and were built in drydocks on Neeltje Jans, where one pillar still stands. After floated into position, pillars were filled with sand. Silt and strong currents cause **corrosion** and damage to mechanisms, doors and foundations. This results in an annual maintenance bill of about €10 million!

Southern: Route 17: The Delta Dams & Schouwen (42 km)

On **Schouwen**, you'll cycle by the lonely **Koudekerke** church tower. According to **local legend**, the village was submerged hundreds of years ago because fishermen captured a **mermaid**, the wife of a King Neptune-type character. He begged the fishermen to give his wife back, but they just laughed. Then he spoke his fatal words, "I'll let your village drown and only the tower will survive!" **Experience** the legend and **climb** to the top of this **Plump Tower** ("Plompe Toren", open daily, free).

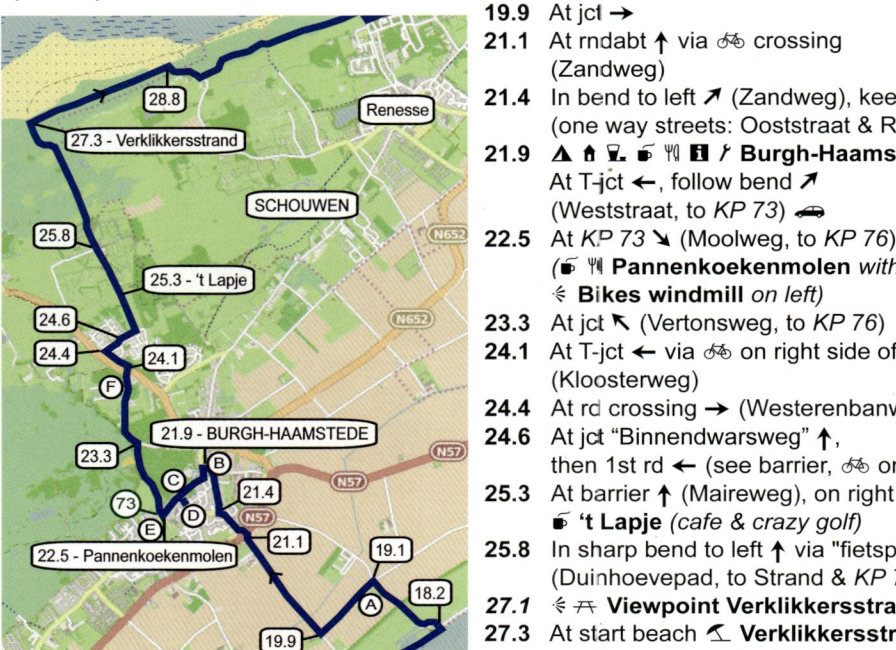

19.1	At jct ← (Brabersweg)
19.9	At jct →
21.1	At rndabt ↑ via 🚴 crossing (Zandweg)
21.4	In bend to left ↗ (Zandweg), keep ↑ (one way streets: Ooststraat & Ring)
21.9	⛺🛏🍴☕🍽ℹ🚲 **Burgh-Haamstede** At T-jct ←, follow bend ↗ (Weststraat, to KP 73) 🚗
22.5	At KP 73 ↘ (Moolweg, to KP 76) (🔒🍴 **Pannenkoekenmolen** with 🚲 **Bikes windmill** on left)
23.3	At jct ↖ (Vertonsweg, to KP 76)
24.1	At T-jct ← via 🚴 on right side of rd (Kloosterweg)
24.4	At rd crossing → (Westerenbanweg)
24.6	At jct "Binnendwarsweg" ↑, then 1st rd ← (see barrier, 🚴 only)
25.3	At barrier ↑ (Maireweg), on right side 🔒 **'t Lapje** (cafe & crazy golf)
25.8	In sharp bend to left ↑ via "fietspad" (Duinhoevepad, to Strand & KP 76)
27.1	🚴 🚻 **Viewpoint Verklikkersstrand**
27.3	At start beach ↙ **Verklikkersstrand** → via gravel 🚴 (to KP 76)

Burgh-Haamstede is the main town on Schouwen, with a pretty high street and church square. Do not miss the **pancake windmill** ("pannenkoekenmolen") with its bikes windmill (see book cover). The remaining ride is mostly via extensive sand dune reserves, including the wide beach **Verklikkersstrand**.

- **28.8** Ep → via concrete path, after crossing dune ridge ← via gravel "fietspad" *(to KP 76)*
- **29.9** At ⚓ **Wilhelminahoeve** ↑ *(to KP 76)*
- **31.0** At ⚓ **Van Renesseweg** → via concrete rd, at bike park ← via gravel *through bike park (!)*, cut through bushes to tarmac rd, ↖ *(to KP 76)*
- **31.7** At KP 76, in sharp bend to right, ↑ via gravel "fietspad" *(to KP 84)*
- **32.4** Ep ↖ via rd (Rampweg, to KP 84) 🚲 (🏠 🛏 🍽 **Zeerust** *hotel-restaurant on corner)*
- **34.3** 1st rd ↑ (to car park & KP 84), after 100m ↖ via 🚲 *(to KP 84)*
- **35.1** At jct KP 84 ← via 🚲 *(to Rotterdam)*
- **35.4** Cross rd ↑ via 🚲 onto dam ridge *(to KP 51)* 🌊 **Brouwersdam**
- **38.4** *(For 🏠 🛏 🍽* **Brouwersdam** *(beach pavillion)* ← *at rd crossing), otherwise* ↑ *(to KP 51)*
- **41.5** End of route *(to continue see page 150)*

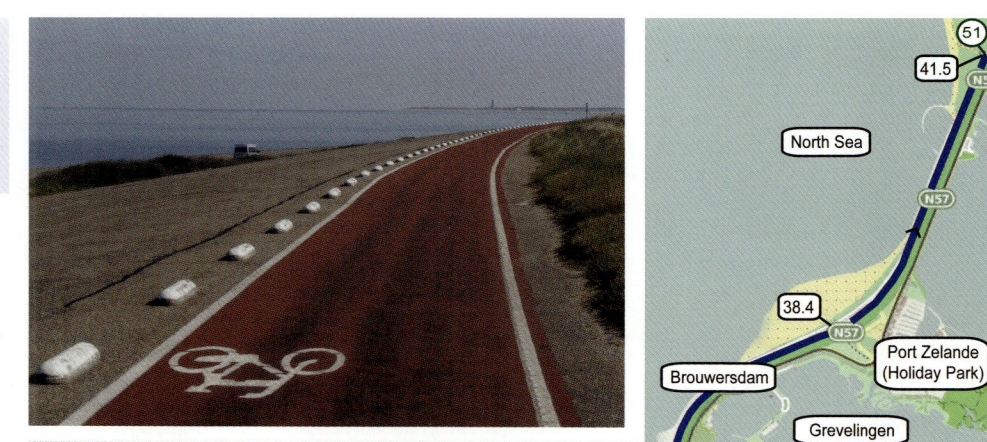

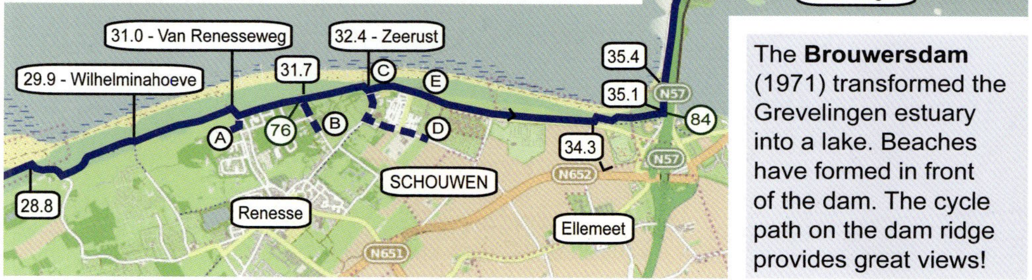

The **Brouwersdam** (1971) transformed the Grevelingen estuary into a lake. Beaches have formed in front of the dam. The cycle path on the dam ridge provides great views!

Southern: Route 18: Goeree & Voorne (42 km)

Stations: None (Vlissingen, route 16 or Hoek van Holland, route 19)
Cycling time: 2.5 - 4 hours (🚴 59%, 🥾 39%, ⛴ 2%)

Goeree and **Voorne** were both isolated islands until the impressive Delta Works dams connected them with the mainland from the 1950s. Windswept reclaimed land, only sheltered from the North Sea by a handful of sand dunes, set the scene for centuries until tourism and the Rotterdam docks extension schemes arrived. On Goeree, **Ouddorp** caters mostly for holidaymakers. The town is a good place to stock up on provisions. **Goedereede** (literally meaning "safe anchorage") is a scenic small town which once had a thriving trading and fishing port. Sedimentation slowly closed the port off from the sea, ending the town's wealth. Buildings are well preserved and you'll feel like you are cycling through an open air museum; lunch on the market square is recommended!

The Market Square of Goedereede (left) and Ouddorp-Haven (above)

- 0.0 (41.5) At KP 51 → into tunnel (to KP 52), then ← (to Ouddorp & KP 52), keep ↑
- 1.8 Ep → via rd (to Ouddorp & KP 52)
- 3.1 At KP 52 ↑ (to KP 58), rd becomes 🚴
- 5.4 At jct ↑ via path 🛒 🍴 **Ouddorp Haven**
- 5.6 Ep ↗ via rd, at KP 58 ← via bridge, then → (to Ouddorp & KP 57) 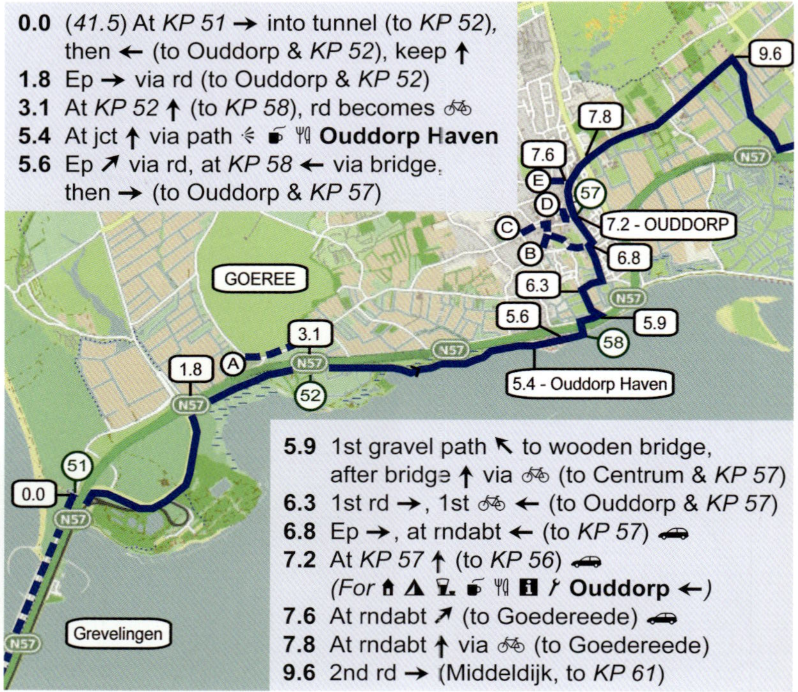
- 5.9 1st gravel path ↖ to wooden bridge, after bridge ↑ via 🚴 (to Centrum & KP 57)
- 6.3 1st rd →, 1st 🚴 ← (to Ouddorp & KP 57)
- 6.8 Ep →, at rndabt ← (to KP 57)
- 7.2 At KP 57 ↑ (to KP 56)
  (For 🏠 ⛺ 🛒 🍴 🍺 ℹ️ ⛽ **Ouddorp** ↓)
- 7.6 At rndabt ↗ (to Goedereede)
- 7.8 At rndabt ↑ via 🚴 (to Goedereede)
- 9.6 2nd rd → (Middeldijk, to KP 61)

- 10.6 1st 🚴 ← (Spuidijk, to *KP 61*)
- 11.4 In 🚴 🏠 ☕ 🛏 **Goedereede** 1st rd → (Pieterstraat), keep ↑ (Markt)
- 11.7 1st tarmac 🚴 ↗ (Kinderdijk, *LF 1b*), keep ↑ (to Havenhoofd)
- 14.0 Ep ↑ via rd into **Havenhoofd** (Haveneind, to Brielle)
- 14.5 Join 🚴 on left side of rd (Meester Snijderweg, to *KP 64*)
- 16.7 After tunnel under main rd ← via 🚴 (to Brielle, *LF 1b*), after bridge keep ↑ onto 🚴 **Haringvlietdam** (🚴 ☕ 🛏 🍴 **Haringvliet Expo** *on right*)

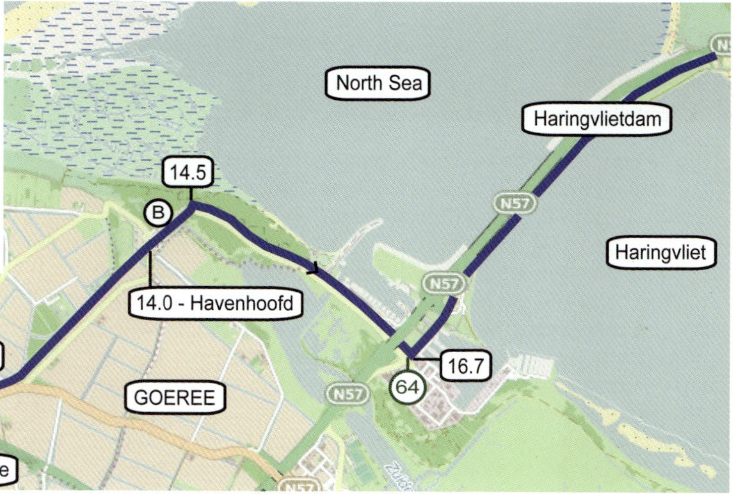

The **Haringvlietdam** (1970) is the main outlet for both Rhine and Meuse Rivers. Its sluices were built on location in the mouth of the Haringvliet estuary in an enormous drydock. The dam brutally stopped fish migration and salt water entering the estuary for over forty years. Only recently, some sluices have been opened to help the ecosystem.

Southern: Route 18: Goeree & Voorne (42 km)

- 21.4 At *KP 21* ↑, 1st rd ← (Onderlangs, to Brielle)
- 22.0 After tunnel, at T-jct ← (Krommeweg)
- 23.5 1st 🚲 ← (to Brielle)
- 24.2 Ep cross rd, ← via 🚲 into tunnel, keep ↑
- 24.8 1st rd → (Bredeweg, later Goolseweg)
- 26.3 1st rd ← (Sliklandseweg)
- 26.9 1st rd ← (Middenweg)
- 27.7 1st rd ← (Sluisweg)
- 29.3 Cross rd, then ← via 🚲 (to *KP 32*)
- 30.0 1st rd ↗ (*KP 32*, Oude Dijk)
- 30.1 ☕ **De Vuijle Vaatdoek (art gallery & cafe)**
- 30.3 In bend ↖ (Oude Dijk), follow 🚲 route

Voorne is the last former coastal island on the southern route. You'll cycle across open polder farmland to **Brielle**. This scenic town is encircled by **fine fortifications**, reflecting its important role in the fight against Spanish rule during the **Dutch war of independence**, which lasted 80 years! Allow time to take in essential Dutch history in the **Historisch Museum** (open Tue-Sun, €4 pp) or to enjoy a stroll in the historic town centre. If you are heading for Hoek of Holland, make sure to leave Brielle by 5.30pm at the latest. It is still a long way to the pedestrian ferry to Hook and if you miss the last ferry around 7pm, you'll be **stuck** in the vast docklands of Rotterdam (see pages 154 and 155).

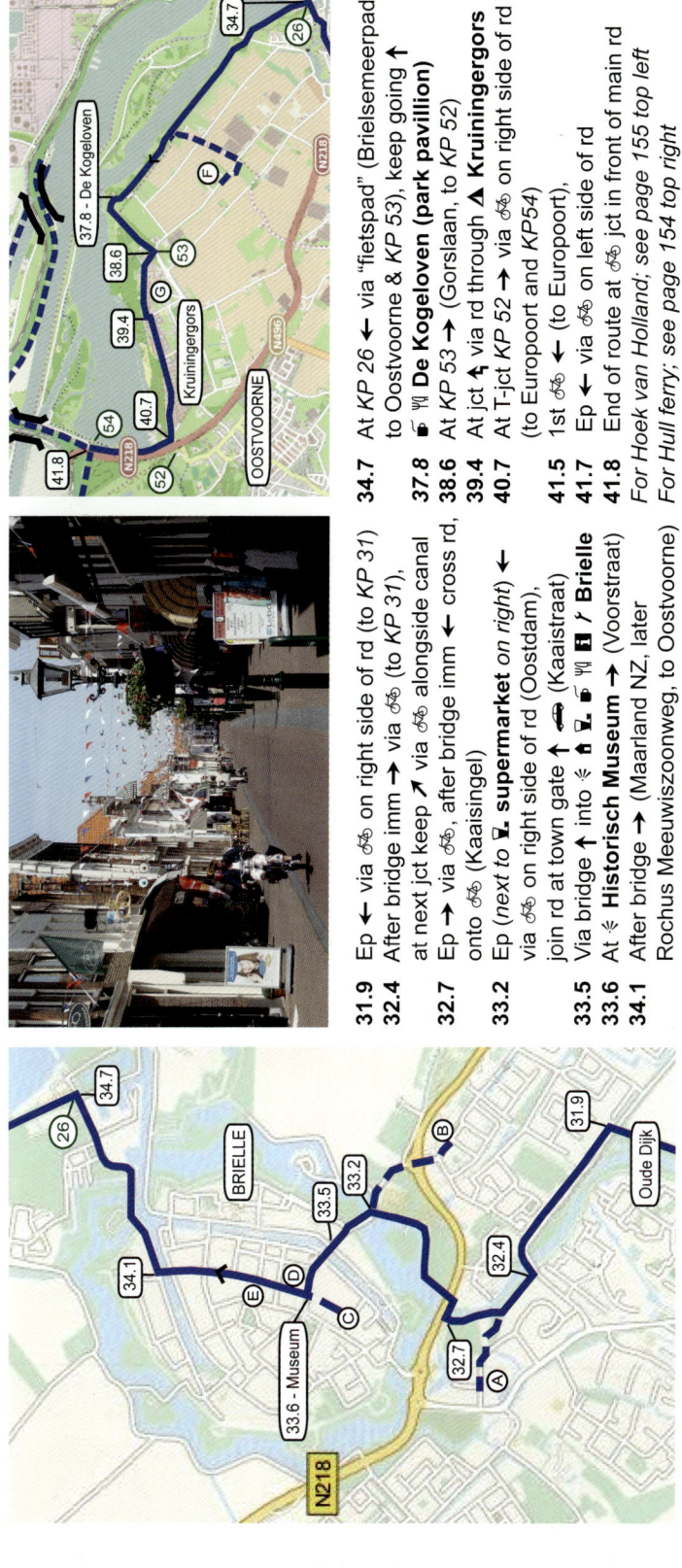

153

31.9	Ep ← via 🚲 on right side of rd (to *KP 31*)
32.4	After bridge imm → via 🚲 (to *KP 31*), at next jct keep ↗ via 🚲 alongside canal
32.7	Ep → via 🚲, after bridge imm ← cross rd, onto 🚲 (Kaaisingel)
33.2	Ep *(next to* 🛒 **supermarket** *on right)* ← via 🚲 on right side of rd (Oostdam), join rd at town gate ↑ 🍴 (Kaaistraat)
33.5	Via bridge ↑ into ⛪ 🏛 🍴 🍽 🏨 🍴 **Brielle**
33.6	At ⛪ **Historisch Museum** → (Voorstraat)
34.1	After bridge → (Maarland NZ, later Rochus Meeuwiszoonweg, to Oostvoorne)
34.7	At *KP 26* ← via "fietspad" (Brielsemeerpad, to Oostvoorne & *KP 53*), keep going ↑
37.8	🍴 🍽 **De Kogeloven (park pavillion)**
38.6	At *KP 53* → (Gorslaan, to *KP 52*)
39.4	At jct ↰ via rd through ▲ **Kruiningergors**
40.7	At T-jct *KP 52* → via 🚲 on right side of rd (to Europoort and *KP54*)
41.5	1st 🚲 ← (to Europoort)
41.7	Ep ← via 🚲 on left side of rd
41.8	End of route at 🚲 jct in front of main rd

For Hoek van Holland; see page 155 top left
For Hull ferry; see page 154 top right

Southern: Route 19: Rotterdam Docklands (13 or 20 km)

Stations: *Hoek van Holland Haven (via ferry from/to Maasvlakte)*
Cycling time: *1 - 2 hours (🚲 98%, 🚶 2%)*

This route serves those who are travelling on our **Southern route** to Hoek van Holland or Hull ferry and those who have to cycle between **"Hook"** and the **Hull ferry**. For the **Randstad Circle route** via **Hook**, see pages 95-96.

It is important to be mentally prepared for the **sheer size** of the **Rotterdam docks**. It is **Europe's biggest harbour**, always expanding into the North Sea on newly reclaimed land. **Europoort** is the eastern part of the port, **Maasvlakte** the newest western section. Even in this surreal landscape you'll find **good cycle routes**, but be prepared for strong **headwinds** and stock up on **provisions** at either Hook, Brielle or the Hull ferry, as there is not much out there on the way! Essential is the **pedestrian ferry** between **Maasvlakte** and **Hook**. It runs daily, once per hour, with the last journey just after 7pm (€4 pp); **don't miss the last ferry from Maasvlakte!**

Route from Hull Ferry:

- **0.0** At terminal, join 🚲 on right side of rd (to "All directions")
- **0.5** After railway, cross rd ↑, then ← via 🚲 on right side of rd
- **2.1** 1st 🚲 ← (to Maasvlakte), onto bridge, next to motorway
- **6.1** Ep reset mileage to 0.0 and continue on page 155 top left!

Route to Hull Ferry: *(from Hook, read page 155 top right side first!)*

- **0.0** (13.7 or 41.8) Join 🚲 north on right side of rd (to Rotterdam)
- **4.0** Ep cross rd, → via 🚲 on left side of rd (to Hull Ferry)
- **5.6** 1st 🚲 →, cross rd and railway (to Hull Ferry)
- **6.1** ⛴ **Hull Ferry Terminal**

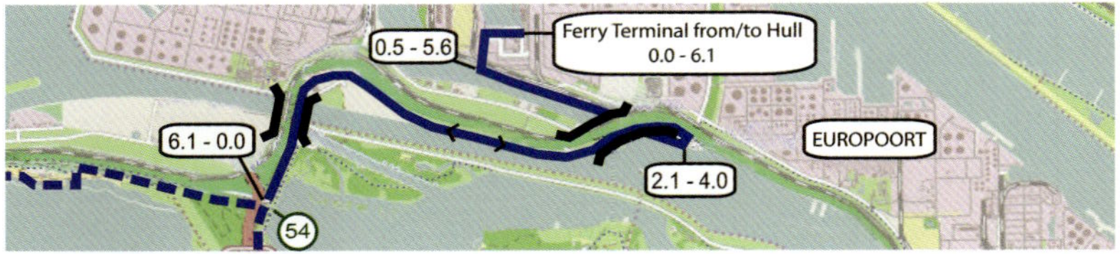

Route to Hook (from Hull ferry):
(continued from previous page)
**Southern route to Hook cyclists;
start reading from here!**

- **0.0** (6.1 or 41.8) Cross rd to 🚲 west (to Hoek van Holland)
- **0.7** 1st 🚲 ← (to Slag Stormvogel)
- **1.5** 🏠 **Slag Stormvogel (cafe)**
- **4.5** At T-jct of *KP 56* ↑ via 🚲 (to Hoek van Holland & *KP 91*)
- **6.2** At *KP 92* → via 🚲 (to Hoek van Holland & *KP 57*), cross motorway viaduct and keep ↑
- **9.8** At 🛈 **Future Land** ↑ via 🚲 (to Hoek van Holland & *KP 57*)
- **13.7 Ferry Landing Maasvlakte**

Route from Hook to Hull ferry:
In Hook, follow signs "RET Fast Ferry"

- **0.0** At **Ferry Landing Maasvlakte**, join 🚲 west, on right side of rd (to Rotterdam & *KP 56 & 92*)
- **3.9** At 🛈 **Future Land** ↑ via 🚲 (to Rotterdam & *KP 92*)
- **7.5** At *KP 92* ← via 🚲 (to Rotterdam & *KP 56*)
- **9.2** At *KP 56* ↑ via a dead end rd, lake on right side (to *KP 54*)
- **12.2** 🏠 **Slag Stormvogel (cafe)**
- **13.0** Ep → via 🚲 (to Rotterdam)
- **13.7** Cross rd, then reset mileage to 0.0 and continue on page 154, top right!

The ride via Maasvlakte is exposed. There are no shelter options, except for the Ferry Landing, where you'll find a shelter with benches and great harbour views (picture left). The cycle path to the Hull ferry is pictured on the right.

Rte	Km	Page	Ref	Town	Name, address and postcode	Info	Phone (+ 31)	Internet	Distance to route & extra directions
A1	0.6	31	A	Amsterdam	MacBike Central Station, Stationsplein 5, 1012 AB	♻ hire	-	www.macbike.nl	0.1 km (at lhts after tunnel →)
A1	0.7	31	B	Amsterdam	Bike 4 U, Gelderse Kade 17hs, 1011 EH	⚐ ♻ hire	020 2335367	www.rentbike4u.com	0.3 km (at Nieuwmarkt ↗ via Zeedijk, 1st ←)
A1	1.1	31	C	Amsterdam	Black Bikes Red Light District, Oudekerksplein 62, 1012 HA	♻ hire	020 6708531	www.black-bikes.com	0.3 km (at rd crossing → via Damstraat)
A1	1.4	31	D	Amsterdam	Damstraat Rent a bike, Damstraat 20-22, 1012 HK	♻ hire	020 6255029	www.rentabike.nl	0.1 km (← via bridge and imm ← via canal)
A1	1.7	31	E	Amsterdam	Stayokay Stadsdoelen (YHA),Kloveniersburgwal 97, 1011 KB	♙ ⛺ hire	020 6246832	www.stayokay.com	0.1 km (after Stopera, at main rd jct →)
A1	2.2	31	F	Amsterdam	MacBike Waterlooplein, Waterlooplein 199, 1011 PG	♻ hire	020 4287005	www.macbike.nl	0.3 km (→ via bridge, 1st rd →)
A1	2.2	31	G	Amsterdam	Green Budget Bikes, Amstel 140, 1017 HE	⚐ ♻ hire	020 4210157	www.greenbudgetbikes.nl	
A2	1.7	32	A	Amsterdam	Topfiets Rent a bike, Eerste Van Campenstraat 56, 1072 BH	♻ hire	020 7891298	www.topfiets.nl	
A2	2.5	32	B	Amsterdam	Black Bikes Leidseplein, Lijnbaansgracht 283, 1017 RM	♻ hire	020 6708531	www.black-bikes.com	0.2 km (← cross rd, 1st bridge ←)
A3	0.0	33	A	Amsterdam	MacBike Leidseplein, Weteringschans 2, 1017 SG	♻ hire	020 5287688	www.macbike.nl	
A3	0.3	33	B	Amsterdam	Green Budget Bikes, Lange Leidsedwarsstraat 103, 1017 NJ	⚐ ♻ hire	020 3413535	www.greenbudgetbikes.nl	0.1 km (at jct →)
A3	1.3	33	C	Amsterdam	Green Budget Bikes, Raadhuisstraat 29, 1016 DC	⚐ ♻ hire	020 3705740	www.greenbudgetbikes.nl	0.2 km (at jct with lhts →)
A3	1.3	33	D	Amsterdam	Bike City, Bloemgracht 70, 1015 TL	⚐ ♻ hire	020 6263721	www.bikecity.nl	0.2 km (←, after bridge →, after bridge ↙)
A3	1.3	33	E	Amsterdam	Holiday Biker (Vakantiefietser), Westerstraat 216, 1015 MS	♻ gear	020 6164091	www.vakantiefietser.nl	0.5 km (see above, then 1st rd →, wide rd ←)
A3	2.1	33	F	Amsterdam	Frederic Rent a bike, Brouwersgracht 78, 1013 GZ	♻ hire	020 6245509	www.frederic.nl	- (after bridge imm → via canalside rd)
A3	2.8	33	G	Amsterdam	OV Fiets Central Station, Stationsplein 12, 1012 AB	⚐ ♻ hire	-	-	0.1 km (→ next to "fietsflat" to station square)
A5	7.2	35	A	Amsterdam	Amsterdamse Bos Fietsverhuur, Bosbaanweg 1, 1182 DA	♻ hire	020 6445473	http://amsterdamsebosfietsverhuur.nl	
A8	2.9	38	A	Amsterdam	Black Bikes Olympic Stadium, Koninginneweg 267, 1075 CW	♻ hire	020 6708531	www.black-bikes.com	0.3 km (← via Zeilstraat)
A9	2.1	39	A	Amsterdam	Stayokay Vondelpark (YHA), Zandpad 5, 1054 GA	♙ ⛺ hire	020 5898996	www.stayokay.com	0.2 km (end Vondelpark ← at lhts, 1st rd ←)
A9	2.1	39	B	Amsterdam	A-Bike, Tesselschadestraat 1e, 1054 ET	♻ hire	020 2181292	www.a-bike.eu	0.1 km (end Vondelpark ← at lhts, 2nd rd ←)
B6	8.8	46	A	Amsterdam	Black Bikes Oostpoort, Land van Cocagneplein 1e, 1093 NB	⚐ ♻ hire	020 6708531	www.black-bikes.com	0.4 km (← at lhts, ↑ viaduct, ← via Peperstr)
B6	11.4	47	A	Amsterdam	MacBike Uil30, Uilenburgerstraat 30, 1011 LR	♻ hire	020 2141000	www.macbike.nl	
B6	12.0	47	B	Amsterdam	MacBike Oosterdokskade, Oosterdokskade 149, 1011 DL	⚐ ♻ hire	020 8115110	www.macbike.nl	0.6 km (at major jct with lhts → under railway)
C1	2.6	49	A	Amsterdam	Black Bikes Stork, Czaar Peterstraat 14, 1018 PR	♻ hire	020 6708531	www.black-bikes.com	0.7 km (at T-jct →, at T-jct ←, after bend ↙)
C1	3.4	49	B	Amsterdam	Stayokay Zeeburg, Timorplein 21, 1094 CC	♙ ⛺ hire	020 5513190	www.stayokay.com	0.5 km (via ramps onto high canal bridge)
C1	5.0	49	C	Amsterdam	Camping Zeeburg, Zuider IJdijk 20, 1095 KN	⛺	020 6944430	www.campingzeeburg.nl	
D1	1.9	57	A	Amsterdam	Camping Vliegenbos, Meeuwenlaan 138, 1022 AM	⛺	020 6368855	www.amsterdam.nl/vliegenbos/	
D2	3.3	58	A	Durgerdam	Camping De Badhoeve, Uitdammerdijk 10, 1026 CP	⛺	020 4904294	www.campingdebadhoeve.nl	
E1	0.3	63	A	Amsterdam	King Bikes, Spuistraat 1c, 1012 SP	♻ hire	020 3301255	www.kingbikes.nl	0.3 km (← next to "fietsflat", at square → ↑)
E1	0.3	63	B	Amsterdam	Yellow Bike, Nieuwezijds Kolk 29, 1012 PV	♻ hire	020 6206940	www.yellowbike.nl	0.4 km (← next to "fietsflat", at square → ↑)
E1	0.7	63	C	Amsterdam	Rent A Bikey, Binnen Wieringerstraat 3, 1013 EA	♻ hire	06 29236913	www.rentabikey.nl	0.1 km (after jct with canal bridge 2nd rd ←)
E4	2.5	69	A	Amsterdam	Amsterdam Rent a bike, Buiksloterweg 5c, 10311 CC	⚐ ♻ hire	06 13998675	http://fietsreparatieamsterdam.nl	- (via free ferry "Buikslotenwegveer")
E4	2.5	69	B	Amsterdam	Amstel Botel, NDSM Pier 3, 1033 RG	♙ ⚓	020 6264247	www.amstelbotel.nl	- (via free ferry to "NDSM" landing)

Rte	Km	Page	Ref	Town	Info	Name, address and postcode	Phone (+ 31)	Internet	Distance to route & extra directions
1	8.0	74	A	Vreeland		B&B De Willigen, Nigtevechtseweg 186-188, 3633 XX	06 51798045	http://dewilligenlogies.nl	-
1	11.0	74	B	Vreeland		Hotel De Nederlanden, Duinkerken 3, 3633 EM	0294 232326	www.nederlanden.nl	-
1	14.5	74	C	Loenen aan de Vecht		B&B Het Huisje aan de Vecht, Mijdensedijk 2, 3632 NV	06 40546221	www.hethuisjeaandevecht.nl	-
1	14.5	74	D	Loenen aan de Vecht		Recreatiecentrum Mijnden, Bloklaan 22a, 1231 AZ	0294 233165	www.mijnden.nl	1.0 km (at KP 25 ←, via ⌀ on right side of rd)
1	14.5	74	E	Loenen aan de Vecht		Camping Fort Spion, Bloklaan 9, 1231 AZ	0294 234932	www.fortspion.nl	2.0 km (at KP 25 ←, via ⌀ on right side of rd)
1	17.0	75	A	Nieuwersluis		Camping Doornenbal, Zandpad 22, 3631 NL	0294 231692	www.camping-doornenbal.nl	-
1	19.0	75	B	Breukelen		Age van 't Hoff Tweewielers, Marijkestraat 22, 3621 DC	0346 261475	www.agevanthoff.nl	0.5 km (at KP 84 →, next jct ⌀, next jct ↑)
1	22.8	75	C	Breukelen		B&B Geesberge, Zandpad 23, 3601 NA	0346 561435	www.geesberge.nl	-
2	1.4	77	A	Maarssen		Ekeris Fietsplezier, Kaatsbaan 32, 3601 ED	0346 286359	www.ekerisfietsplezier.nl	0.2 km (at KP 46 ↑, at T-jct ↑ to shops area)
2	5.3	77	B	Oud-Zuilen		B&B Klein Zuylenburg, Dorpsstraat 1, 3611 AD	06 20738375	www.kleinzuylenburg.nl	-
2	5.3	77	B	Oud-Zuilen		B&B Logement Swaenenvecht, Dorpsstraat 16a, 3611 AE	06 38102922	www.swaenen-vecht.nl	-
2	9.4	77	C	Utrecht		B&B Het Gekroonde Visje, Lauwerecht 129, 3515 GR	06 12968776	http://hetgekroondevisje.nl	-
2	9.6	78	A	Utrecht		Huijsen Tweewielers, Draaiweg 5, 3515 EJ	030 2719881	www.huijsentweewielers.nl	0.1 km (← via Draaiweg)
2	10.3	78	B	Utrecht		B&B Aan de Singel, Van Asch van Wijckskade 14, 3512 VP	030 2935032	www.aandesingelvanutrecht.nl	0.2 km (after ⌀ bridge, at Nijntje Pleintje ←)
2	10.4	78	C	Utrecht		Mary K Hotel, Oude Gracht 25, 3511 AB	030 2304888	www.marykhotel.com	-
2	11.3	78	D	Utrecht		Hotel Dom, Domstraat 4, 3512 JB	030 2324242	www.hoteldom.nl	-
2	11.5	78	E	Utrecht		B&B Bij de Jongens, Donkere Gaard 4 bis, 3511 KW	030 2977977	http://bnbbijdejongens.nl	0.1 km (just before bridge "Oude Gracht" ←)
2	12.5	78	F	Utrecht	hire	Fietsenstalling Laag Catharijne, Catharijnesingel 28, 3511 GB	030 2316780	www.laagcatharijne.nl	0.2 km (→ via Smakkelaarsveld, 1st rd →)
2	12.8	78	G	Utrecht		Park Plaza Hotel Utrecht, Westplein 50, 3531 BL	030 2925200	www.parkplaza.com	0.1 km (after tunnel, 1st rd →)
2	13.0	78	H	Utrecht		Hotel NH Utrecht, Jaarbeursplein 24, 3521 AR	030 2977977	www.nh-hotels.nl/hotel/nh-utrecht	0.1 km (← at lhts, 1st rd ←)
2	14.0	79	A	Utrecht		Ton van den IJssel, Laan van Nieuw Guinea 30, 3531 JK	030 2932679	www.tonvandenijssel.nl	0.2 km (→ via locks bridge, ↖ Groeneweg)
2	21.3	79	B	Utrecht		B&B Buitenhof, Enghlaan 4, 3543 BD	030 6774526	www.bedandbreakfastdebuitenhof.nl	-
2	25.3	79	C	Haarzuilens		B&B Brink 10, Brink 10, 3455 SE	06 23783323	www.haarzuilens.net/bed-breakfast.htm	-
3	6.0	81	A	Woerden		B&B Mourits Hoeve, Breeveld 15, 3445 BA	0348 419674	http://mouritshoeve.nl	-
3	7.3	81	B	Woerden		B&B Hoeve De Posthoorn, Breeveld 7, 3445 BA	0348 448507	www.hoevedeposthoorn.nl	-
3	10.3	81	C	Woerden		Tweewielercentrum Hans Voorn, Voorstraat 12, 3441 CL	0348 412456	-	0.7 km (↑ via Rijnstraat)
3	10.3	81	C	Woerden		B&B Bed & Brood Groenendaal, Groenendaal 7, 3441 BC	0348 402825	www.bedenbroodgroenendaal.nl	0.8 km (↑ via Rijnstraat, ← via Korte Jans St)
3	15.2	82	A	Snelrewaard		De Boerderij, Zuid-Linschoterzandweg15, 3425 EM	0348 421199	www.natuurcampingdeboerderij.nl	0.6 km (cross stream via foot bridge, then →)
3	15.2	82	B	Snelrewaard		De Oude Boomgaard, Zuid-Linschoterzandweg 21, 3425 EM	0348 560071	www.oude-boomgaard.nl	0.8 km (cross stream via foot bridge, then →)
3	19.8	82	C	Oudewater		Hotel Abrona, Broeckerstraat 20, 3421 BL	0348 567456	http://hotelrestaurantabrona.nl	0.1 km (→ via Broeckerstraat)
3	19.9	82	D	Oudewater		Wooldrik Tweewielers, Rootstraat 38, 3421 AW	0348 560660	www.wooldriktweewielers.nl	0.1 km (→ via Rootstraat)
3	23.6	83	A	Hekendorp		Camping De Boomgaard, Hekendorpsebuurt 22, 3467 PD	06 22264434	http://campingdeboogaard.nl	-
3	23.7	83	B	Hekendorp		Camping De Mulderije, Hekendorpsebuurt 33, 3467 PA	0348 563233	www.demulderije.nl	-

Rte	Km	Page	Ref	Town	Info	Name, address and postcode	Phone (+ 31)	Internet	Distance to route & extra directions
4	0.5	85	A	Gouda	✓	Van Leeuwen Tweewielers, BurgMartenssingel 100, 2806 CX	0182 513520	www.vanleeuwen2wielers.nl	0.3 km (at lhts →)
4	0.9	85	B	Gouda	♠ ✗	Hotel De Utrechtsche Dom, Geuzenstraat 6, 2801 XV	0182 528833	www.hotelgouda.nl	-
4	5.5	85	C	Gouda	✓ ᧢ hire	Rep 26, Nieuwehaven 147, 2801 CV	0182 689753	www.rep26.nl	0.5 km (on station route, see map)
4	1.4	85	D	Gouda	✓ ᧢ hire	Fietspoint Oldenburger, Stationsplein 10, 2801 AK	0182 519751	www.fietspoint.com	0.7 km (in station building, see map)
4	1.4	85	E	Gouda	♠ ✗	B&B Aan de Gouwe, Lage Gouwe 114, 2801 LK	06 47787590	www.bbgouda.nl	0.2 km (before bridge over canal →)
4	1.7	85	F	Gouda	♠ ✗	Hotel De Keizerskroon, Keizerstraat 31, 2801 NJ	0182 528096	www.hotelkeizerskroon.nl	-
4	1.9	85	G	Gouda	♠ ✗	B&B De Kamer Hiermaast, Kominsteeg 1, 2801 NN	0182 582855	www.dekamerhiernaast.nl	0.1 km (← via Peperstraat)
4	20.7	87	A	Krimpen a/d Lek	✓	B&B Het Klippennest, Onder de Waal 20, 2931 AS	0180 550255	www.klippennest.org	-
4	21.2	87	B	Krimpen a/d Lek	✓	Fietswereld Mica, Hoofdstraat 21, 2931 CE	0180 552325	www.fietswereldmica.nl	0.4 km (at jct of ferry →)
4	21.9	87	C	Kinderdijk	✓	B&B Kiwok, Molenstraat 145, 2961 AK	078 6912041	www.kiwok.nl	0.2 km (at KP 3 → via rd)
4	32.2	88	A	Streefkerk	◬ ✗	Camping Landhoeve, Lekdijk 15, 2957 CA	0184 684137	www.landhoeve.com	0.8 km (↑, at T-jct ← via dyke rd)
4	32.2	88	B	Streefkerk	♠ ✗	B&B Op de Lekdijk, Lekdijk 11, 2957 CA	0184 685557	www.opdelekdijk.nl	0.5 km (↑, at T-jct ← via dyke rd)
4	41.2	88	C	Schoonhoven	◬ ✗	Camping De Bovenstad, Hogedijk 110, 2861 GD	0182 382641	www.campingdebovenstad.nl	-
4	43.9	88	D	Schoonhoven	♠ ✗	Hotel Belvedere, Lekdijk-West 4, 2871 MK	0182 325222	www.hotelbelvedere.nl	0.2 km (↑, 1st rd →)
4	44.1	88	E	Schoonhoven	♠ ✗	B&B Den Bonten Osch, Lange Weistraat 6c, 2871 BM	06 10153509	www.denbontenosch.nl	0.7 km (→ Lopikerstr, end moat ↓, 1st →)
4	44.4	88	F	Schoonhoven	♠ ✗	B&B In de oude praktijk, Nassaukade 11b, 2871 AR	0182 320410	http://indeoudepraktijk-bb.nl	0.9 km (→ Lopikerstr, end moat ↓, 2nd →)
4	44.4	88	G	Schoonhoven	♠ ✗	B&B Villa Voorncamp, Lopikerweg 48b, 2871 AV	0182 385794	www.villavoorncamp.nl	-
4	44.4	88	H	Schoonhoven	✓	Bike Totaal Boom, Kerkstraat 9, 2871 ED	0182 329555	http://boomtweewielers.nl	-
4	54.0	89	A	Haastrecht	♠ ✗	Slingerland Fietsen, Hoogstraat 142, 2851 BK	0182 502452	www.slingerland-fietsen.nl	0.1 km (do NOT turn right, but go ↑)
4	54.0	89	B	Haastrecht	⌐	Hotel Over de Brug, Veerlaan 1, 2851 BV	0182 501210	www.hoteloverdebrug.nl	-
5	13.8	91	A	Zevenhuizen	✓	Bike Totaal Boode, Dorpsstraat 103, 2761 AN	0180 634788	www.biketotaalboode.nl	-
5	14.0	91	B	Zevenhuizen	◬ ✗	Camping Koormmolen, Tweemanspolder 6a, 2761 ED	0180 631654	www.koormmolen.nl	1.5 km (at KP 12 ↓)
5	28.9	92	A	Berkel en Rodenrijs	◬ ✗	Bike Totaal Leo Smit, Rodenijseweg 309, 2651 BS	010 5112421	www.biketotaalleosmit.nl	0.5 km (1st rd →, at next jct ←)
5	37.0	92	B	Delft	♠ ✗	De Abtswoudse Hoeve, Rotterdamseweg 215, 2629 HE	015 2561202	www.navah.nl	-
5	41.0	93	A	Delft	♠ ✗	Hotel Vermeer, Molslaan 18, 2611 RM	015 2126466	www.hotelvermeer.nl	0.4 km (see walking route from "De Veste")
5	41.0	93	B	Delft	✓	Rijwielsporthuis Piet Vonk, Voldersgracht 20, 2611 EV	015 2123252	www.pietvonk.nl	0.6 km (see walking route from "De Veste")
5	41.0	93	C	Delft	♠ ✗	Bridges House, Oude Delft 74, 2611 CD	015 2124036	http://bridgeshouse.nl	0.7 km (see walking route from "De Veste")
5	41.0	93	D	Delft	♠ ✗	Hotel Royal Bridges, Koornmarkt 55-65, 2611 EC	015 3643787	www.royalbridges.nl	0.5 km (see walking route from "De Veste")
5	41.0	93	E	Delft	♠ ✗	Hotel Leeuwenbrug, Koornmarkt 16, 2611 EE	015 2147741	www.leeuwenbrug.nl	0.5 km (see walking route from "De Veste")
5	41.0	93	F	Delft	♠ ✗	B&B Prinsenstad, Achterom 86, 2611 PS	015 3808693	www.prinsenstad.com	0.3 km (see walking route from "De Veste")
5	2.7	94	A	Den Hoorn	✓	Paul Willemsen, Woudseweg 6, 2635 CC	015 2614976	http://paulwillemsen.nl	-
5	5.6	94	B	Schipluiden	✓	Van Dijk B&B, Vlaardingsekade 2, 2636 BA	06 53817820	www.bedenbreakfastvandijk.nl	- (at T-jct KP 56 ↑, do not cross bridge)
5	5.6	94	C	Schipluiden	✓	Rijwielhandel Van den Bosch, Dorpsstraat 11, 2636 CC	015 3808252	http://rijwielhandelvandenbosch.nl	0.1 km (after bridge →)

Rte	Km	Page	Ref	Town	Info	Name, address and postcode	Phone (+ 31)	Internet	Distance to route & extra directions
5	15.9	95	A	Naaldwijk	♞ ⛽	Fletcher Hotel Carlton, Tiendweg 20, 2671 SB	0174 272625	www.hotelcarlton.nl	0.1 km (after jct with lhts, 1st rd ←, 1st rd ↓)
6	0.3	96	A	Hoek van Holland	♞ ⛽	Grand Hotel Hoek van Holland, Rietdijkstraat 96, 3151 GK	0174 388145	www.grandhotelhoekvanholland.nl	- (on corner of central square)
6	0.4	96	B	Hoek van Holland	⚑ ⛽ hire	Van Leeuwen Tweewielers, Prins Hendrikstraat 203, 3151 AH	0174 387895	www.petervanleeuwentweewielers.nl	0.1 km (keep ↑)
6	0.4	96	C	Hoek van Holland	♞ ⛽	Langeslag B&B, Prins Hendrikstraat 190a, 3151 AT	06 44402237	http://langeslag.bedandbreakfasthoekvanholland.com	0.2 km (keep ↑)
6	1.0	96	D	Hoek van Holland	♞ ⛽	Hotel 't Seepaerd, Harwichweg 210, 3151 BR	06 51828570	www.seepaerd.nl	-
6	2.0	96	E	Hoek van Holland	⛺ ⛽	Camping Hoek van Holland, Wierstraat 100, 3151 VP	0174 382550	www.rotterdam.nlcampinghoekvanholland.nl	-
6	3.3	97	A	's Gravenzande	⛺ ⛽	Camping Jagtveld, Nieuwlandsedijk 41, 2691 KV	0174 413479	http://campingjagtveld.nl	-
6	3.6	97	B	's Gravenzande	⛺ ⛽	Camping Vlugtenburg, 't Louwtje 10, 2691 KR	0174 412420	www.vlugtenburg.nl	-
6	22.6	100	A	Den Haag (The Hague)	♞ ⛽	Easy Hotel, Parkstraat 31, 2514 JD	070 2113635	http://easyhotelbenelux.com/the-hague	-
6	23.1	100	B	Den Haag (The Hague)	♞ ⛽	Hotel Corona, Buitenhof 39-42, 2513 AH	070 3637930	www.hampshire-hotels.com	0.5 km (see map, in basement of station)
6	0.7	100	C	Den Haag (The Hague)	⚑ ⛽ hire	Rijwielshop Den Haag, Julianaplein 10, 2595 AA	070 3853235	www.rijwielshopdenhaag.nl	0.6 km (see map, via rd under station bridges)
6	0.7	100	D	Den Haag (The Hague)	⚑ ⛽ hire	Rijwielshop Centraal, Lekstraat 21-25, 2515 XA	070 3830039	www.rijwielshopcentraal.nl	0.7 km (see map, via rd under station bridges)
6	0.7	100	D	Den Haag (The Hague)	⚑ ⛽ hire	De Vroome Bikes, Lekstraat 83, 2515 XB	06 54215986	www.devroomebikes.nl	1.3 km (see map, via route to Scheveningen)
6	4.2	101	A	Den Haag (Scheveningen)	♞ ⛽	B&B Emma aan Zee, Harstenhoekweg 151, 2587 SH	070 3557345	http://bbemma.nl	1.7 km (see map, via Alkmaarsestraat)
6	4.2	101	B	Den Haag (Scheveningen)	♞ ⛽	Hotel Duinzicht, Alkmaarsestraat 6a, 2587 RN	070 3506999	www.hotelduinzicht.com	1.8 km (see map, via Alkmaarsestraat)
6	4.2	101	C	Den Haag (Scheveningen)	♞ ⛽	Hotel Gevers, Gevers Deynootweg 1302, 2586 HP	070 3552606	www.hotelgevers.nl	2.3 km (see map, to guarded bike park)
6	4.2	101	D	Den Haag (Scheveningen)	♞ ⛽	Hotel Aquarius, Zeekant 110, 2586 JJ	070 3543543	www.aquarius-hotel.nl	2.3 km (see map, to guarded bike park)
6	4.2	101	D	Den Haag (Scheveningen)	♞ ⛽	Strand Hotel, Zeekant 111, 2586 JJ	070 3540193	www.strandhotel-scheveningen.nl	2.3 km (see map, to guarded bike park)
7	6.8	103	A	Wassenaarse Slag	♞ ⛽	Hotel Duinoord, Wassenaarseslag 26, 2242 PJ	070 5119332	www.hotelduinoord.nl	-
7	11.5	104	A	Katwijk	⛺ ⛽	Camping De Zuidduinen, Zuidduinseweg 1, 2225 JS	071 4014750	www.zuidduinen.nl	- (use side entrance directly on ⛽)
7	12.6	104	B	Katwijk	⚑	Profile Paul, Driepiassenweg 1, 2225 JH	071 4013256	-	0.2 km (at lighthouse → via Vuurbaakplein)
7	12.7	104	C	Katwijk	♞ ⛽	Bed & Breakfast aan het strand, Boulevard 129, 2225 HC	071 4013890	www.bedandbreakfastaanstrand.nl	-
7	12.8	104	D	Katwijk	♞ ⛽	Bed & Breakfast Katwijk, Andreasplein 4, 2225 GR	071 8873114	www.bedandbreakfastkatwijk.nl	0.1 km (→ via Andreasplein)
7	13.3	104	E	Katwijk	♞ ⛽	Hotel Seahorse, Boulevard 14, 2522 AA	071 4015921	www.hotelseahorse.nl	-
7	13.5	104	F	Katwijk	♞ ⛽	Hotel Zee en Duin, Boulevard 5, 2225 AA	071 4013320	www.zeeenduin.nl	-
7	13.6	104	G	Katwijk	♞ ⛽	Hotel Savoy, Boulevard 1, 2225 AA	071 4015645	www.hotelsavoy.nl	-
7	13.9	104	H	Katwijk	⛺ ⛽	Camping De Noordduinen, Campingweg 1, 2221 EW	071 4025295	www.noordduinen.nl	- (← across car park)
7	18.5	105	A	Noordwijk	⚑ ⛽ hire	Profile Mooijekind, Schoolstraat 45, 2202 HD	071 3612826	-	0.3 km (3rd rd → Lage Wurft, T-jct ↓, 1st →)
7	18.5	105	B	Noordwijk	♞ ⛽	Hotel aan zee, Parallel Boulevard 206, 2202 HT	071 3612919	www.hotelaanzee.nl	0.2 km (3rd rd → Lage Wurft, T-jct ↓)
7	18.5	105	C	Noordwijk	⛺ ⛽	Flying Pig Beach Hostel, Parallel Boulevard 208, 2202 HT	071 3622533	www.flyingpig.nl	0.2 km (3rd rd → Lage Wurft, T-jct ↓)
7	19.0	105	D	Noordwijk	♞ ⛽	Pension Maaike, Van Uffordstraat 96, 2202 NK	071 3621455	www.pensionmaaike.nl	0.3 km (↑, follow next bend to right, T-jct ↓)
7	35.0	107	A	Zandvoort	♞ ⛽	B&B Zeespiegel, Boulevard Paulus Loot 69, 2042 AE	06 29259654	http://bbzeespiegel.nl	0.2 km (← via Frederik Hendrikstraat, →)
7	35.6	107	B	Zandvoort	♞ ⛽	Pension De Schelp, Marisstraat 14, 2042 AK	06 37221411	www.pensiondeschelp.com	-

Rte	Km	Page	Ref	Town	Name, address and postcode	Info	Phone (+ 31)	Internet	Distance to route & extra directions
7	35.7	107	C	Zandvoort	Pension De Watertoren, Thorbeckestraat 38, 2042 GM	⌂ ⌐	023 5730457	www.pensiondewatertoren.com	-
7	36.0	107	D	Zandvoort	B&B Spaanstra, Engelbertstraat 12, 2042 KN	⌂ ⌐	023 5712610	www.spaanstra.nl	0.4 km (→ to Station, ↑ via Zeestraat, 3rd ↗)
7	36.0	107	E	Zandvoort	Behind the beach Bike Rentals, Haltestraat 51, 2042 LL	⌕ hire	023 8224746	http://behindthebeach.nl	0.5 km (→ to Station, ↑ via Zeestraat, 3rd ↘)
7	36.0	107	E	Zandvoort	Versteege Wielersport, Haltestraat 31, 2042 LK	⌕ ⌕ hire	023 5714499	www.versteegewielersport.nl/	0.5 km (→ to Station, ↑ via Zeestraat, 3rd ↘)
7	36.4	107	F	Zandvoort	Pension Het Zeehuis, Mezgerstraat 36, 2041 HC	⌂ ⌐	023 5717195	www.zeehuiszandvoort.nl	0.2 km (after sharp bend to the left, 2nd rd ↑)
7	39.6	108	A	Bloemendaal aan Zee	Camping De Lakens, Zeeweg 60, 2051 EC	⌂ ⌐	023 5411570	www.campingdelakens.nl	0.6 km (↑ via ⌕, stay on left side of main rd)
7	39.6	108	B	Bloemendaal aan Zee	Camping Bloemendaal, Zeeweg 72, 2051 EC	⌂ ⌐	023 5732178	www.campingbloemendaal.nl	0.6 km (↑ via ⌕, stay on left side of main rd)
7	45.0	109	A	Overveen	Hotel Loetje, Bloemendaalseweg 260, 2051 GN	⌂ ⌐	023 5277457	http://overveen.loetje.com/hotel-loatje/	-
7	46.2	109	B	Haarlem	Seref Rijwielhandel, Zijlweg 117 zw, 2013 DG	⌐	023 5327732	www.seref.nl/	-
7	46.6	109	C	Haarlem	Hotel Die Raeckse, Raaks 1-3, 2011 VA	⌂ ⌐	023 5326629	www.hoteldieraeckse.com	0.2 km (after cycle bridge imm →, 1st ↓)
7	46.8	109	D	Haarlem	B&B Hotel Malts, Zijlstraat 56-58, 2011 TP	⌂ ⌐	023 5512385	www.maltshotel.nl	- (on south west side of square)
7	47.1	109	E	Haarlem	Hotel Amadeus, Grote Markt 10, 2011 RD	⌂ ⌐	023 5324530	www.amadeus-hotel.com	- (on north east side of square)
7	47.1	109	F	Haarlem	Hotel Carillon, Grote Markt 27, 2011 RC	⌂ ⌐	023 5310591	www.hotelcarillon.com	- (on north east side of square)
7	47.1	109	G	Haarlem	De Fietsfanaat, Parklaan 47, 2011 KR	⌐ ⌕ hire	023 5421195	www.defietsfanaat.nl	0.4 km (on square ←, via Jansstaat, ← at lhts)
8	0.0	111	A	Voorhout	Hotel Boerhaave, Herenstraat 57, 2215 KE	⌂ ⌐	0252 211483	www.boerhaave-voorhout.nl	0.2 km (from south end of station platform →)
8	8.9	111	B	Lisse	Hotel De Duif, Westerdreef 49, 2161 EN	⌂ ⌐	0252 410076	www.hoteldeduif.nl	0.5 km (→, pass Keukenhof on left, ↗ at lhts)
8	8.9	111	C	Lisse	Profile Rijperkerk, Koninginneweg 83, 2161 ZB	⌐	0252 413671	-	0.8 km (→, pass Keukenhof on left, ↑ at lhts)
8	8.9	111	D	Lisse	Hotel De Nachtegaal, Heereweg 10, 2161 AG	⌂ ⌐	0252 433030	www.nachtegaal.nl	1.0 km (→, pass Keukenhof on left, ← at lhts)
8	0.8	112	A	Noordwijkerhout	Stayokay Noordwijk (YHA), Langevelderlaan 45, 2204 BC	⌂ ⌐	0252 372920	www.stayokay.com	-
8	2.5	112	B	Noordwijkerhout	Camping Sollasi, Duinschooten 12, 2211 ZC	⌂ ⌐	0252 374460	www.sollasi.nl	-
8	7.0	112	C	Bennebroek	Giant Store van Bakel, Bennebroekerlaan 83, 2121 GS	⌐	023 5846473	www.vanbakel.nl	0.5 km (keep ↑, at T-jct ←)
9	3.6	114	A	Haarlem	Stayokay Haarlem (YHA), Jan Gijzenpad 3, 2024 CL	⌂ ⌐	023 5373793	www.stayokay.com	1.6 km (← on right side of canal, to KP 34)
9	0.5	116	A	IJmuiden	Hotel Augusta, Oranjestraat 98, 1975 DD	⌂ ⌐	0255 514217	www.augusta.nl	0.3 km (2 x 1st rd ←, but NOT → up slope!)
9	1.0	116	B	IJmuiden	B&B Het Wellnest, Havenkade 7, 1973 AH	⌂ ⌐	06 12612583	www.hetwelnest.nl	0.1 km (→ at mdabt)
9	1.5	116	C	IJmuiden	Rijwielspecialist Kok, Kennemerlaan 61, 1972 EH	⌐	0255 515368	www.kok-ijmuiden.nl	-
9	1.6	116	C	IJmuiden	Hotel Royal, Houtmanstraat 2-4, 1972 EE	⌂ ⌐	0255 533807	www.hotelroyal-ijmuiden.nl	- (← via Houtmanstraat)
9	1.6	116	C	IJmuiden	Hotel Velsen, Kennemerlaan 119, 1972 ES	⌂ ⌐	0255 515368	www.hotelvelsen.nl	-
9	4.3	116	D	Driehuis	Camping Schoonenberg, Driehuizerkerkweg 15d, 1981 EH	⌂ ⌐	0255 523998	www.campingschoonenberg.nl	0.3 km (at mdabt KP 4 via quiet rd to KP 3)
9	4.5	116	E	Driehuis	B&B Noordzee, PC Hooftlaan 11, 1985 BE	⌂ ⌐	0255 540433	www.bbnoordzee.nl	0.2 km (← via Schaepmanlaan, 1st rd ↘)
9	6.5	116	F	Santpoort-Noord	B&B De Jachtkamer, Duin en Kruidbergerweg 76, 2071 LE	⌂ ⌐	023 5371558	www.dejachtkamer.com	0.3 km (via drive between house no 72 -74)
9	3.9	117	A	Spaarnwoude	Droompark Buitenhuizen, Buitenhuizerweg 2, 1981 LK	⌂ ⌐	023 5383726	www.droomparken.nl/buitenhuizen/	1.0 km (↘ at KP 11 onto bridge, 1st rd ↓)
9	5.9	117	B	Nauerna	B&B De Bedstee, Zaandammerweg 36b, 1566 PG	⌂ ⌐	06 11763449	www.bbdebedstee.nl	0.2 km (← at KP 67)
9	9.6	117	C	Westzaan	Hotel De Prins Westzaan, Kerkbuurt 31, 1551 AB	⌂ ⌐	075 6281972	www.deprins-westzaan.nl	0.1 km (→ into main street with some shops)

Rte	Km	Page	Ref	Town	Info	Name, address and postcode	Phone (+ 31)	Internet	Distance to route & extra directions
10	3.7	118	A	Marken		Hotel Hof van Marken, Buurt II 15, 1156 BC	0299 601300	www.hofvanmarken.nl	0.2 km (opposite Marken Express Ferry →)
10	4.2	118	B	Monnickendam		Camping Hemmeland, Jachthaven Hemmeland, 1141 LA	0299 655555	www.hemmeland.nl	0.2 km (→ via entrance "Hemmeland")
10	5.0	118	C	Monnickendam		Ber Koning, Noordeinde 12, 1141 AM	0299 651267	www.berkoning.nl	-
10	5.1	118	C	Monnickendam		B&B De Reederij, Havenstraat 4, 1141 AW	06 10235902	www.dereederij.nl	0.1 km (→ via Brugstraat)
10	5.2	118	C	Monnickendam		Hotel Posthoorn, Noordeinde 41-43, 1141 AG	0299 654598	www.posthoorn.eu	-
10	5.4	118	D	Monnickendam		Hotel Lake Land, Jachthaven 1, 1141 AV	0299 653751	www.lakeland.nl	0.3 km (at end of historic town →)
10	12.3	119	A	Volendam		Hotel Old Dutch, Haven 142, 1131 EW	0299 399888	www.olddutch.nl	-
10	12.4	119	A	Volendam		Hotel Van den Hogen, Haven 106, 1131 EV	0299 363775	www.hogen.nl	-
10	0.0	119	B	Volendam		Hotel Spaander, Haven 15-19, 1131 EP	0299 363595	www.hotelspaander.nl	0.1 km (→ via quay side)
10	4.3	119	C	Edam		Hotel De Harmonie, Voorhaven 94, 1135 BT	0299 371664	www.harmonie-edam.nl	-
10	4.7	119	D	Edam		Speciaalzaak Ronald Schot, Grote Kerkstraat 7, 1135 BC	0299 371155	www.ronaldschot.nl	0.1 km (at Damplein → via Grote Kerkstraat)
10	4.7	119	E	Edam		L'Auberge Dam Hotel, Keizersgracht 1, 1135 AZ	0299 371766	www.damhotel.nl	- (at Damplein ↖ via bridge)
10	4.7	119	F	Edam		Hotel Fortuna, Spuistraat 3, 1135 AV	0299 371671	www.fortuna-edam.nl	0.1 km (at Damplein ↑, next jct ←)
10	5.1	119	G	Edam	hire	Ton Tweewielers, Schepenmakersdijk 6, 1135 AG	0299 371922	www.tontweewielers.nl	0.3 km (follow bend ↑, after bridge imm ←)
10	8.0	120	A	Middelie		B&B Waterland, Axwijk 7, 1472 GA	0299 621716	www.bedandbreakfastwaterland.nl	0.3 km (at jct Middelie →)
10	8.0	120	B	Middelie		Hotel 't Wapen van Middelie, Brink 1, 1472 GB	0299 621376	www.hetwapenvanmiddelie.nl	0.2 km (at jct Middelie →)
10	15.3	120	C	Oosthuizen		Pension Zonneweelde, Oosteinde 87, 1474 ME	0299 403907	www.zonneweelde.nl	-
10	15.8	120	D	Oosthuizen		B&B Het Kerkje van Etersheim, Etersheim 10, 1474 MT	0299 403907	www.hetkerkjevanetersheim.nl	-
10	17.4	120	E	Schardam		Camping De Eenhoorn, Burgerwoudweg 1, 1476 NE	06 53798020	www.campingdeeenhoorn.nl	-
10	22.2	121	A	Hoorn		B&B Koetshuis De Hulk, De Hulk 19, 1622 DZ	06 10810653	www.koetshuisdehulk.nl	-
11	0.0	122	A	Hoorn		Hotel De Posthoorn, Breed 23, 1621 KA	0229 214057	http://hotelposthoorn.nl	0.1 km (↑ at jct of start of route)
11	0.0	122	A	Hoorn		Hotel De Keizerskroon, Breed 31, 1621 KA	0229 212771	www.keizerskroonhoorn.nl	- (on arrival at central square imm ←)
11	0.6	122	B	Hoorn		B&B Grote Noord, Grote Noord 3, 1621 KD	06 28719018	www.bedandbreakfastgrotenoord.nl	-
11	1.4	122	C	Hoorn		Hotel De Magneet, Kleine Oost 5, 1621 GR	0229 215021	www.hoteldemagneet.nl	-
11	4.6	123	A	Schellinkhout		B&B Zuidwest7, Zuiderdijk 60a, 1697 KG	0229 210390	www.zuidwest7.nl/indexeng.html	-
11	5.8	123	B	Schellinkhout		B&B 't Langhuus, Dorpsstraat 121, 1697 KH	0229 852684	www.hetlanghuus.nl	0.3 km (at KP 62 ↘ down from dyke, imm →)
11	7.5	123	C	Wijdenes		Minicamping De Appelhoek, Zuiderdijk 46, 1608 MV	0229 501150	www.appelhoek.nl	-
11	20.6	124	A	Broekerhaven		Camping Broekerhaven, Zuiderdijk 1b, 1611 MC	0228 511987	www.campingbroekerhaven.nl	0.2 km (↑ at KP 28 via ⟲, after bridge →)
11	25.4	125	A	Enkhuizen		Camping De Vest, Noorderweg 31, 1601 PC	0228 321221	www.campingdevest.nl	-
11	25.5	125	B	Enkhuizen		Camping Enkhuizerzand, Kooizandweg 4, 1601 LK	0228 317289	www.campingenkhuizerzand.nl	0.2 km (where path gets to old city wall, go ↘)
11	26.8	125	C	Enkhuizen		B&B Appelo, Breedstraat 96, 1601 KE	0228 318877	http://appelo-bedandbreakfast.nl	0.2 km (after bridge ← and imm →)
11	26.9	125	D	Enkhuizen		B&B 't Vissershuis, Zuider Havendijk 63, 1601 JA	06 17429669	www.tvissershuis.nl	0.1 km (↑)
11	27.2	125	E	Enkhuizen		Hotel Du Passage, Paktuinen 8, 1601 GD	0228 312462	http://www.hoteldupassage.nl	0.2 km (→ via Voorstraat, 1st rd →)

Rte	Km	Page	Ref	Town	info	Name, address and postcode	Phone (+ 31)	Internet	Distance to route & extra directions
11	27.2	125	F	Enkhuizen		Hotel De Port van Cleve, Dijk 74-76, 1601 GK	0228 312510	http://deportvancleve.nl	0.2 km (→ via Voorstraat, after bridge →)
11	27.2	125	G	Enkhuizen		John Brandhof Tweewielers, Westerstraat 25, 1601 AB	0228 325571	www.johnbrandhofftweewielers.nl	0.6 km (→ via Voorstraat, ↑, → Westerstraat)
11	27.2	125	G	Enkhuizen		Dekker Tweewielers, Nieuwstraat 2, 1601 JJ	0228 312961	www.dekker-tweewielers.nl	0.8 km (→ via Voorstraat, ↑, → Westerstraat)
11	27.4	125	H	Enkhuizen		B&B Bakker, Van Loosenpark 1, 1601 EP	0228 315469	www.bedandbreakfastenkhuizen.nl	0.4 km (after viaduct, 1st ⌀, 1st rd ↓)
12	0.8	127	A	Lelystad		B&B Huis van Steen, Lommerrijk 2, 8241 AZ	0320 280990	www.huisvansteen.nl	-
12	3.5	128	A	Lelystad		Hotel De Lange Jammer, Pioniersstraat 15, 8245 PD	0320 260415	www.delangejammer.nl	-
12	7.1	128	B	Lelystad		Camping 't Opperfje, Uilenweg 11, 8245 AB	0320 253693	www.opperfje.nl	1.8 km (at KP 23 ↓, 1st rd ↓)
12	44.4	129	A	Almere Poort		Camping Marina Muiderzand, IJmeerdijk 4, 1361 AA	036 5369151	www.marinamuiderzand.nl	2.2 km (keep ↑ via lakeside ⌀)
12	48.8	129	B	Muiderberg		B&B Onder Zeil, Flevolaan 18, 1399 HG	0294 261027	http://bedandbreakfastmuiderberg.nl	-
12	49.1	129	B	Muiderberg		Hotel Het Rechthuis, Googweg 11, 1399 EP	0294 261323	www.hotelhetrechthuis.nl	0.2 km (at KP 17 ↓, 1st rd ↓ through park)
13	5.5	130	A	Breukelen		B&B Geesberge, Zandpad 23, 3601 NA	0346 561435	www.geesberge.nl	-
13	5.1	131	A	Tienhoven		B&B Tienhoven, Dwarsdijk 20, 3612 AP	0346 579400	http://benb-tienhoven.nl	0.3 km (1st rd →)
13	13.0	131	B	Hollandsche Rading		Camping Fazantenhof, Karnemelksweg 1a, 3739 LA	06 10484896	www.campingfazantenhof.nl	0.4 km (at T-jct KP 98 →, after 350 m ↓)
13	14.8	131	C	Lage Vuursche		Hotel De Kastanjehof, Kloosterlaan 1, 3749 AJ	035 6668248	www.dekastanjehof.nl	- (from car park ← and imm ← again)
13	15.0	131	D	Lage Vuursche		Camping & Hotel Puur, Koudelaan 25, 3723 ME	035 6669785	http://puurlv.nl	0.8 km (at end of village →)
13	19.5	131	E	Soest		B&B Soest, Veenzoom 6, 3766 ME	035 6011555	www.bbsoest.nl	0.4 km (at KP 61 ↓, cross rd ↑, keep to rd)
13	20.6	131	F	Soest		Stayokay Soest (YHA), Bosstraat 16, 3766 AG	035 6012296	www.stayokay.com	0.7 km (→ via Bosstraat)
13	20.9	131	G	Soest		Buitenplaats De Eerste Aanleg, De Zoom 7, 3766 LR	035 6037732	www.buitenplaatsdeeerstaanleg.nl	0.5 km (in front of railway crossing →)
13	25.9	132	A	Soesterberg		Kontakt der Kontinenten, Amersfoortsestraat 20, 3769 AS	0346 351755	www.kontaktderkontinenten.nl	0.4 km (at KP 53 ↓, keep ↑ and join ⌀)
13	20.2	134	A	Leersum		B&B De Darthuizer Molen, Molenweg 1, 3956 NR	0343 454824	www.darthuizermolen.nl	0.3 km (↙ via sandy rd, 1st sandy rd →)
13	20.8	134	B	Leersum		B&B Klein Groenbergen, Nieuwe Steeg 18, 3956 RD	0343 410156	www.kleingroenbergen.nl	1.0 km (at jct ↗ follow ⌀ routes)
13	20.8	134	C	Leersum		Camping De Boterbloem, Ameronger Wetering 2, 3958 MD	0343 451757	www.boterbloem.com	2.0 km (at jct ↗ follow ⌀ routes, at T-jct →)
13	22.1	134	D	Leersum		Pater Bike Totaal, Rijksstraatweg 131, 3956 CL	0343 451371	http://pater.biketotaal.nl	-
13	23.7	134	E	Amerongen		B&B De Utrechtse Heuvelrug, Wilhelminaweg 52a, 3958 CP	0343 461051	http://amerongen.greup.com	0.5 km (at mdabt → via N225)
13	24.5	134	F	Amerongen		B&B 't Gasthuys, Gasthuisstraat 1-3, 3958 BL	06 46752009	www.het-gasthuys.nl	0.3 km (↑ to castle, opposite castle ←)
13	29.0	135	A	Betuwe		Camping van Sijll, Rijnstraat 72, 4031 KM (Ingen)	0344 601485	www.campingvansijll.nl	0.8 km (at KP 77 ↓, 1st rd ↓)
13	36.9	135	B	Rhenen		Roosenboom, Nieuwe Veenendaalseweg 32, 3911 ML	0317 613372	www.roseboomtweewielers.nl	0.6 km (at mdabt ↑)
14	0.8	136	A	Rhenen		Hotel 't Paviljoen, Grebbeweg 103-105, 3911 AV	0317 619003	http://paviljoen.nl	-
14	4.4	136	B	Opheusden		B&B Veerhuis Opheusden, Veerweg 1, 4043 JV	0488 441207	www.veerhuis-opheusden.nl	-
14	5.8	136	C	Opheusden		Van den Dikkenberg Tweewielers, Hamsestraat 36, 4043 LH	0488 441376	www.dikkenbergtweewielers.nl	0.6 km (at jct after shops →)
14	20.9	137	A	Slijk-Ewijk		B&B De Zwaluw, Dorpsstraat 81, 6677 PJ	0481 372692	www.dezwaluw.eu	0.1 km (← into village)
14	20.9	137	B	Slijk-Ewijk		B&B De Remketting, Fabriciuspark 15, 6677 PN	0481 481737	http://deremketting.nl	0.1 km (← into village, at cross roads →)
14	22.7	137	C	Oosterhout		Camping De Grote Altena, Waaldijk 39, 6678 MC	0481 481200	www.campingdegrotealtena.nl	-

Rte	Km	Page	Ref	Town	Info	Name, address and postcode	Phone	Internet	Distance to route & extra directions
15	0.0	139	A	Nijmegen	⚲ ⊖ hire	Rijwielshop Nijmegen, Stationsplein 7, 6512 AB	024 3229618	www.rijwielshopnijmegen.nl	- (underground under station square!)
15	0.6	139	A	Nijmegen	♠ ♣	B&B De Prince, Lange Hezelstraat 42-44, 6511 CK	024 3604510	http://deprince.nl	- (Restrictions during Four Days Marches!)
15	0.6	139	B	Nijmegen	♠ ♣	B&B Nijmegen, Lange Hezelstraat 43a, 6511 CC	024 3773568	www.bed-and-breakfast-nijmegen.nl	- (Restrictions during Four Days Marches!)
15	1.0	139	C	Nijmegen	♠ ♣	Hotel Atlanta, Grote Markt 38, 6511 KB	024 3603000	http://atlanta-hotel.nl	- (Restrictions during Four Days Marches!)
15	1.0	139	D	Nijmegen	♠ ♣	B&B In-credible, Hertogstraat 1, 6511 RV	024 3220498	www.in-credible.nl	- (Restrictions during Four Days Marches!)
15	1.5	139	E	Nijmegen	♠ ♣	Hotel Courage, Waalkade 108-112, 6511 XR	024 3604970	www.hotelcourage-waalkade.nl	- (Restrictions during Four Days Marches!)
15	1.5	139	F	Nijmegen	♠ ♣	B&B Opoe Sientje (On River Shipl), Lindenberghaven	06 13624255	www.opoesientje.nl	- (Restrictions during Four Days Marches!)
15	6.1	140	A	Beek	♠ ♣	Hotel Sous les Eglises, Rijksstraatweg 124, 6573 DD	024 6841850	www.souslesseglises.nl	- (Restrictions during Four Days Marches!)
15	6.2	140	A	Beek	♠ ♣	Hotel Spijker, Rijksstraatweg 191, 6573 CP	024 6841295	www.hotelspijker.nl	- (Restrictions during Four Days Marches!)
15	8.5	141	A	Berg en Dal	⛺ ⚓	Minicamping Flierenberg, Zevenheuvelenweg 57, 6571 CH	024 6841481	www.campingdegrooteflierenberg.nl	- (Restrictions during Four Days Marches!)
15	9.3	141	B	Beek en Dal	⛺ ⚓	Camping Nederrijkswald, Zevenheuvelenweg 47, 6571 CH	024 6841782	www.nederrijkswald.nl	- (Restrictions during Four Days Marches!)
15	10.7	141	C	Groesbeek	⛺ ⚓ ♠	Minicamping De Hoge Hof, Derdebaan 14, 6561 KH	024 3971225	www.dehogehof.com	- (Restrictions during Four Days Marches!)
15	11.5	141	D	Groesbeek	⛺ ⚓ ♠	Minicamping De Klos, De Klos 4, 6561 KD	06 22104640	www.campingdeklos.nl	- (Restrictions during Four Days Marches!)
15	0.1	141	E	Groesbeek	⛺ ⚓ ♠	Camping De Oude Molen, Wylerbaan 2a, 6561 KR	024 3971715	www.oudemolen.nl	- (Restrictions during Four Days Marches!)
16	2.1	142	A	Vlissingen	♠ ♣	Hotel Pension Lousiana, Nieuwendijk 25, 4381 BV	0118 413554	www.hotel-louisiana.nl	0.3 km (ep → via rd next to harbour)
16	2.1	142	A	Vlissingen	♠ ♣	Hotel Zilt, Nieuwendijk 37-39, 4381 BW	0118 410921	www.hotel-zilt.nl	0.3 km (ep → via rd next to harbour)
16	2.1	142	B	Vlissingen	♠ ♣	B&B De Kleyne Wereld, Nieuwstraat 24, 4381 CT	06 175563863	www.dekleynewereld.nl	0.1 km (ep →; imm ← via Sarazijnstraat)
16	2.2	142	C	Vlissingen	♠ ♣	Hotel Bonaventure, Beursplein 7, 4381 CA	0118 414766	www.hotel-bonaventure.nl	-
16	3.0	142	D	Vlissingen	♠ ♣	Pension Marijke, Coosje Buskenstraat 88, 4381 LG	0118 415062	www.pensionmarijke.nl	0.2 km (at jct on promenade ↗)
16	8.1	143	A	Dishoek	♠ ♣	Pension Duinlust, Dishoek 18, 4371 NS	0118 551534	www.duinlustdishoek.nl	-
16	11.8	143	A	Zoutelande	♠ ♣	Duinhotel Zomerlust, Duinweg 44, 4374 EG	0118 561261	www.duinhotelzomerlust.nl	-
16	12.3	144	A	Zoutelande	♠ ♣	Hotel Valkenhof, Zuidstraat 9-11, 4374 AJ	0118 561252	www.dunehotels.nl	0.1 km (→ into Zuidstraat)
16	13.5	144	B	Zoutelande	♠ ♣	Hotel De Distel, Westkapelseweg 1, 4374 BA	0118 562040	www.dunehotels.nl	-
16	13.7	144	C	Zoutelande	♠ ♣	Duinhotel Haga, Westkapelseweg 17, 4374 BA	0118 561823	www.duinhotelhaga.nl	-
16	17.1	144	D	Westkapelle	♠ ♣	B&B Huis De Kreek, De Casembrootstraat 18, 4361 AT	0118 570763	www.huisdekreek.nl	0.6 km (at T-jct ←, d'Arke)
16	17.1	144	D	Westkapelle	⚲	Daalhuizen Onderhoud, De Casembrootstraat 29, 4361 AS	0118 572275	www.daalhuizenfietsonderhoud.nl	0.6 km (at T-jct ←, d'Arke)
16	17.5	144	E	Westkapelle	♠ ♣	Hotel De Valk, Zuidstraat 97, 4361 AH	0118 571294	www.devalkhotel.nl	0.5 km (from museum → via high street)
16	21.6	144	F	Domburg	⛺ ⚓ ♠	Camping Noordduin, Schelpweg 17a, 4357 RG	0118 582666	www.campingnoordduin.nl	0.2 km (at T-jct → via main rd)
16	22.3	144	G	Domburg	⛺ ⚓ ♠	Minicamping 't Veldehof, Trommelweg 4, 4357 RH	0118 582557	www.veldehof.nl	-
16	25.2	145	A	Domburg	♠ ♣	B&B De Dorsvloer, Singel 26, 4357 BW	0118 750223	www.dedorsvloer.nl	0.2 km (at T-jct ↓)
16	25.2	145	A	Domburg	⚲ ⊖ hire	Akkerdaas Tweewielers, Weststraat 2b, 4357 BM	0118 581105	http://akkerdaastweewielers.com	0.1 km (← via high street)
16	25.5	145	B	Domburg	♠ ♣	B&B De Lijsterhof, Weststraat 11a, 4357 BL	0118 750223	www.delijsterhof.nl	0.2 km (← via high street)
16	25.6	145	C	Domburg	♠ ♣	Hotel Viewegen, 't Groentje 10, 4357 BC	0118 583393	www.viewegen.eu	-

Rte	Km	Page	Ref	Town	Info	Name, address and postcode	Phone	Internet	Distance to route & extra directions
16	27.2	145	D	Domburg		Stayokay Domburg (YHA), Duinvlietweg 8, 4356 ND	0118 581254	www.stayokay.com	0.2 km (on Duinvlietweg, 1st driveway →)
16	32.3	145	E	Vrouwenpolder - Breezand		Camping Oranjezon, Koningin Emmaweg 16a, 4354 KD	0118 591549	www.oranjezon.nl	-
16	34.3	145	F	Vrouwenpolder - Breezand		Mini Camping Schorre, Vroondijk 2, 4354 NN	0118 594473	www.schorre.nl	-
17	0.0	146	A	Vrouwenpolder - Breezand		Hotel Duinoord, Breezand 65, 4354 NL	0118 591346	www.hotel-duinoord.nl	-
17	19.2	148	A	Burgh-Haamstede		Mini Camping Veldvreugd, Brabersweg 4-5, 4328 NN	0111 651225	www.veldvreugd.nl	-
17	21.9	148	B	Burgh-Haamstede		Hotel Bom, Noordstraat 2, 4328 AL	0111 652229	www.hotel-bom.nl	-
17	22.2	148	C	Burgh-Haamstede		B&B De Lindehof, Julianastraat 21, 4328 AR	0111 651834	www.pensiondelindehof.nl	0.1 km (← into Bernhardstraat)
17	22.2	148	D	Burgh-Haamstede		B&B Zeeland aan Zee, Burghseweg 44, 4428 LB	0111 407879	www.zeelandaanzee.com	-
17	22.2	148	E	Burgh-Haamstede	hire	Bike Totaal Verton, Kerkstraat 1, 4328 LH	0111 651324	www.vertonbiketotaal.nl	0.3 km (at Pannenkoekenmolen ↑ to Burgh)
17	24.0	148	F	Burgh-Haamstede		Camping In de Boogerd, Vertonsweg 2, 4328 GL	0111 653672	www.indeboogerd.nl	-
17	31.0	149	A	Renesse		Hotel De Zeeuwse Stromen, Duinwekken 5, 4325 GL	0111 462040	www.zeeuwsestromen.nl	0.1 km (ignore bike park, ↑ onto rd, 1st →)
17	31.7	149	B	Renesse		Camping Duinhoeve, Scholderlaan 8, 4325 EP	0111 461309	www.campingduinhoeve.nl	0.3 km (at KP 76 →)
17	32.4	149	C	Renesse		Pension Zeerust, Rampweg 1, 4325 LG	0111 461390	www.pczeerust.nl	-
17	32.4	149	D	Renesse		Camping De Kempe, Korte Moermondsweg 17, 4325 LB	0111 462540	www.dekempe.nl	0.6 km (join rd →, 1st rd →)
17	32.7	149	E	Renesse		B&B aan Zee, Rampweg 9, 4325 LG	0111 407804	www.bbaanzeeland.nl	-
18	3.1	150	A	Ouddorp		Camping Zuidhoek, Westduinweg 1, 3253 LV	0187 681823	www.campingzuidhoek.n	0.5 km (at KP 52 ←, 1st rd ←)
18	6.8	150	B	Ouddorp		B&B De Smousenhoek, Hazersweg 23, 3253 XE	0187 687151	www.desmousenhoek.nl	0.4 km (ep →, T-jct ←)
18	6.8	150	C	Ouddorp		Pension Ouddorp, Dorpsweg 26, 3253 AH	0187 681724	www.pensionouddorp.nl	0.6 km (ep ←, T-jct →, follow bend ←)
18	6.8	150	C	Ouddorp		Akershoek Fietsen, Dorpsweg 27, 3253 AG	0187 681704	www.akershoekfietsen.nl	0.6 km (ep ←, T-jct →, follow bend ←)
18	7.2	150	D	Ouddorp		Hotel Akershoek, Boompjes 1, 3253 AC	0187 681437	www.hotelakershoek.nl	0.3 km (←, follow bend ←, 1st ←)
18	7.6	150	E	Ouddorp		B&B 't Meulweegje, Molenweg 12, 3253 AM	0187 664746	-	0.1 km (at mdabt ↖)
18	11.5	151	A	Goedereede		Hotel De Gouden Leeuw, Markt 11, 3252 BC	0187 491371	www.hoteldegoudenleeuw.net	-
18	11.5	151	A	Goedereede		B&B Goedereede, Markt 13, 3252 BC	0187 841508	http://bbgoeree.nl	-
18	14.1	151	A	Havenhoofd		Haveneind B&B, Haveneind 1, 3252 LN	0187 750772	www.haveneind.nl	-
18	26.9	152	A	Hellevoetsluis		B&B Landleven, Langeweg 2, 3222 LD	0181 329064	www.bedandbreakfastlandleven.nl	0.5 km (keep ↑ via Langeweg)
18	30.0	152	B	Brielle		Fietsplus van Oudenaarden, 't Woud 4, 3232 LN	0181 413351	www.fietsplusvanoudenaarden.nl	1.0 km (keep on ⌒ of main rd, 2nd rd ↓, →)
18	32.5	153	A	Brielle		B&B Buiten de Vest, Matthijsenlaan 2b, 3232 ED	0181 412069	www.buitendevest.nl	0.3 km (at jct of paths, keep ↖, ep →)
18	33.2	153	B	Brielle		Bastion Hotel Brielle-Europoort, Amer 1, 3232 HA	0181 416588	www.bastionhotels.nl	0.2 km (ep →, at mdabt ↑)
18	33.6	153	C	Brielle		Atlas Hotel Brielle, Nobelstraat 20, 3231 BC	0181 413455	www.atlas-hotels.com	0.1 km (at Historisch Museum ←)
18	33.6	153	D	Brielle		Fletcher Hotel De Zalm, Voorstraat 6-8, 3231 BJ	0181 413388	www.hoteldezalm.nl	-
18	33.8	153	E	Brielle		Hotel De Nymph, Voorstraat 45, 3231 BE	0181 415230	www.hotelbrielle.nl	-
18	36.7	153	F	Oostvoorne		Modjo Kerto, Bollaarsdijk 5, 3233 LB	06 10891796	www.modjo-kerto.nl	1.0 km (from ⌒, 2nd exit ← onto rd, T-jct →)
18	39.4	153	G	Oostvoorne		Kruiningergors, Gorsplein 2, 3233 XC	0181 482711	www.molecaten.nl/kruininger-gors	-

Cycling in Amsterdam and The Netherlands

The very best routes in the cyclist's paradise

Eric van der Horst

www.eoscycling.com

Cycling in Amsterdam and The Netherlands
The very best routes in the cyclist's paradise

Dedicated to my grandparents Jaap and Mies van der Horst, who never owned a car, loved cycling and knew many of the routes in this book (see pictures page 12).

Published by EOS Cycling Holidays Ltd, Barnstaple, Devon, United Kingdom
www.eoscycling.com
www.cyclinginholland.com
Twitter: @DutchmanCycling or @EOSCyclingUK

ISBN: 978-0-9576617-1-4

Copyright © Eric van der Horst, 2015

Disclaimer: The publisher and author have done their best to ensure the accuracy of all the information in this guidebook and on the internet. However, they can accept no responsibility for any loss, injury or inconvenience sustained by any traveller as a result of information or advice contained in the guidebook, via additional products such as GPS-tracks and/or on the internet.

The maps in this book are made available under the Open Database License: http://opendatacommons.org/licenses/odbl/1.0/. Any rights in individual contents of the database are licensed under the Database Contents License: http://opendatacommons.org/licenses/dbcl/1.0/ - See more at: http://opendatacommons.org/licenses/odbl/#sthash.PXqWKVpE.dpuf. Design of detailed town maps courtesy of MapQuest (www.mapquest.com). Note that only the maps in this book are made publicly available according to the "Share Alike" principle, see www.openstreetmap.org. On all other content, copyright applies. Whilst every effort has been made to ensure the accuracy of all content, Eric van der Horst, EOS Cycling Holidays Ltd, OpenStreetMap and MapQuest cannot be held responsible for any errors or omissions. The representation of a road, track or path is no evidence of the existence of a public right of way.

Dutch cycling facts (see pages 4, 12, 13, 14 and 15) sourced from The Dutch Cyclists Union (De Fietsersbond, www.fietsersbond.nl), "In the city of bikes" by Pete Jordan (HarperCollins Publishers, New York, USA, 2013) and "How the Dutch got their cycle paths" by Mark Wagenbuur ("Bicycle Dutch" on YouTube and Wordpress).

All photography by Eric van der Horst, except for some pictures on the front cover (Eleanore Hamaker), pages 1 and 113 (Dirk van Rens), page 4 (Berno Brosschol), page 12 (Van der Horst family archives), pages 15, 36, 38, 46 and 105 (Bert van der Horst), page 20 (Silvia Pilger), page 24 (Ellen Beckering), page 26 (Bart ten Harkel), page 28 (Inge Hollander), pages 53 and 67 (Dawn Connor), page 56 (Martijn Tuinman), pages 108, 111, 113, 122, 131 and 139 (Wikimedia Commons), page 133 (Eric Keetels) and page 143 (Peter Tol). The publisher endeavoured to contact copyright holders of the historic pictures on pages 13 and 14. If you have the copyright on these pictures, contact us.

The author wishes to thank Martin Whitfield for all his advice, Martijn Tuinman and Eric Keetels for the "surveying fun", Rob Olijkan of Bikecity for the surveying bike and his wife Dawn and children Lucas and Oscar for their support.

Printed by Toptown Printers, Barnstaple, Devon, United Kingdom (www.toptown.co.uk).

About the author

"Cycling Dutchman" Eric van der Horst went on his first cycling holiday when he was 16. It took him over 15 years to explore the full extent of the Dutch cycle route network. The routes in this guidebook represent his personal local favorites. Eric also travelled the world by bike and cycled in many different countries. Today, he lives in England and works as a cycle route consultant, Bikeability instructor and author. Follow him on Twitter @DutchmanCycling or http://thecyclingdutchman.blogspot.com.

Appeal to readers

This book contains 1,064 kms (656 miles) of routes. We need your help to keep everything up-to-date. Please report any changes you find and share experiences via Twitter @DutchmanCycling. You can also contact us via our websites (see top left). We publish all important changes on the updates page of the website.